I0763089

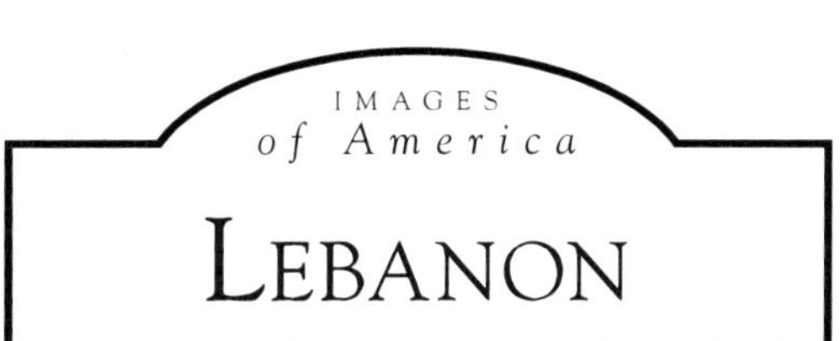
IMAGES
of America
LEBANON

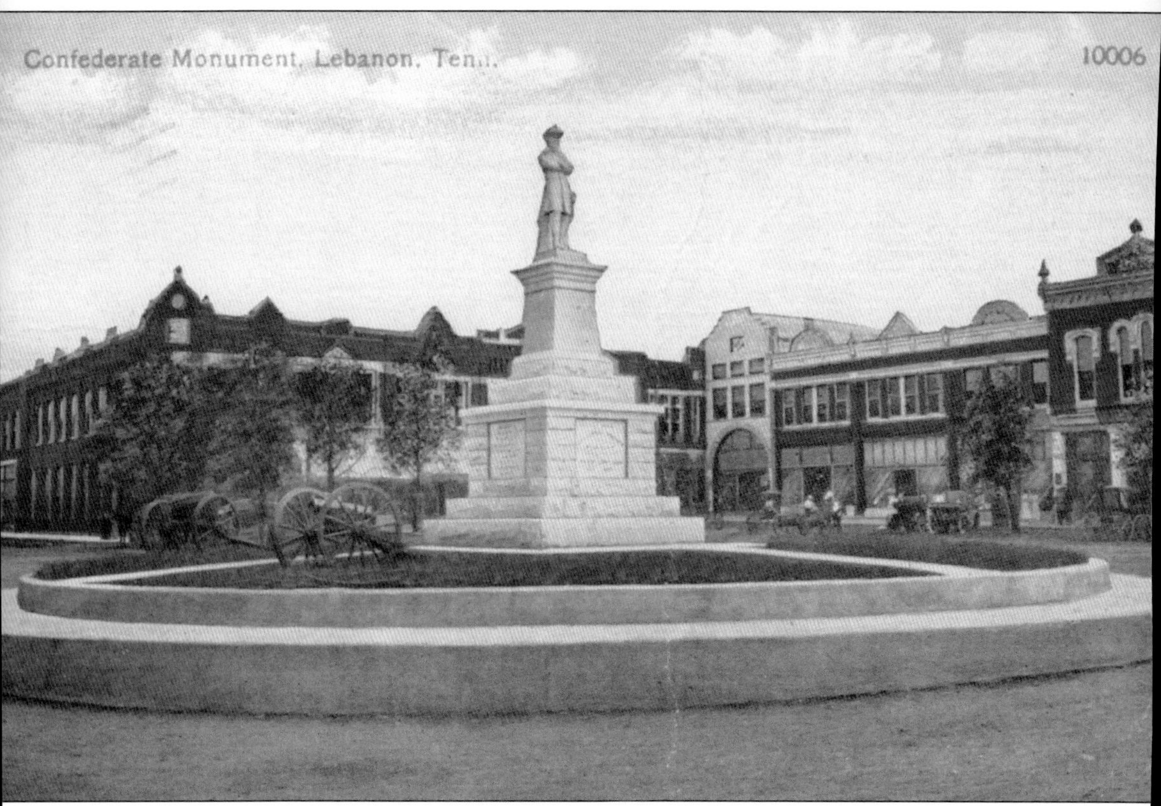

This postcard view of Lebanon's Public Square from 1914 is a familiar sight. Although taken 100 years ago, the monument to Gen. Robert Hatton and the buildings in the southeast corner of the Square are still mostly intact. Before this, though, the Public Square was quite a different place. A courthouse stood in its center, and buildings were constructed and destroyed by fire in an ever-changing landscape. (Courtesy of the Ridley Wills Postcard Collection, Cumberland University.)

On the Cover: Outings to Hunters Point, on the Cumberland River north of Lebanon, were a popular activity with the town's social set in the late 1890s. This photograph taken by I.W.P. Buchanan includes, from left to right, (on the ground) Judge Nathan Green Jr. and Bill Slate, driver; (first row on top), unidentified, Sarah Dodson Ferrell, unidentified, Alice Williamson Hooker, and Willie Buchanan; (second row on top) Martha Martin Burke, unidentified, Martha Williamson Bone, and Johnnie Lester. (Courtesy of the I.W.P. Buchanan Collection.)

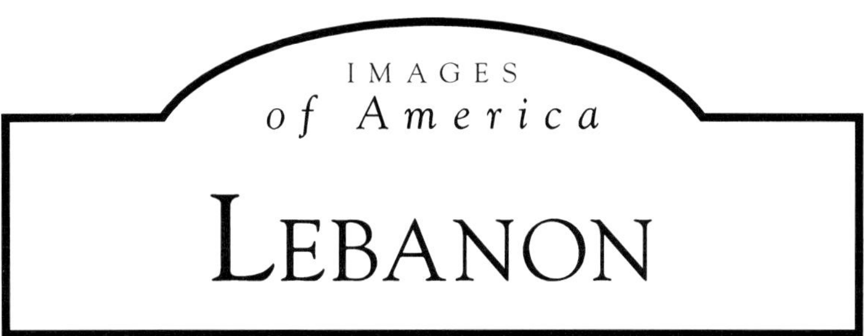

Kim Jackson Parks for Historic Lebanon

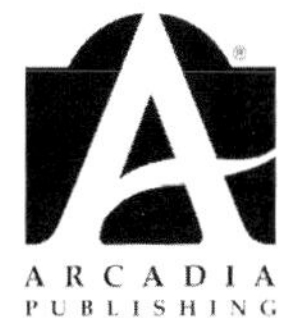

ISBN 978-1-4671-1298-7

Published by Arcadia Publishing
Charleston, South Carolina

Printed in the United States of America

Library of Congress Control Number: 2014939396

For all general information, please contact Arcadia Publishing:
Telephone 843-853-2070
Fax 843-853-0044
E-mail sales@arcadiapublishing.com
For customer service and orders:
Toll-Free 1-888-313-2665

Visit us on the Internet at www.arcadiapublishing.com

To the Lebanon community for their continued support of Historic Lebanon and the fulfillment of our mission.

Contents

ACKNOWLEDGMENTS

This book was made possible by the resources, advice, and encouragement of the following: Historic Lebanon board of directors, C. Tracey Parks, Thomas Partlow and Linda Granstaff at the Wilson County Archives, Phil Carter, Eloise Hitchcock at the Cumberland University Vise Library and Stockton Archives, Rob Hosier, Castle Heights Military Academy Alumni Association, Debbie Jessen, City of Lebanon, Sam Hatcher, W.P. Bone, Tom Clemmons, Hubert Clemmons, Edward L. Thackston, David Brooks and Ligon and Bobo Funeral Home, Marilyn and Hattie Bryant, Partlow Funeral Home, Ken Thomson, Mary Harris, Tennessee State Library and Archives, T.A. Bryan, Hale Moss and Wilson County Promotions, Ellen Campbell Marsh and the Campbell family, Rick Bell, Charles and Elaine Bell, Wilson County Civic League, Wilson County Black History Associates, Hollis McClanahan, Tick Bryan, and Liz Gurley of Arcadia Publishing.

The images in this volume appear courtesy of the City of Lebanon Museum and History Center (CLMHC), the Ridley Wills Postcard Collection at Cumberland University (RWPCCU), the I.W.P. Buchanan Collection (BC), the Stockton Archives at Vise Library at Cumberland University (CU), the Castle Heights Military Academy Alumni Association (CHMA), the Wilson County Archives (WCA), Tennessee State Library and Archives (TSLA), Library of Congress (LC), and others as noted.

INTRODUCTION

On November 13, 1801, Wilson County commissioners Christopher Cooper, Alanson Trigg, Matthew Figures, John Harpole, and John Doak were empowered with finding a location for the newly formed county's seat. A site east of Barton's Creek on a bountiful spring surrounded by a grove of cedar trees was selected and named Lebanon for the Biblical land of cedars. A total of 40 acres, including the spring, was purchased from James Menees. Lebanon was laid out with one acre reserved for a public square, and the town's first lots were sold at auction on August 16, 1802, with choice ones bringing $33 each. The town's first hotel opened for business in 1803, the same year William Allen opened a store. The Wilson County Courthouse followed. Built of cedar, it stood on the west side of the Square.

Lebanon was chartered in 1807, the same year it elected its first mayor, Edmund Crutcher, and its first postmaster, John Alcorn. In its position as the county seat, Lebanon was a center for the official business of the county as well as a transportation hub. A total of 11 turnpikes radiated out of Lebanon, including the roads to Knoxville, Nashville, and Murfreesboro, each of which had served as the state capital by 1819.

Politics and politicians played their role in shaping the town. Future president Andrew Jackson established a store in Lebanon long before his national political career. Sam Houston began his first law practice in Lebanon, and James Chamberlain "Lean Jimmy" Jones, running as a Whig, managed to defeat future president James K. Polk in both 1841 and 1843 to become the first Tennessee-born citizen elected governor of Tennessee.

Lebanon at its half-century mark had all the elements expected in a town of its size. The opening of Cumberland University, as well as a fine preparatory school and a female college, earned the town a reputation as a center for education. The 1853 *Nashville and State of Tennessee General Commercial Directory* noted, "No town of its size in the West or South has done more, perhaps, not as much, for the cause of education." These schools and the addition of Cumberland's law school in 1847 afforded the town amenities and cultural opportunities not often found in a town of its size.

Lebanon businessmen and farmers were also factors in the advancement of the town. Both sawmills and gristmills played a large role in the economy in the first half of the 19th century. The abundance of local cedar and other timber fueled the sawmills, while locally grown grain forwarded the production of the flour mills. The Lester Mill was noted for the quality of its flour, which was shipped to the British market. The production of cotton and wool in the county made the manufacturing of cloth an important trade, with two mills employing over 500 people and producing 1,000 yards of cloth a day.

The Civil War slowed progress for Lebanon, as well as for the rest of the South. Growth during the Reconstruction years was slow, but Lebanon sustained itself. One note of progress was the start of rail service to the town in 1869. By the turn of the 20th century, Lebanon entered a growth period not seen since well before the war. The addition of a second railroad in 1902, the

Tennessee Central, added to the momentum. The same year, Castle Heights School began its influence on the town, lasting for the next 84 years. The Gulf Red Cedar Pencil Factory relocated to Lebanon in 1908, along with 200 workers and their families. Soon to follow was the Lebanon Woolen Mills.

Lebanon now had the makings of a progressive town. One constant problem that stood in the way of expansion was the town spring, namely the fact that the spring was still the only source of the town's water. Since Lebanon's founding, the spring had been fundamental in shaping the growth of the town. On one hand, it was an asset, an ever-flowing source of drinking water. On the other hand, it created many problems. Roads had to cross the creek leading to the spring. If bridges were not available, the creek had to be forged. This led to undesirable conditions during many months of the year. Not only was the spring the source of the town's drinking supply, it was also used to water livestock and power the mills. The early minutes of the board of aldermen's meetings are scattered with references to the screening of the spring, fines for washing hogs in the creek, and regulations on the use of the spring. In the first years of the town, citizens gathered their water directly from the spring. Stone steps leading down to the source were installed in 1824. In 1887, pipe was installed to carry the water directly to homes and businesses, but the spring, with all of its problems, was still the source of the water. A solution was reached in 1908, with the Cedar City Mills agreeing to town use of its two wells on South Maple Street. These wells were used until the need for more capacity led the town to the Cumberland River for its water source in 1932.

Another important event, in 1908, was the qualification for free delivery of the mail. Receipts of mail, as well as the town's population, had grown enough to reach this milestone. Sen. Cordell Hull's guidance and influence brought federal appropriation for a post office building. Delivery requirements necessitated improvements such as new sidewalks and the numbering of houses and businesses. With the addition of the federal post office and the ongoing success of local industries and businesses, Lebanon continued to grow. Agriculture also played a significant role in Lebanon in these years. First Monday mule day sales, as well as the production of wool and grain, were notable.

Conditions would change dramatically during World War II, but Lebanon played a most important role for the country when Cumberland University was selected as the headquarters for the Tennessee Maneuvers in preparation of an Allied invasion of Europe.

Progressive leadership in the years following World War II facilitated the creation of the first industrial park in 1952. Larger industry followed, and Lebanon flourished. Other important advances included the commercial airport and updated technology for telephones, the creation of state highway routes through Lebanon, and the completion of Interstate 40 south of town.

Just as the first turnpikes and post roads had influenced antebellum Lebanon, transportation infrastructure continued to play a major role in its advancement. One local industry would use this framework to position itself on the growing interstate system and create a successful business model in 1969. Cracker Barrel Old Country Store continues to be headquartered in Lebanon today, with its founder influenced by the culture of entrepreneurship and progressiveness found in Lebanon since its beginning.

Lebanon's first 167 years, from 1802 to 1969, are highlighted in this book. This is not intended to be a complete history but rather an introduction to entice the reader to a further study and exploration of the history of the town and its citizens.

—Kim Jackson Parks
Lebanon, Tennessee
May 2014

One

Early Lebanon

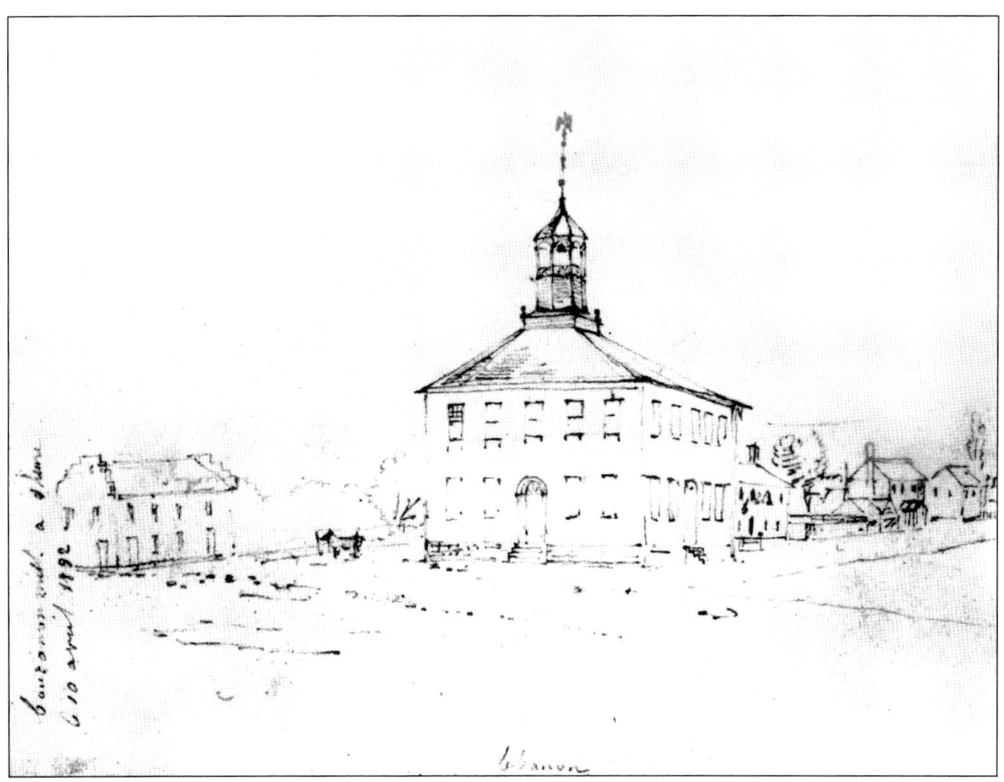

Wilson County's second courthouse was built in the center of the Lebanon Square in 1811 at a cost of $500. Constructed of brick with a hipped roof and a cupola, it would stand for 31 years. This sketch, dated 1832, is the only known image of the structure. It was found in the journal of the French-born Charles A. Lesuer. (CLMHC.)

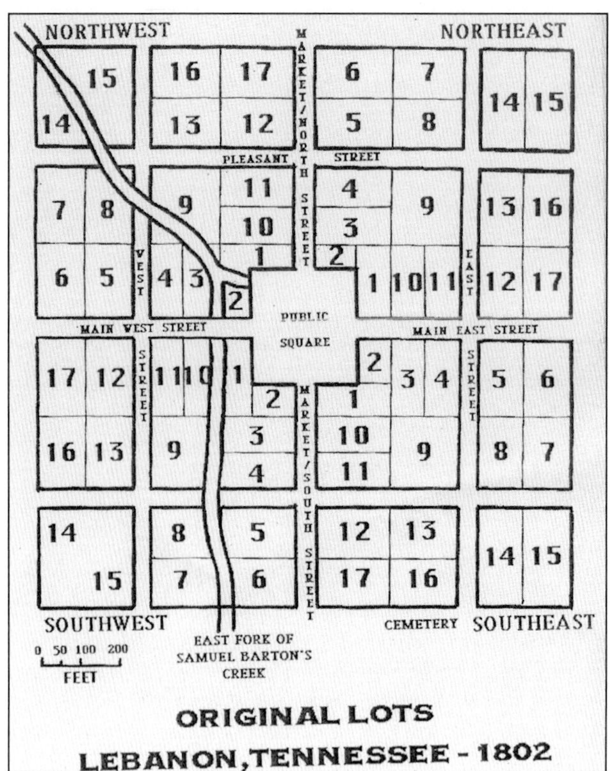

The Wilson County Court, on November 13, 1801, empowered its five commissioners to choose a site for the county seat and purchase 40 acres to lay out a town. One acre would be reserved for a public square and the rest sold as town lots. This map, created by James Victor Miller, shows the layout of the town as created with an auction on August 16, 1802. Lot No. 4 of the southwest quadrant is the site purchased on that day by Andrew Jackson. (WCA.)

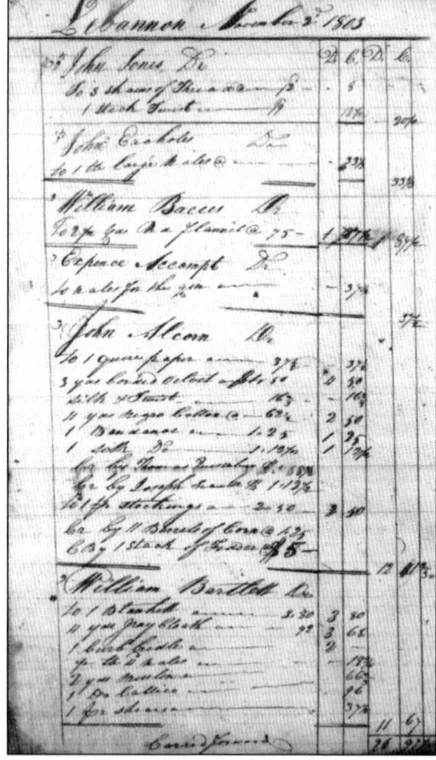

The account book kept by the firm Jackson & Company recorded sales from its mercantile store in Lebanon. Andrew Jackson and John Hutchings, Jackson's nephew, entered into a partnership to operate the store at Lebanon in February 1802 and acquired two lots on the Public Square in furtherance of the enterprise in August of the same year. Additional stores were located at Gallatin and at Jackson's home, Hunter's Hill. (TSLA.)

William Strickland, architect of the Tennessee State Capitol, designed Wilson County's third courthouse. Authorized in 1846 and completed in 1848, this courthouse stood on the south side of the Public Square. A fire on the night of December 13, 1881, destroyed the brick building. This is the only building in Lebanon to be documented in Strickland's architectural sketchbook. (CLMHC.)

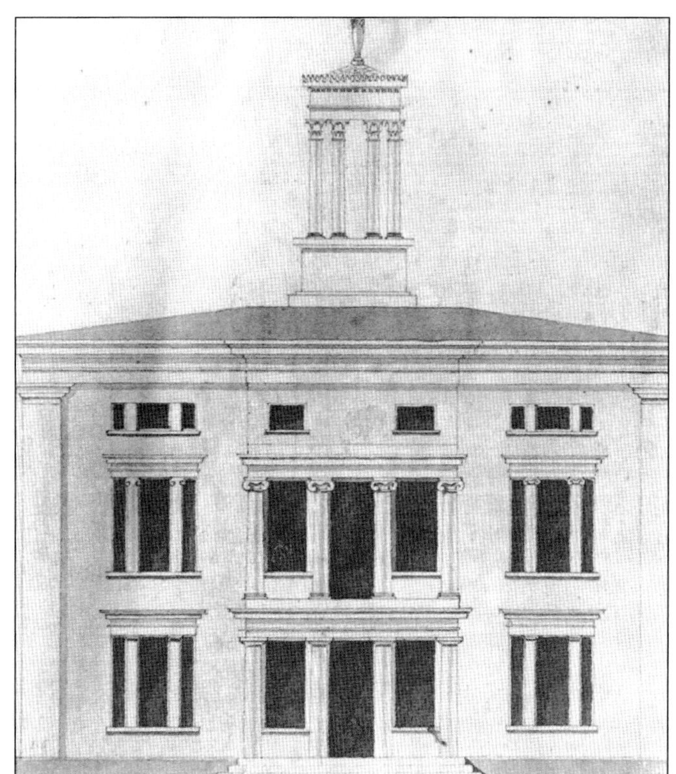

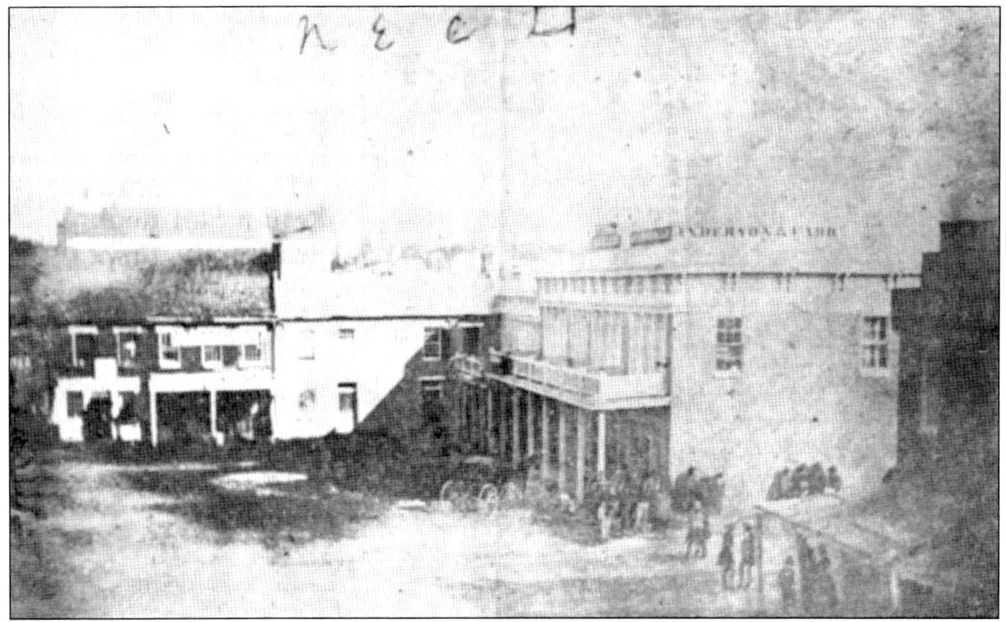

This earliest known photograph of the Public Square shows the northeast corner in 1859. The Cumberland Presbyterian Church, on the corner of North Cumberland and Market Streets, its second location, can be seen over the store roofs to the left. From its earliest days, the Square has been the county's center of commerce. This section was destroyed by fire in 1886 and again in 1923. (CLMHC.)

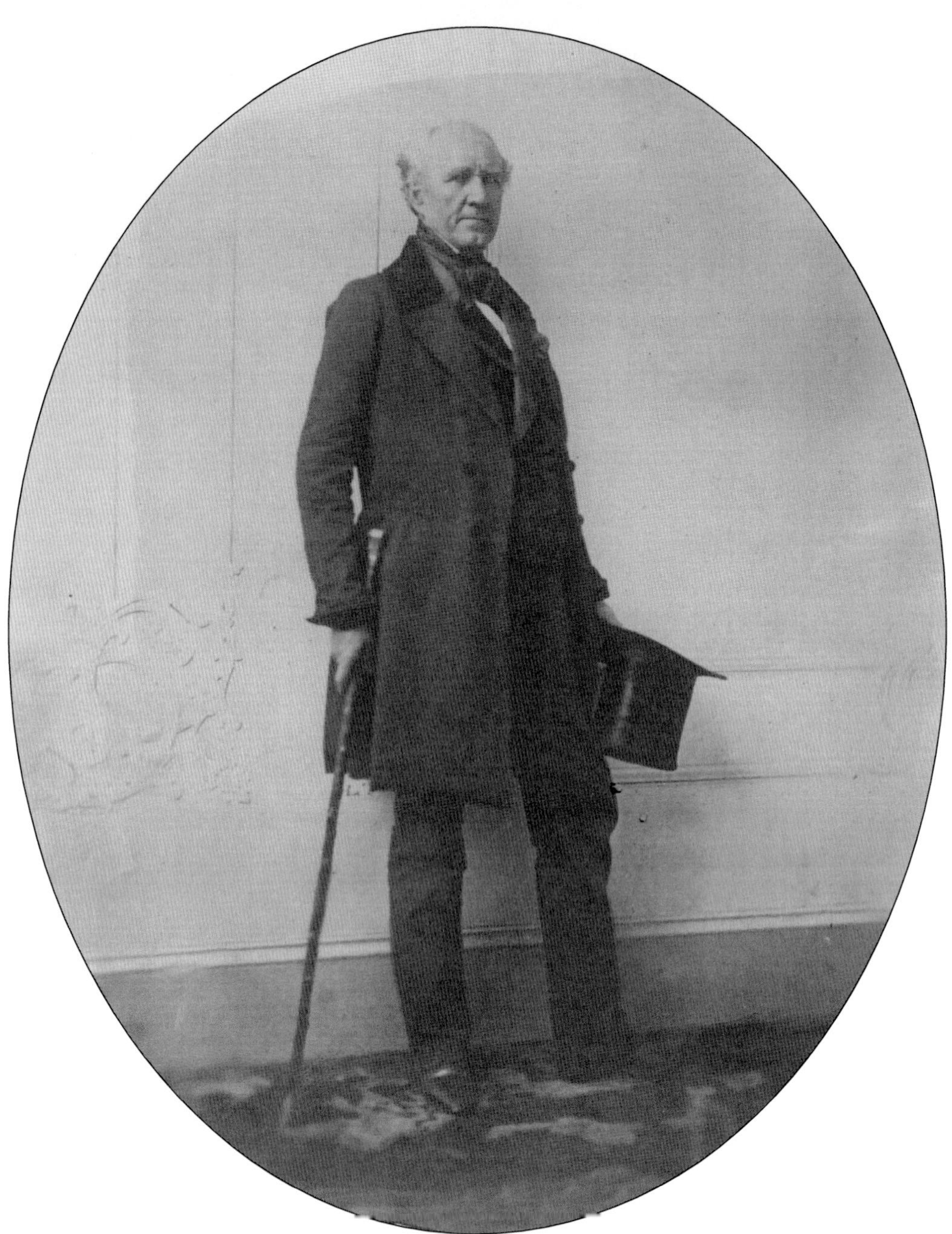

One of Lebanon's most famous residents, Sam Houston (1793–1863), came to the town in 1818 to establish his first law office. The office was located in a small cabin on East Main Street, which he rented from Isaac Golloday, the town's postmaster. Houston moved to Nashville the following year upon winning the office of attorney general. In 1827, Houston was elected governor of Tennessee, but he resigned the office in 1829. By 1832, he entered Texas and helped lead the movement for independence, being elected president of the Republic of Texas in 1836. When one of Golloday's sons became ill in Huntsville, Texas, in 1852, Houston came to his bedside and greeted the young man, saying, "If you are the son of Isaac Golloday, I recognize you a child of an early and true friend," proof of Houston's lifelong affection for friends made in Lebanon. (LC.)

This brick building, constructed in 1831, was the original meetinghouse for the Cumberland Presbyterian Church. It stood at 316 North Cumberland Street. In May 1842, its pastor, Rev. George Donnell, served as chairman of the committee in charge of selecting the location for a new Cumberland University. The school held its first classes in this structure from September 1842 until February 1844. (BC.)

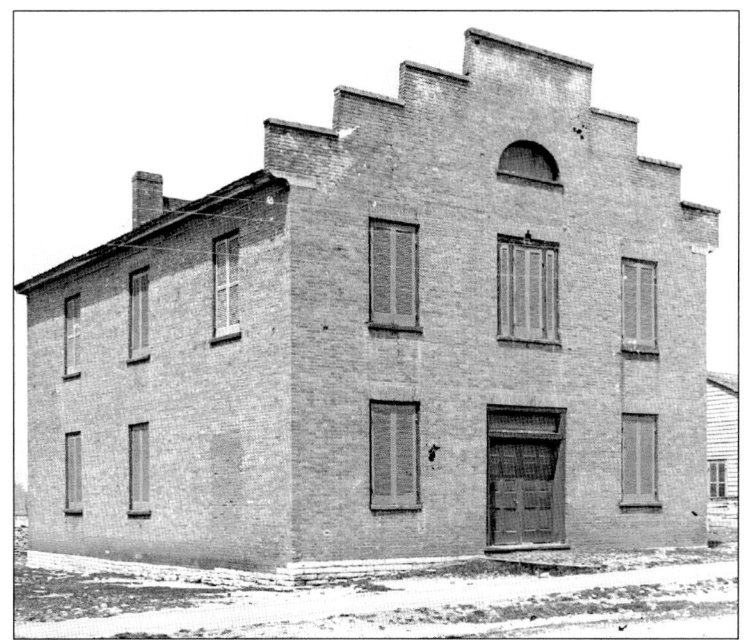

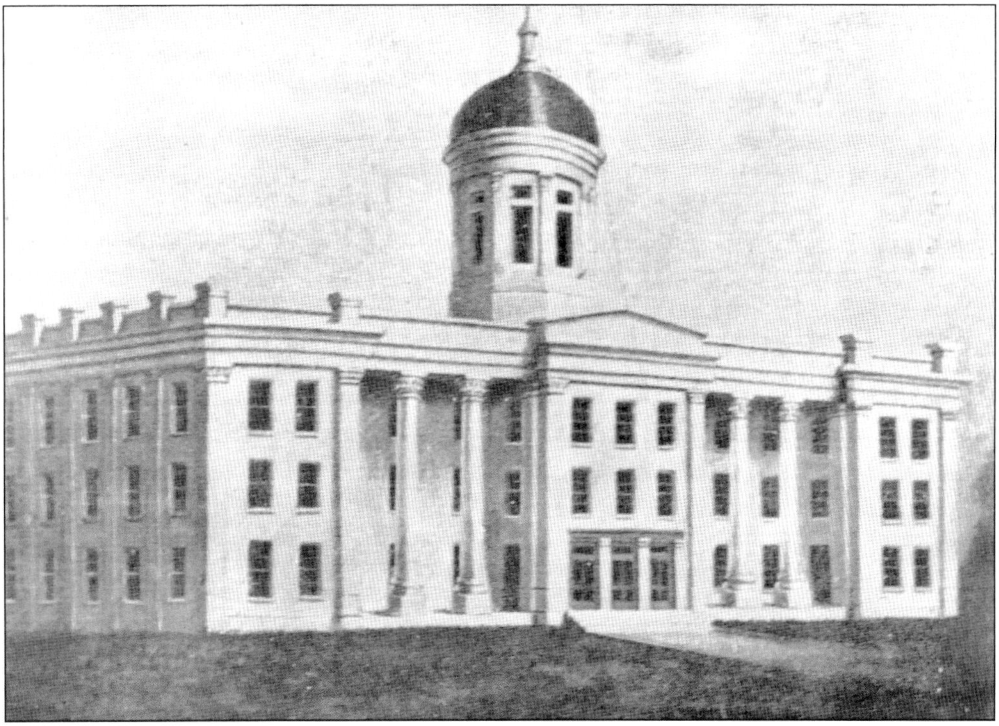

Cumberland University's first campus was located on the southeast corner of College and East Spring Streets. Construction began in 1842, and the finished building was 110 feet long and 40 feet wide. This was expanded with two spacious wings, a colonnade, and a cupola in 1859, making it the largest college edifice in the state. This building was burned on September 4, 1864, by Confederate forces. (CU.)

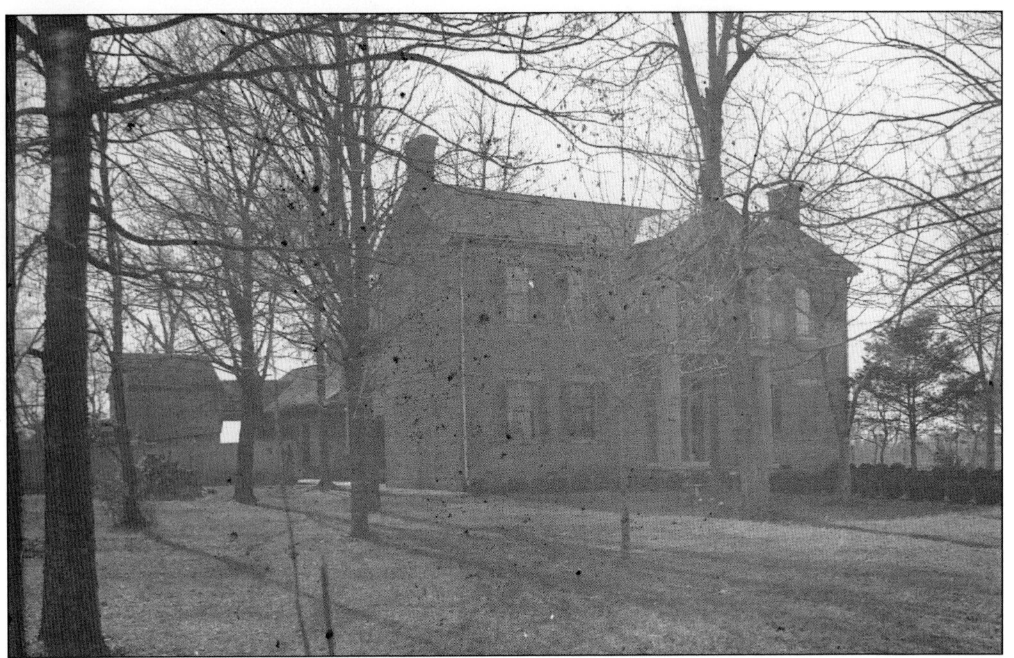

Franceway "Francis" Ranna Cossitt (1790–1863) built this two-story brick home shortly after arriving in Lebanon to serve as Cumberland University's first president in 1842. It stood on the south side of West Main Street in the 400 block until it was razed for the construction of McClain Elementary School in 1923. (BC.)

LEBANON INN.

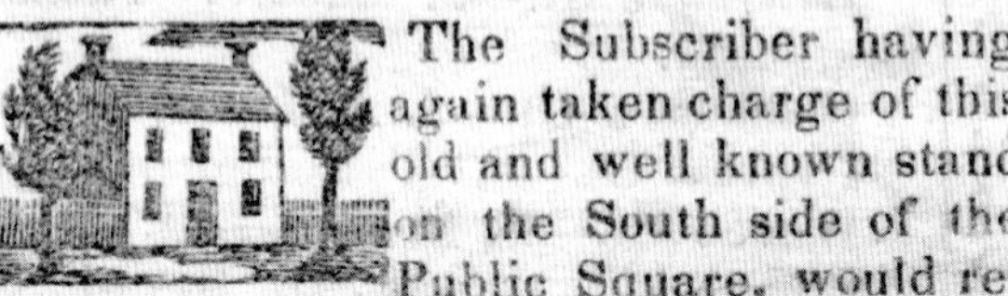

The Subscriber having again taken charge of this old and well known stand on the South side of the Public Square, would respectfully announce to his old friends and the public generally that he is now prepared to accommodate them in a man-equal to any House in the place, and at very moderate rates. His stables are ample. and he pledges himself they shall be constantly furnished with whatever the country produces.

N. B. Travellers, gentlemen of the Bar or others wishing it, can be furnished with private rooms with fire, &c. In short, no pains will be spared to render every accommodation to all who may give him a call.

L. SYPERT.

Lebanon, Jan. 24 1840.

This advertisement for the Lebanon Inn first appeared in a January 24, 1840, issue of the *Lebanon Chronicle*, a local newspaper published by W.P. McClain. L. Sypert's inn on the south side of the Public Square was conveniently located near the courthouse. Lebanon's position as county seat necessitated the ready availability of lodging places in the town. (Courtesy of Edward L. Thackston.)

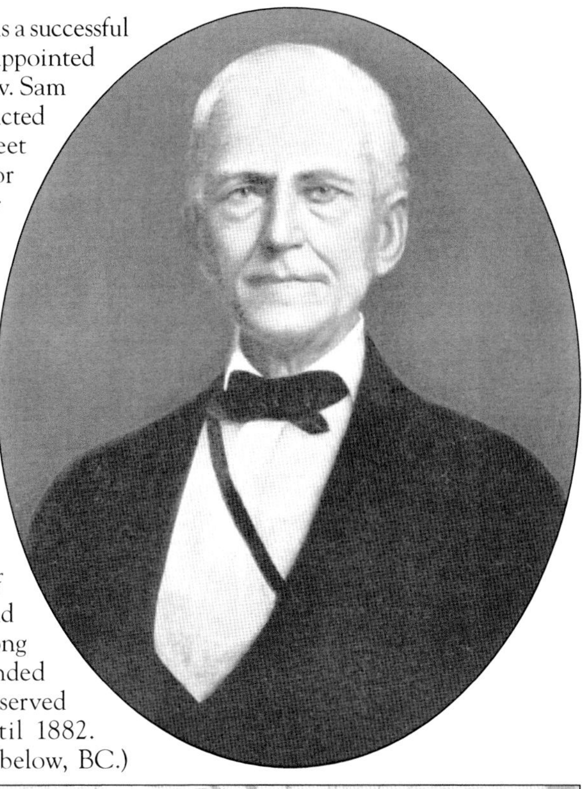

Robert Looney Caruthers (1800–1882) was a successful Lebanon lawyer in 1827 when he was appointed the sixth district attorney general by Gov. Sam Houston. The following year, he constructed a fine brick house on West Main Street (below), which remained his home for the rest of his life. His political career included election to the Tennessee House of Representatives in 1835, a term in the US House of Representatives from 1841 to 1843, and appointment to the Tennessee Supreme Court in 1852, when he replaced Judge Nathan Green Sr. Caruthers was elected governor of Tennessee in 1863 but did not take office, as Federal troops occupied Nashville, preventing the general assembly from convening. He was a founder of Cumberland University, was elected president of its first board of trustees in 1842, and served in this office until his death. Along with his brother Abraham, he cofounded Cumberland's law school in 1847, and served as a professor of law from 1868 until 1882. (Right, courtesy of C. Tracey Parks; below, BC.)

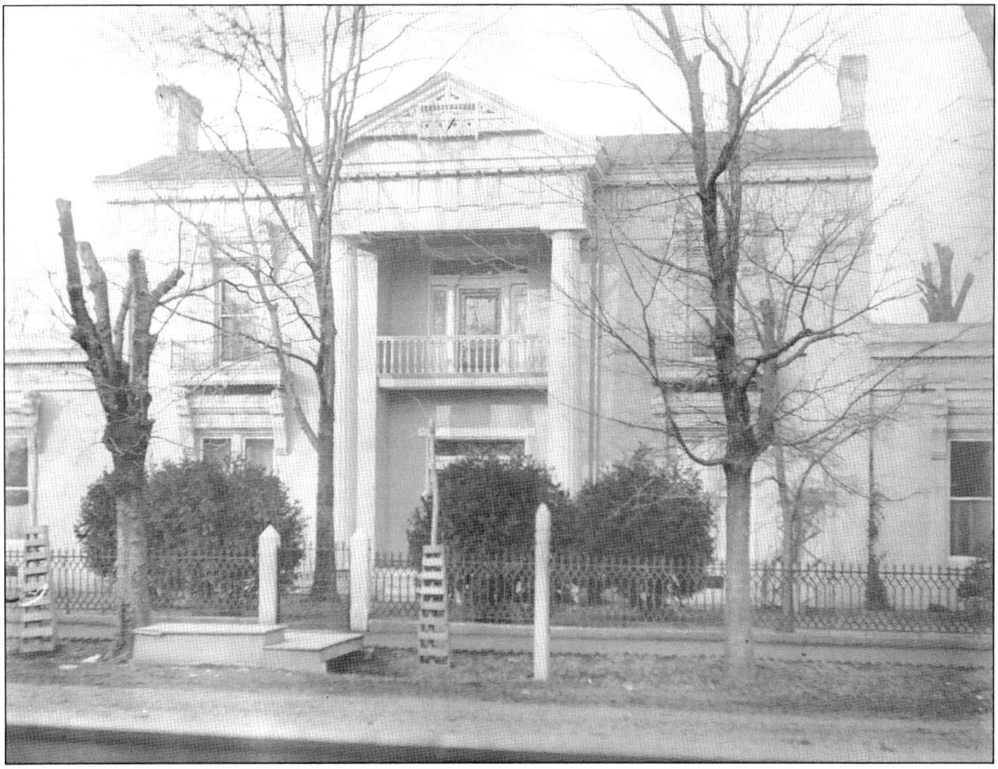

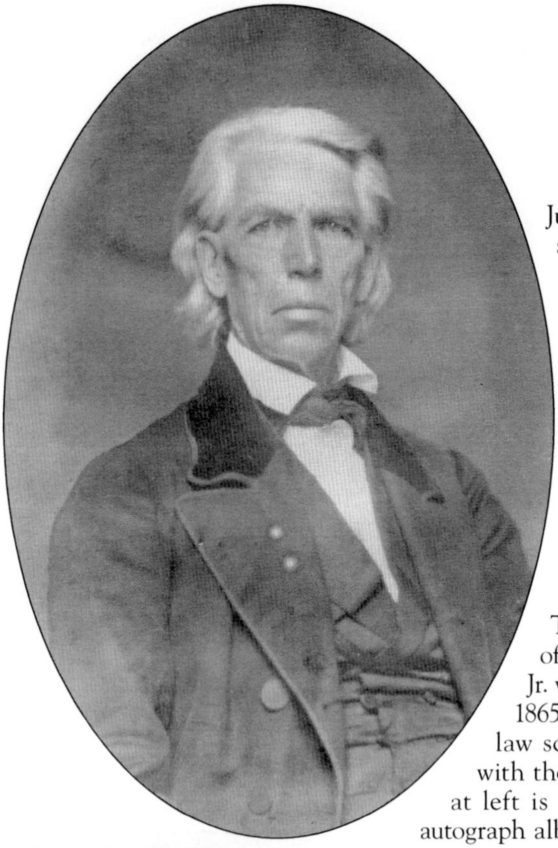

Judge Nathan Green Sr. (1792–1866) had served on the Tennessee Supreme Court for 21 years before his retirement in 1852, at which time he accepted a professorship to teach law at Cumberland University. Preceding his tenure on the Supreme Court, Green had been chancellor of the East Tennessee Division of the court while a resident of Franklin County. Green moved to Lebanon and, in May 1850, purchased six acres on the north side of the turnpike leading to Nashville, where he constructed a two-story home (below) about a mile west of the Public Square. Though Green, who had fought in the War of 1812, opposed secession, his son Nathan Jr. would join the Confederacy. In September 1865, father and son reestablished Cumberland's law school, which had closed in April 1861 with the outbreak of hostilities. The photograph at left is from an 1860 Cumberland University autograph album. (Both courtesy of C. Tracey Parks.)

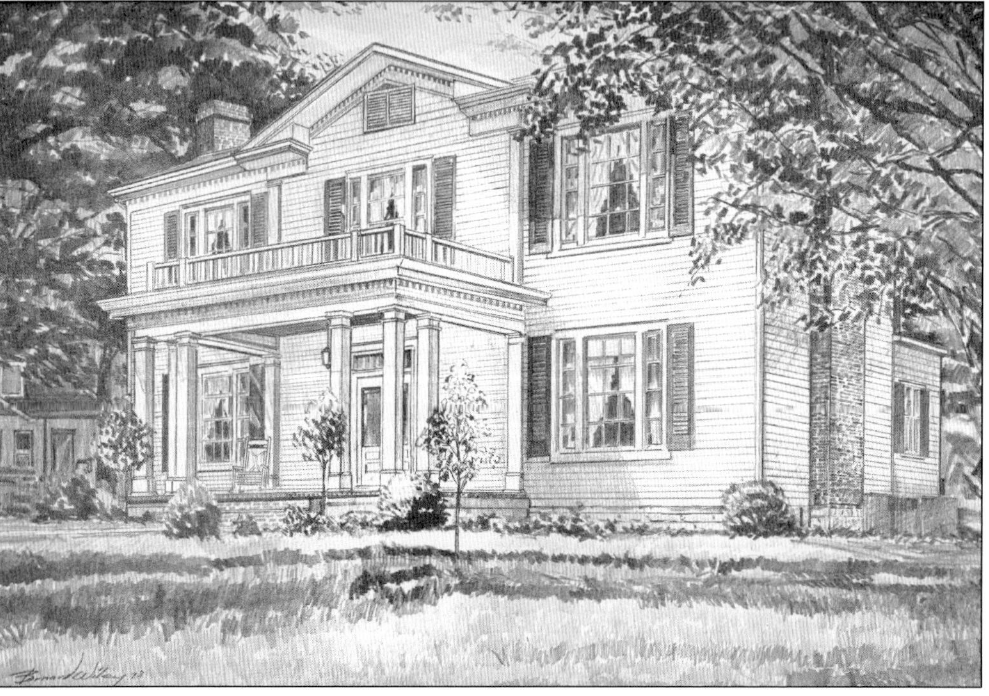

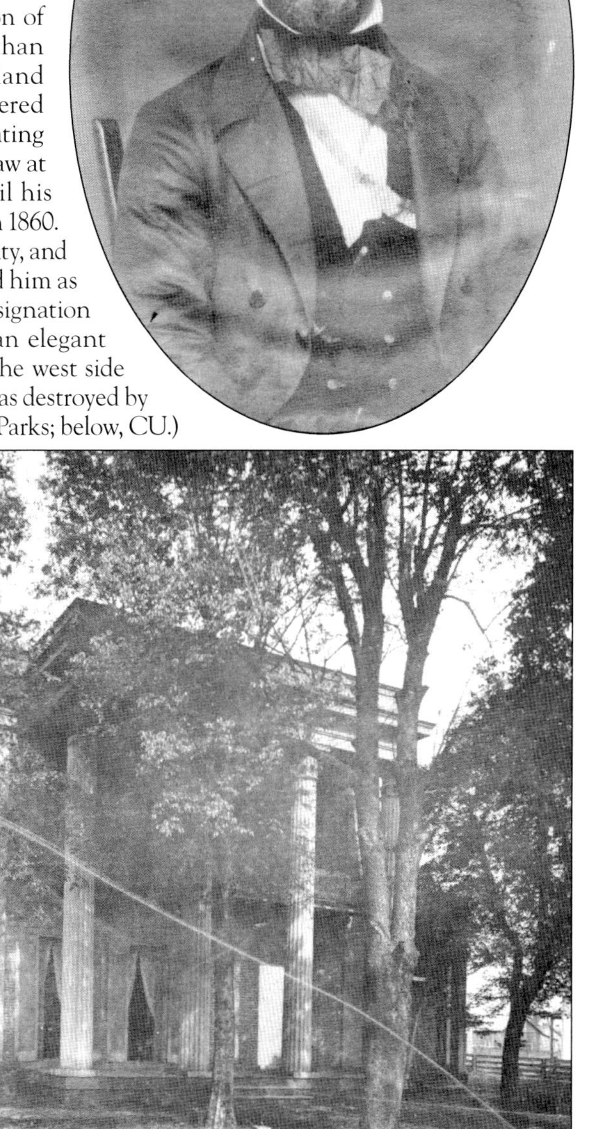

Judge Nathan Green Jr. (1827–1919), son of Tennessee Supreme Court justice Nathan Green Sr., graduated from Cumberland University in 1847, whereupon he entered the newly established law school, graduating in 1849 with Robert Hatton. He taught law at Cumberland continually from 1856 until his death. The photograph at right was taken in 1860. In 1873, he was elected to head the university, and the board of trustees officially designated him as chancellor, a position he held until his resignation in 1902. Green Jr. made his home in an elegant two-story brick house (below) built on the west side of South Greenwood Street. The house was destroyed by fire in 1912. (Right, courtesy of C. Tracey Parks; below, CU.)

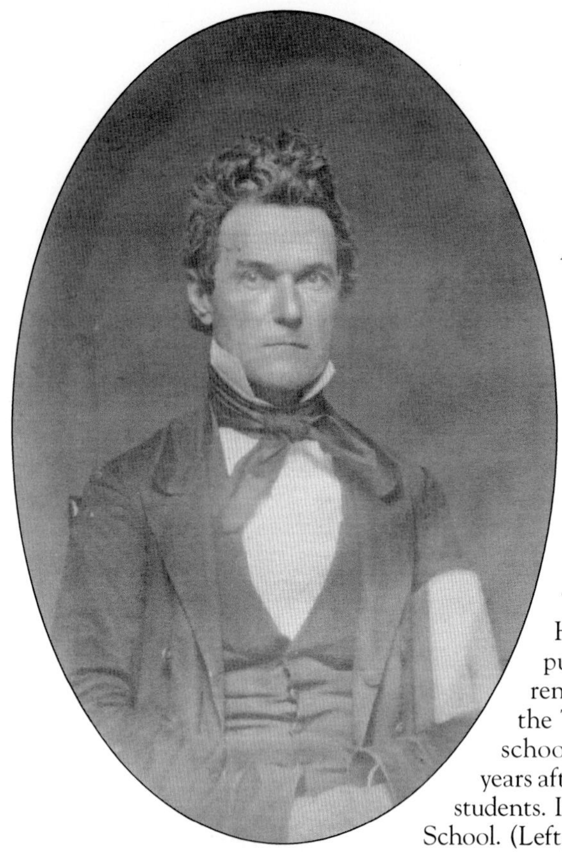

Abraham Caruthers (1803–1862) cofounded Cumberland University's law school with his brother Robert in 1847. His inaugural address at the university's fourth commencement that year publicly made the case for establishing a law school and set out its operational plan. It would be the first law school in Tennessee. Caruthers wrote *A History of a Law Suit*, which became a primary text for the school. He resided on a farm one mile west of town on the south side of the turnpike. The photograph at left was taken in 1860. His brick house (below) and 60 acres were purchased by the university in 1869 and renamed Divinity Hall, serving as home for the Theological School until 1896, when the school moved to Memorial Hall. For several years after 1896, Divinity Hall boarded theological students. It was later sold to Castle Heights Military School. (Left, courtesy of C. Tracey Parks; below, CU.)

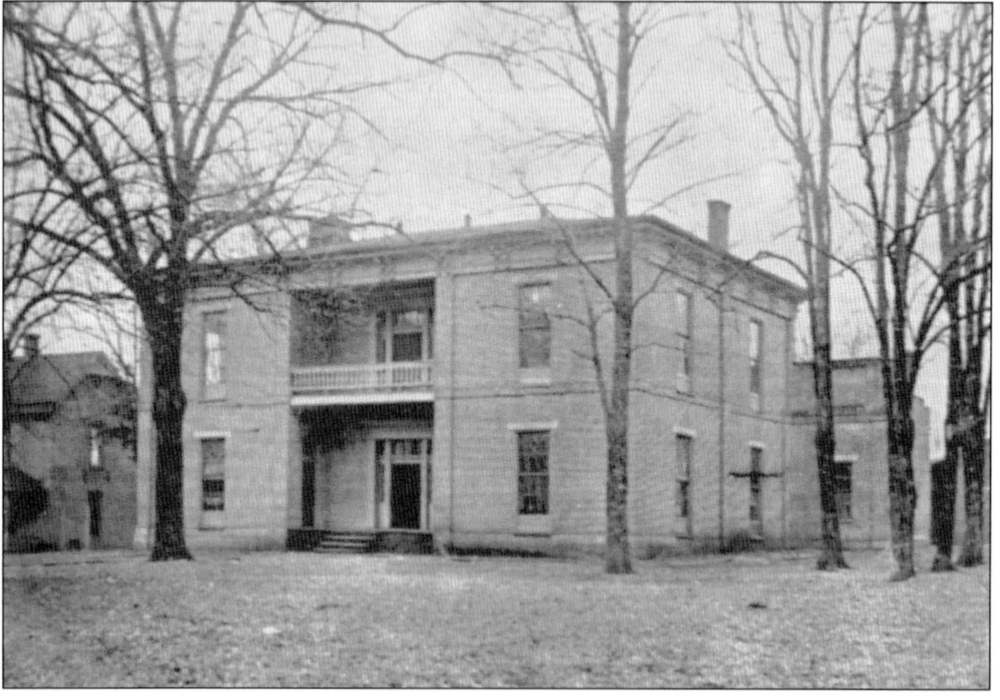

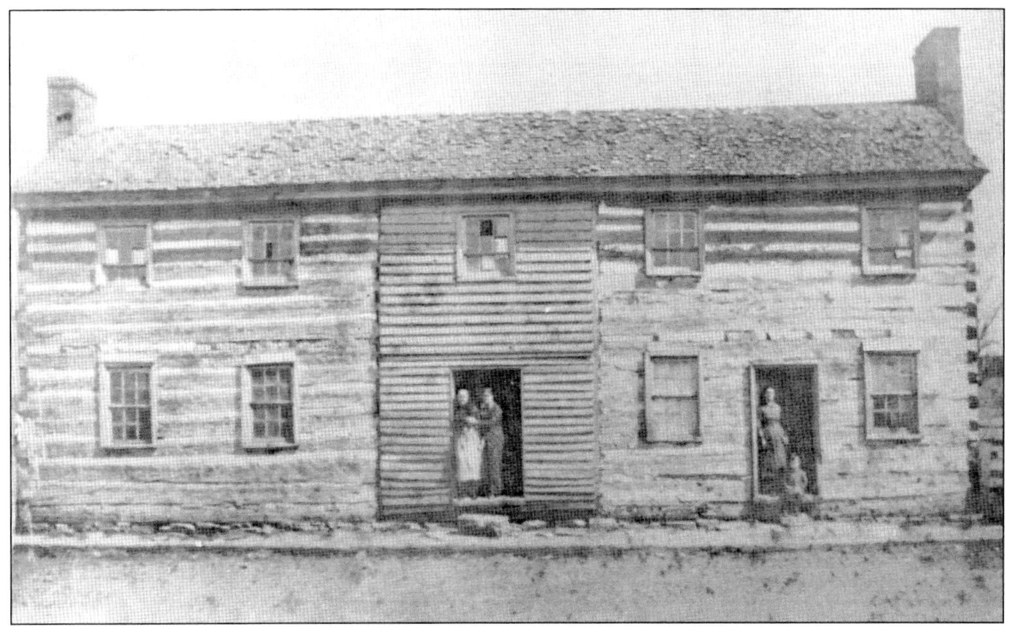

This type of cedar log structure, from around 1840, is typical of early buildings in Lebanon. Used as a meeting place for the congregation of the Lebanon Christian Church starting in the mid-1840s, this building was located at the corner of South Cumberland and Gay Streets, the present site of Shenandoah Mills. The church worshipped here for 30 years before moving to South College Street. (CLMHC.)

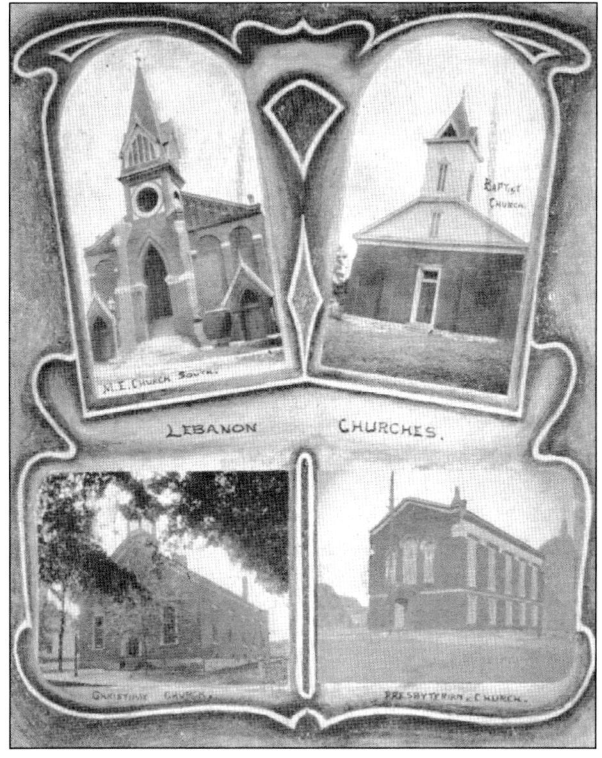

Lebanon's early churches are shown in this postcard view from 1906. They are, clockwise from upper left, First Methodist Church, East Main Street, constructed in 1856; First Baptist Church, East Main Street, built in 1849; Cumberland Presbyterian Church, in its second location, 201 North Cumberland Street, built in 1855; and the Lebanon Christian Church, at its second location, South College Street, constructed in 1874. James Drake's 1879 *Historical Sketch of Wilson County, Tennessee* records Methodists, Baptists, Cumberland Presbyterians, and Christian churches as the principal religious denominations in the county. By 1906, the First Church of Nazarene and the Church of God were also present. Churches within the town included four African American churches, as well as six others. (RWPCCU.)

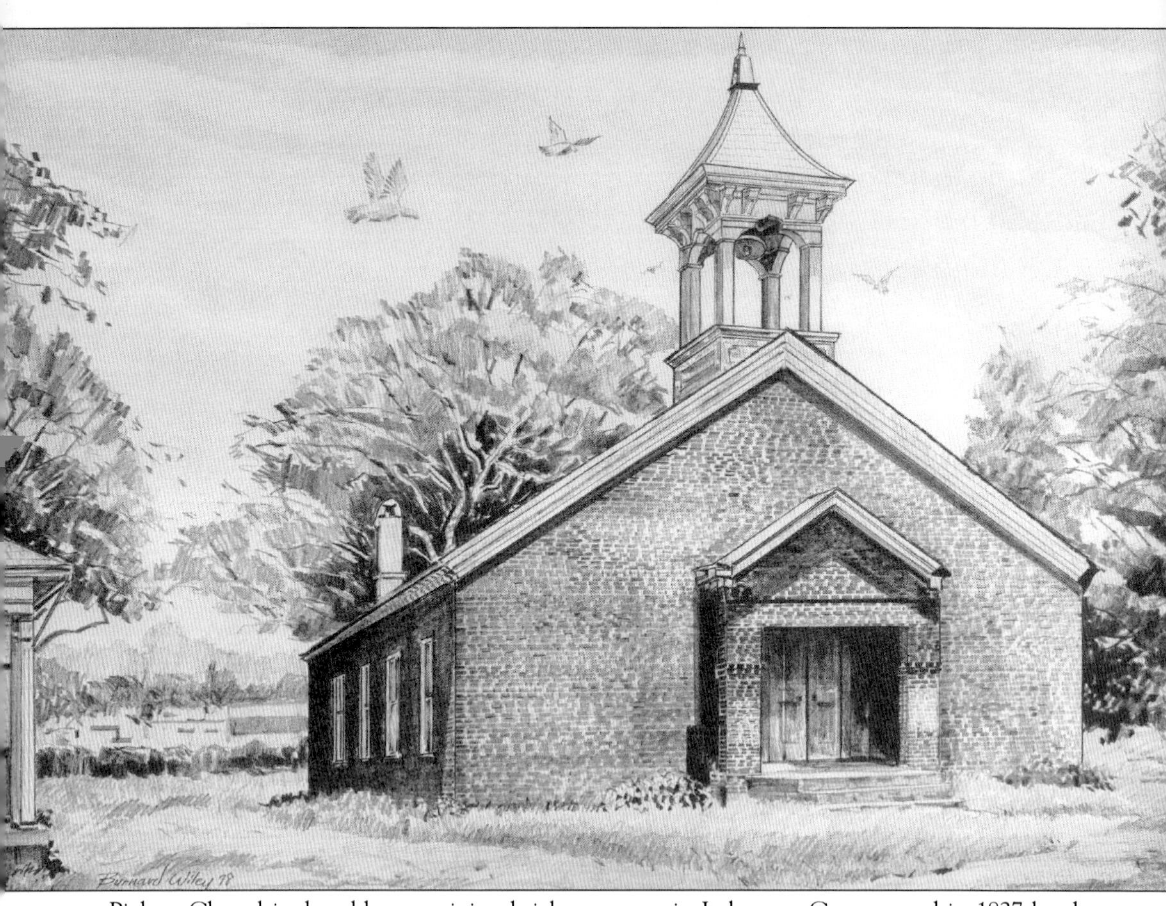

Pickett Chapel is the oldest surviving brick structure in Lebanon. Constructed in 1827 by the Methodist congregation, it is thought to be the first church built in town. White and black congregants worshipped together within the structure, with slaves and free blacks segregated to the balcony. By 1856, the church had outgrown the building and moved to a newly constructed building on East Main Street, and the African American congregation continued to worship in this chapel. On July 18, 1866, the African American Methodists purchased the building. Just one year removed from the Civil War, the $1,500 of debt acquired was a symbol of faith and courage for the newly freed congregants. The new church was named Pickett Chapel Methodist Episcopal Church in honor of its first minister, Rev. Calvin Pickett. In 1973, the church relocated to a new home on Glover Street. Listed in the National Register of Historic Places in 1977, the chapel is now owned by the Wilson County Black History Associates, who are actively pursuing its restoration. (Courtesy of the Roy Bailey African-American History Museum.)

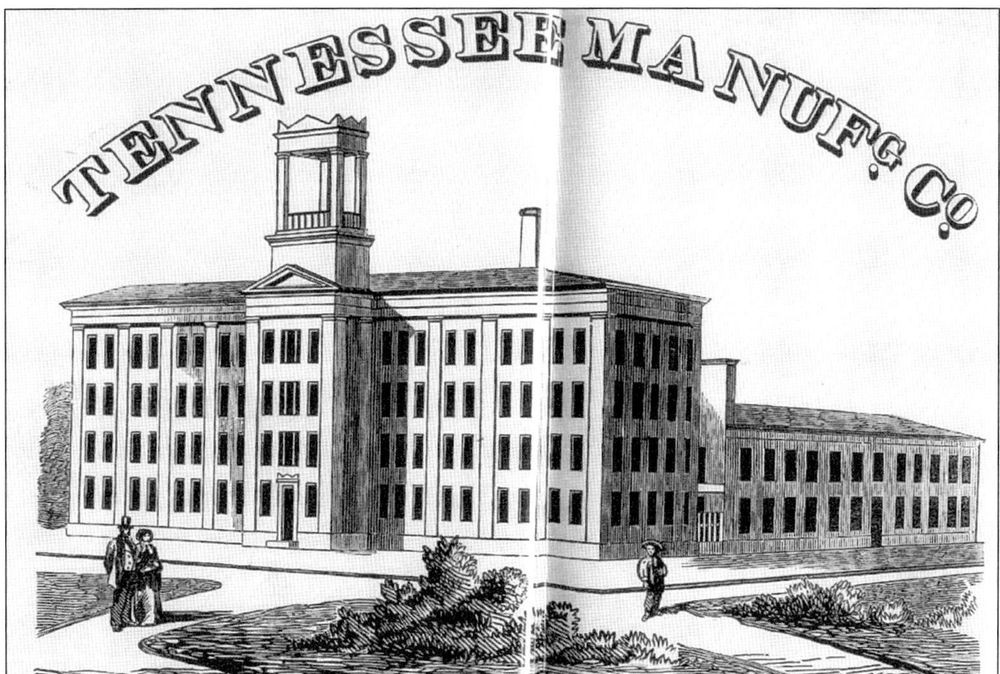

Antebellum Lebanon was home to several large manufacturing concerns. The Tennessee Manufacturing Company, established in 1844, was located on the north side of town. With over 500 employees, it produced cotton and woolen goods. Most of the workers were white women and girls, as well as some slaves hired out from their owners. By 1846, the company was producing 1,000 yards of cloth a day. (CLMHC.)

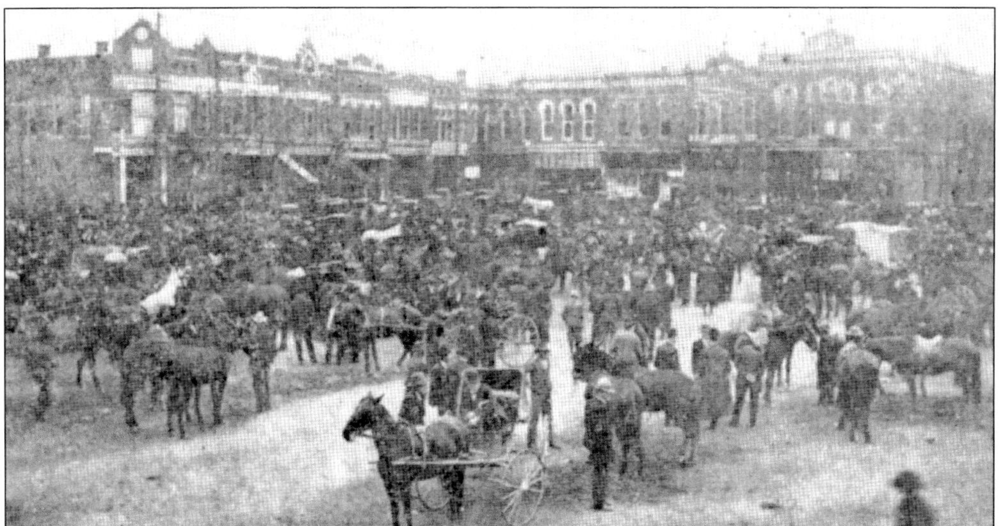

Along with manufacturing, agriculture played a major role in the economy of Wilson County and Lebanon. First Monday mule day sales on the Public Square were a constant until 1939, when the state highway department shut them down for obstructing traffic. The street livestock market was quite a lively scene; respectful ladies were careful to avoid the Square for at least two days afterwards. This photograph is from a First Monday in 1909, shortly before a fire destroyed the southeast corner of the Square. (CLMHC.)

William Bowen Campbell (1807–1867) was elected the 16th governor of Tennessee in 1851. He had gained earlier fame as colonel of the 1st Tennessee Volunteers in the Mexican border campaign. The regiment would earn a reputation as the "Bloody First." Campbell moved to Lebanon in 1853 to assume the duties of the president of the Bank of Middle Tennessee. He and his wife, Frances Owen Campbell, purchased a home on the Coles Ferry Pike, which they named Camp Bell (below). During the Civil War, Campbell held to his convictions of a unified nation, serving in the Union Army as a brigadier general. He did not hold this position for long, however; he resigned after a few weeks for health reasons and to recuse himself from fighting against neighbors and friends. He was elected to the US Congress from Wilson County in 1866. Campbell was recognized for his actions as a public servant and soldier when Fort Campbell, Kentucky, was named in his honor. (Both courtesy of Ellen Campbell Marsh and the Campbell family.)

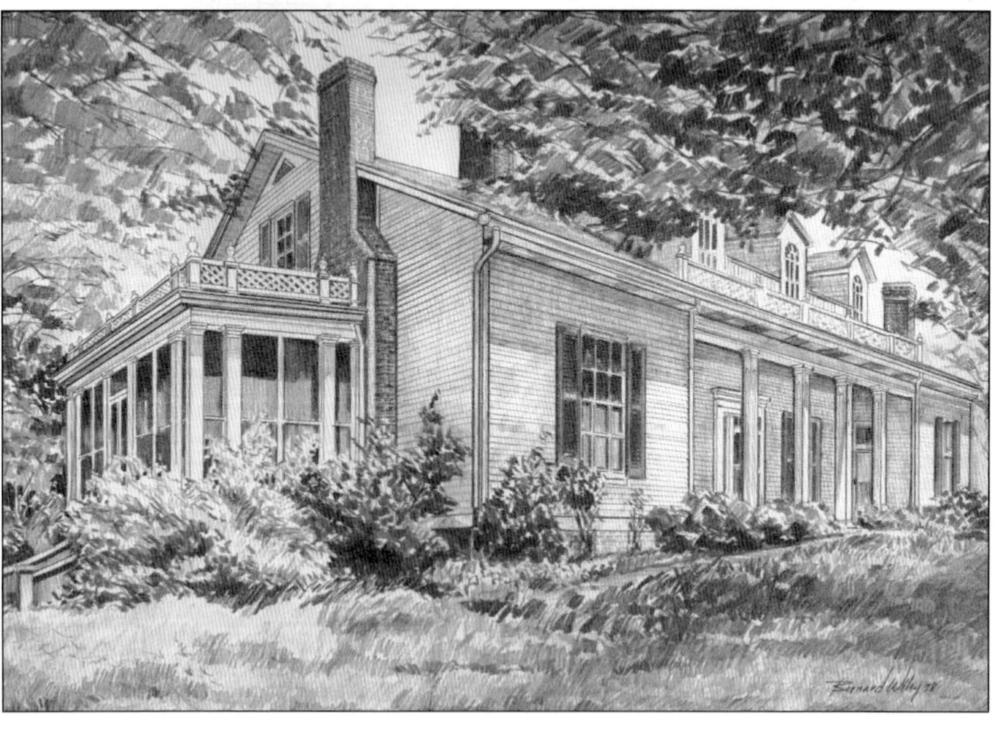

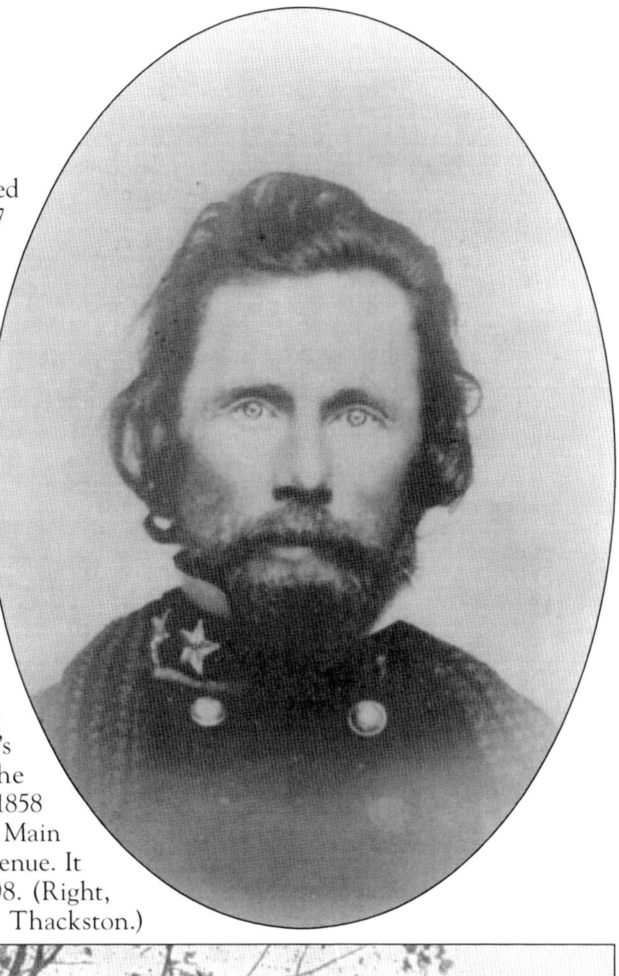

Robert Hatton (1826–1862) graduated from Cumberland University in 1847 and enrolled in the law school in 1848. Although called away from attending school, he continued his studies and received his license to practice law in 1850, returning to Lebanon to form a law partnership with Col. Jordan Stokes. In 1852, Hatton married Sophie K. Reilly of Williamson County and dissolved his partnership with Stokes, forming a new one with Nathan Green Jr. This partnership continued until 1855, the year Hatton was elected the Wilson County representative to the state general assembly. In 1861, Hatton was elected to the US House of Representative from Tennessee's fifth congressional district. The Hatton home (below) was built in 1858 and stood on the north side of West Main Street near present-day Hatton Avenue. It was destroyed by fire in April 1908. (Right, LC; below, courtesy of Edward L. Thackston.)

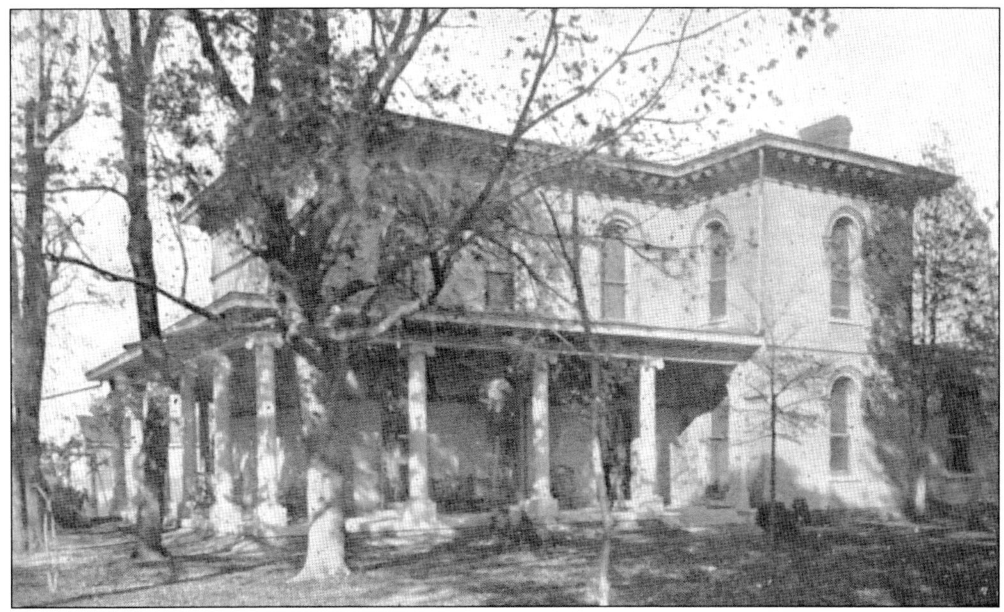

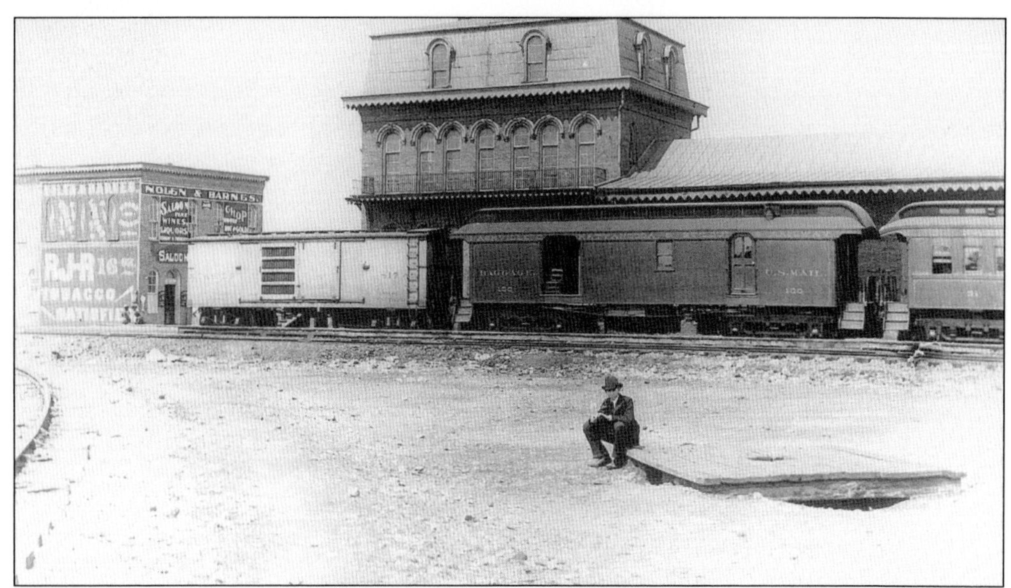

On July 4, 1869, construction began for the Tennessee & Pacific Railroad, the first railroad to service Lebanon. *The History of Wilson County, Its Land, Its Life* describes the location as "in open country about half mile south of the Lebanon Square." Judge Robert L. Caruthers moved the first spade of dirt. A four-story depot was completed for passengers and office space, seen in the photograph above. The Nashville, Chattanooga & St. Louis Railway (NC&StL) acquired the line in 1877, and in 1916, the old depot was abandoned and a new depot built closer to the Square. Below, a locomotive and railroad cars from the NC&StL are seen approaching the Lebanon station in 1896. (CLMHC.)

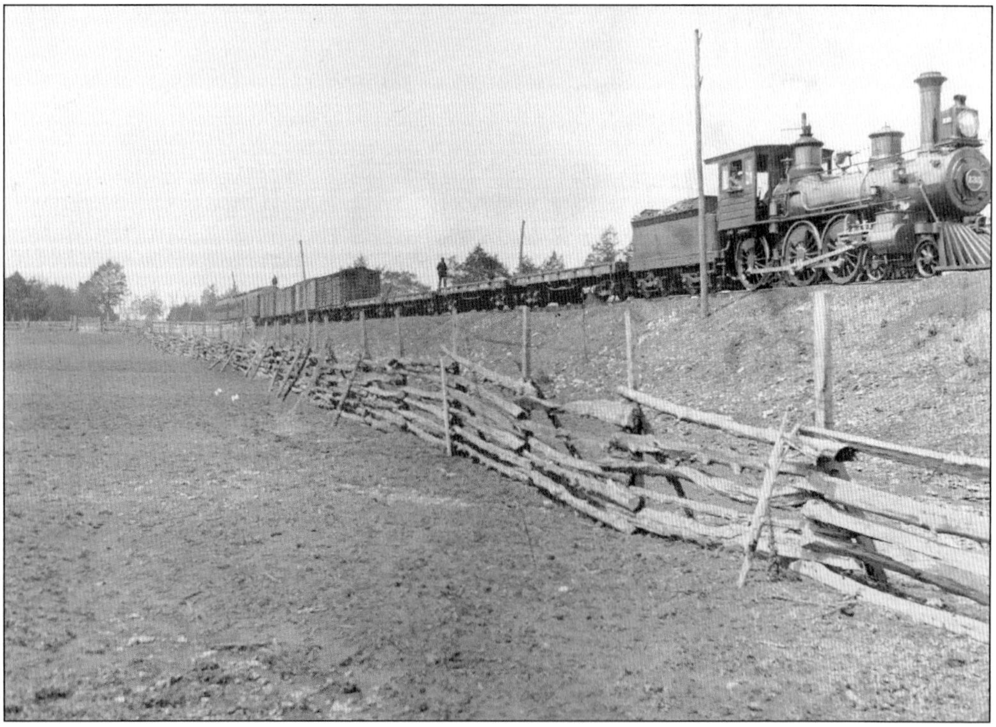

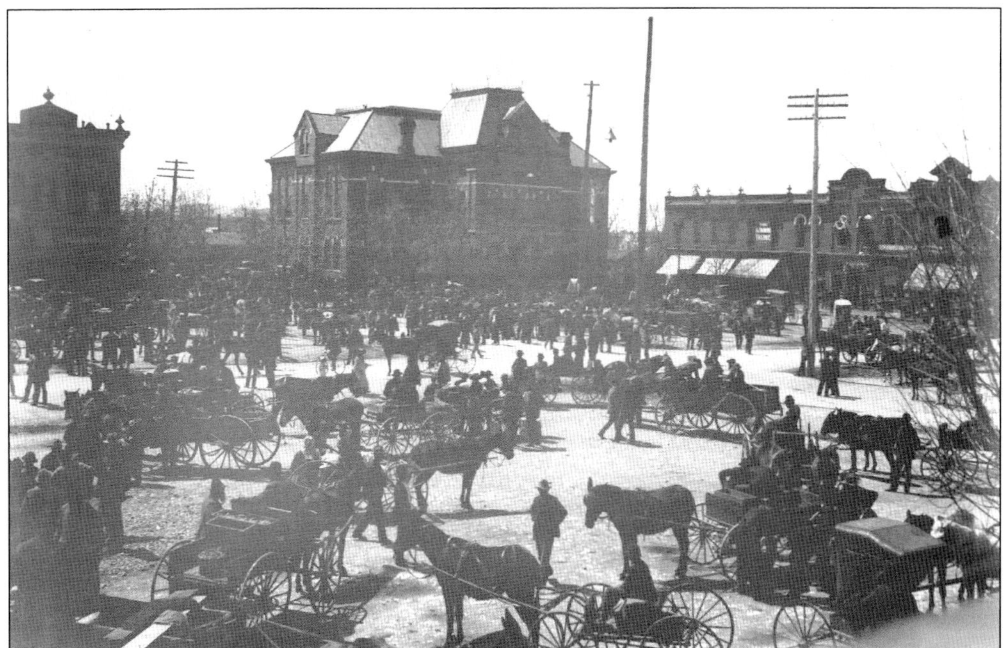

Wilson County's fourth courthouse was completed in 1884 on the site of the Strickland-designed courthouse that burned in 1881. Built at a cost of $18,306, it contained two large courtrooms and offices for county officials. An impressive brick structure with a mansard roof, it stood until it was demolished in 1968. (BC.)

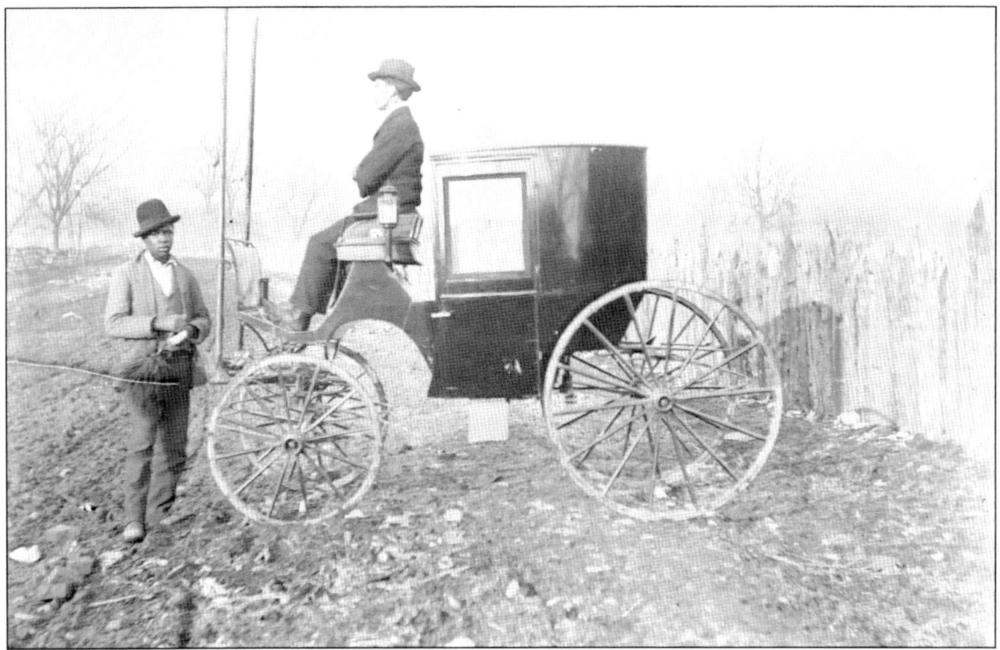

Lebanon, as described by James V. Drake in *An Historical Sketch of Wilson County, Tennessee, From its First Settlement to the Present Time* in 1879, supported three carriage and wagon shops, two saddle and harness shops, and three blacksmith shops. These were necessary to acquire and maintain the mode of transportation of the times; an example is illustrated here. (CU.)

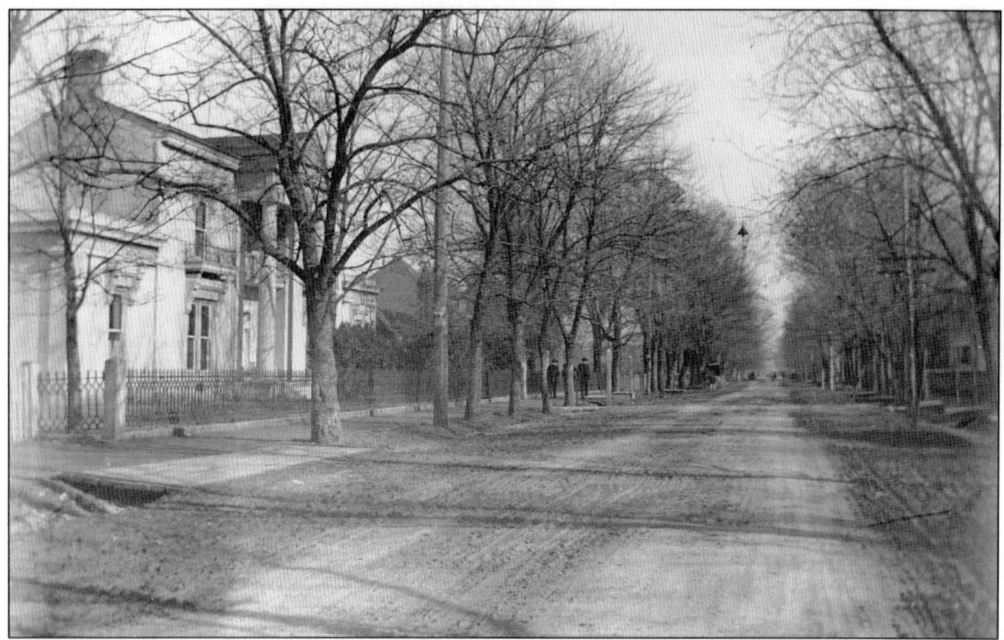

In the first half of the 19th century, West Main Street began filling with many fine, stately homes. The photograph above, looking east from Greenwood Street in the 1890s, shows the Robert L. Caruthers home to the left and the many trees that lined the street. According to Eastin Morris in his *Tennessee Gazetter*, Lebanon was known as a beautiful small town, "with its white limestone roads and dark evergreen trees." Even though this area was the site of fine homes, open pastureland could also be found in its midst. Nearby, on the corner of West Main and Greenwood Streets, Benjamin Foster had pastureland for cattle as late as the 1910s. This mix of farming and "neighborhood" was common. In fact, most homes in the city had space for livestock and cultivation. The photograph below shows a cattle drive through Lebanon in 1896. (Both, BC.)

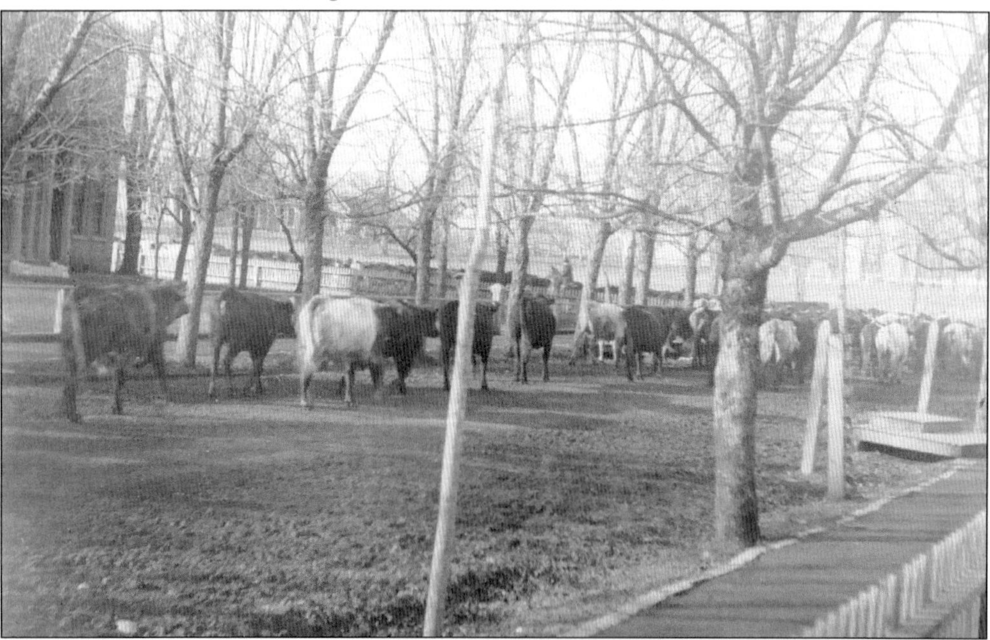

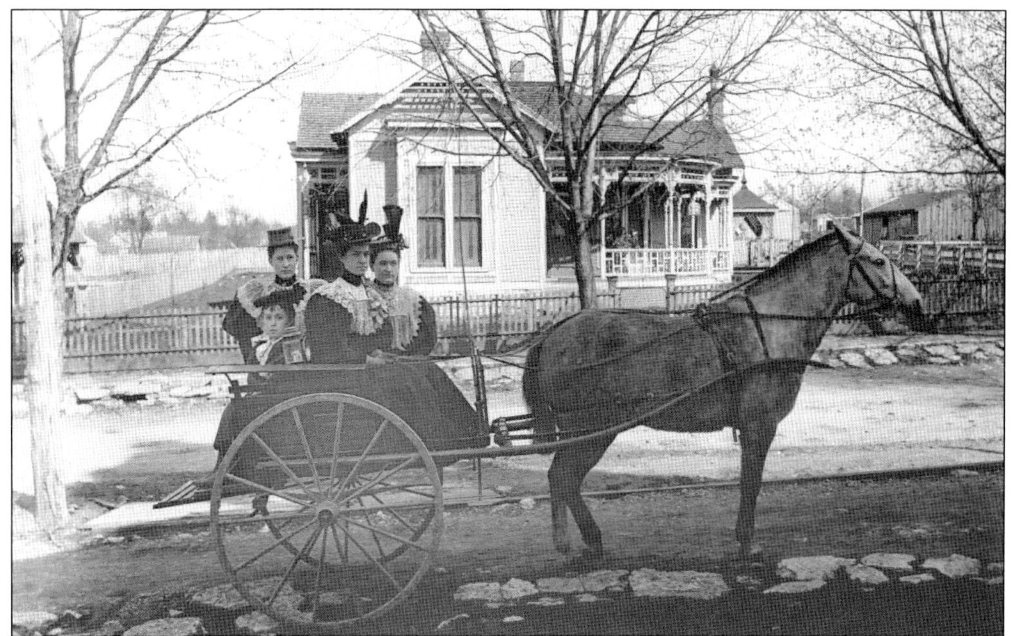

Lebanon's growth during this time was not to the west, as in current times, but instead centered around the Square and Cumberland University's first campus on College Street. Pictured in 1894 are, from left to right, (first row) Bessie Weir Doak and Alice Williamson Bone; (second row) Amy Weir and Martha Martin Burke. The ladies are enjoying a carriage ride in front of the Weir home, at 133 South College Street. (BC.)

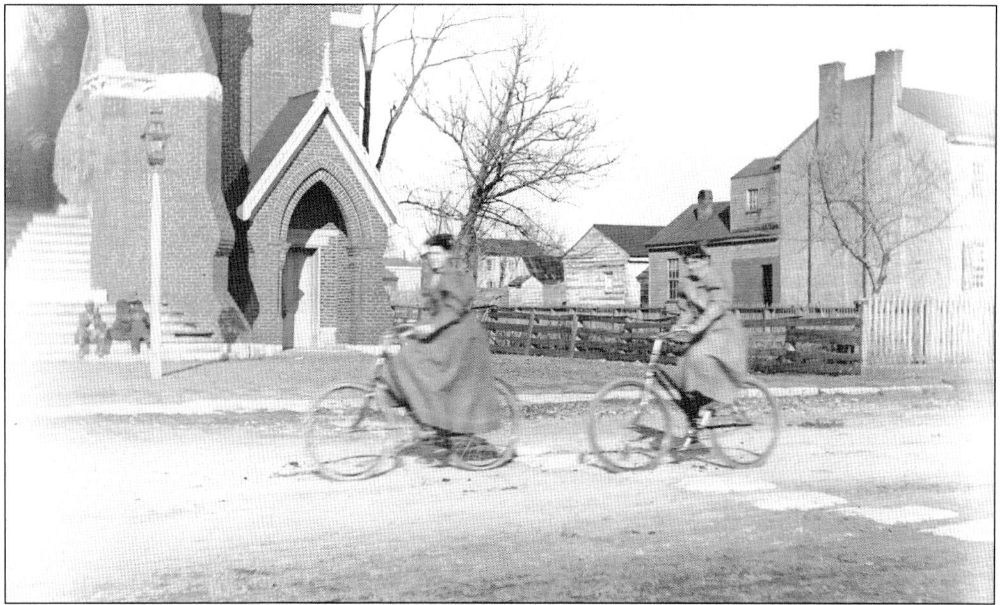

East Main Street was also a thriving place in early Lebanon. Churches, schools, fine homes, and the county jail were all located here as early as 1832. In this photograph, Alice Williamson Hooker and Emma Beard ride their bicycles in front of the First Methodist Church (left) and the county jail (right). The jail burned in 1896 and was rebuilt on a lot just south of the courthouse on the Square. (BC.)

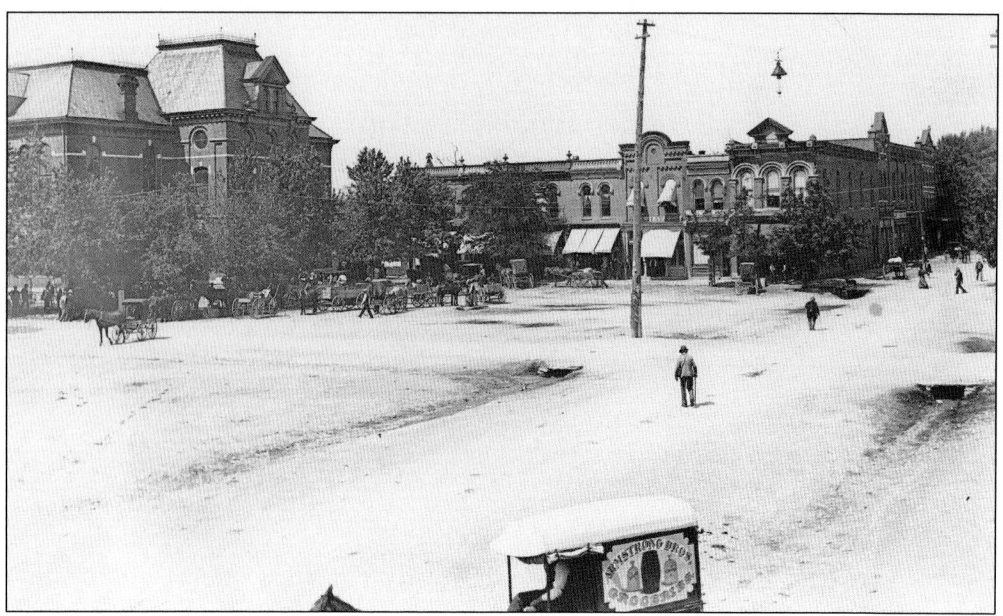

In the third quarter of the 19th century, Lebanon's Public Square was beginning to slowly thrive again. After suffering two major fires in which two blocks of business were destroyed, times were improving. By James Drake's account in 1879, some of the enterprises Lebanon had were six dry goods stores, three drug and book stores, ten family groceries, two hardware stores, one merchant tailor, two millinery shops, three tin and stove shops, two jewelry shops, one bakery and confectionary, two furniture stores, two undertakers, three barbershops, four hotels, two national banks, two newspapers, and five saloons. Most, if not all, of these establishments were located on the Public Square or a block off it. The photograph above shows the courthouse and the southwest side of the Square, and the photograph below shows the northeast corner during a monthly mule day sale or sweet potato day. Both were taken in 1896. (Both, BC.)

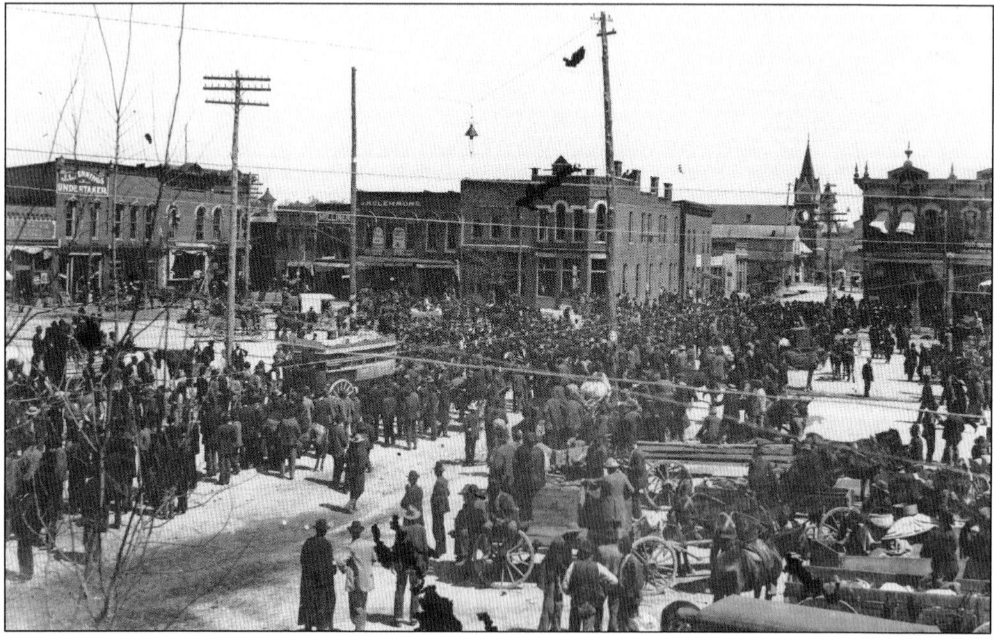

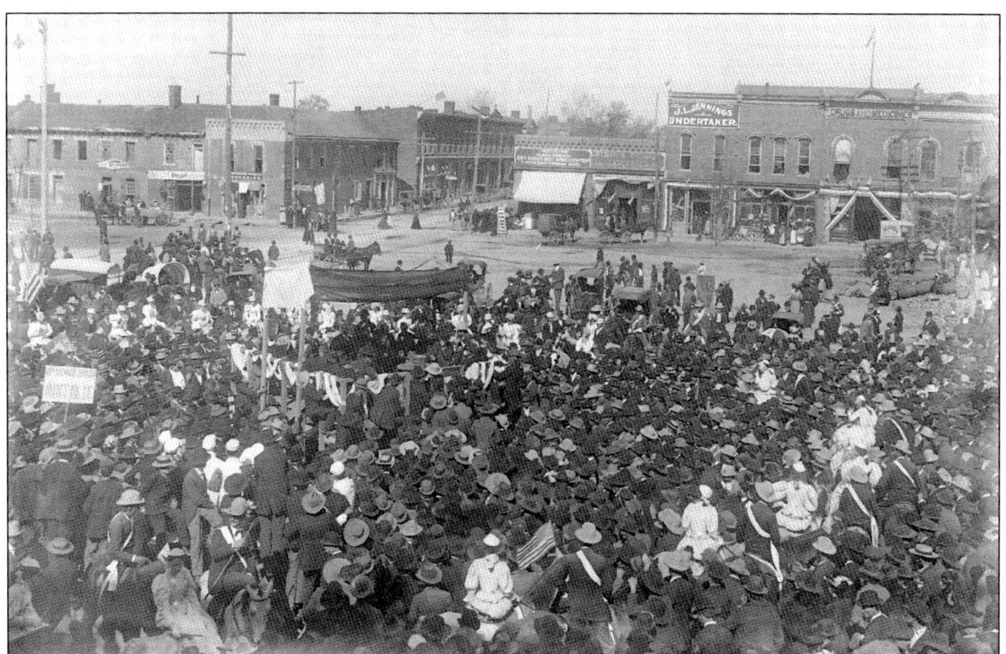

Lebanon's Public Square was not only a center of commerce; it was also often the site of political rallies. The photograph above captures a stop on the Square during William Jennings Bryan's presidential campaign in 1896. Bryan, the Democratic nominee, campaigned on the Free Silver platform, advocating the free coinage of silver at a ratio of 16:1, silver to gold. The young ladies on horseback circling the speaker platform, one in gold and sixteen in white, illustrated this populist ideal during his campaign stops. The photograph below, from 1896, shows the southeast quadrant of the Square with an electrical pole to the left. Lebanon's first phone line from Nashville was run in 1882, and the first electrical lights were turned on in 1880. Also seen in the left background are the First Methodist Church and First Baptist Church, both on East Main Street. (Both, BC.)

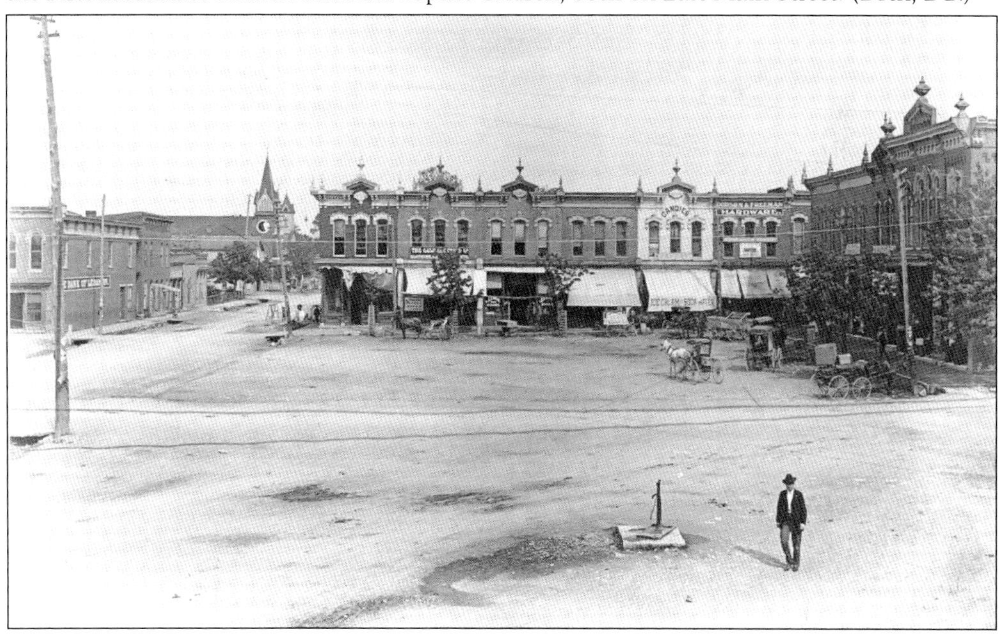

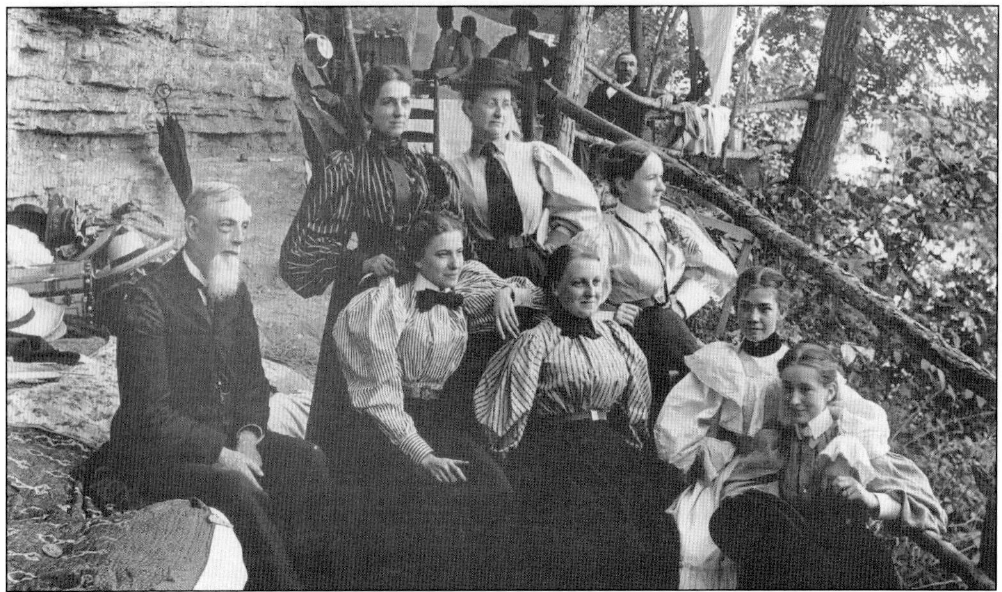

Judge Nathan Green Jr. was one of Lebanon's most prominent citizens. Respected as a professor of law, he was also known for his gregarious personality and active social life. One frequent activity was an adventure to Weir's Castle, at Hunter's Point on the Cumberland River. In the photograph above, Green is shown with, from left to right, (first row) unidentified, Mary Prewitt, Bessie Weir Doak, and Martha Martin Burke; (second row) ? Fitzgerald, Mary Fonville, and Alice Williamson Hooker. The ladies were day visitors, with the men staying on to camp sometimes for as long as two weeks in the summer. The photograph below shows the makings of the camp with the men under a shelter to the back. Men who participated in the camp included Ben Dillard, I.W.P. Buchanan, Bob Weir, J.M. Fakes, and Amzi Hooker. (Both, BC.)

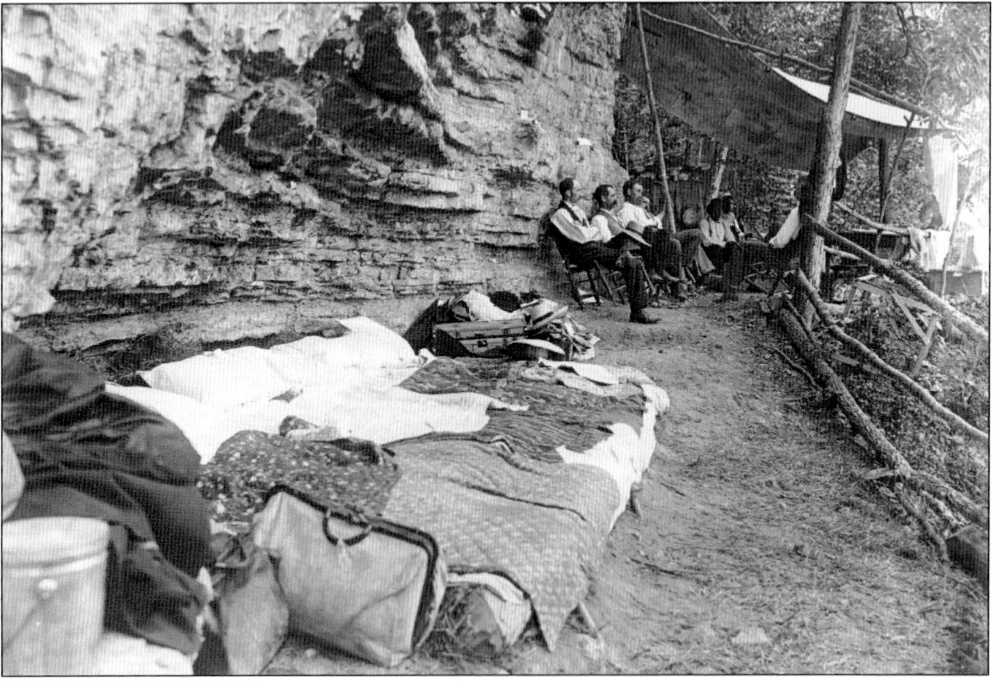

Isaac William Pleasant "I.W.P." Buchanan (1866–1943) came to Lebanon as a child when his father, Dr. A.H. Buchanan, accepted a teaching position at Cumberland University. Buchanan received his bachelor's and doctorate degrees from Cumberland and served as a professor of mathematics at the school from 1894 to 1898. Buchanan was a natural at mathematical and mechanical applications. He held several patents and, in addition to founding the Castle Heights School in 1901, designed its Main Administration building. Buchanan married Willie Conn Elkins in 1892. They are pictured at right, standing behind their camera. One of Buchanan's hobbies was photography. Below, a sketch by Burnard Wiley shows the Buchanan home at 428 West Main Street. The Queen Anne–style Victorian house is a George Barber design. Barber was a well-known American architect headquartered in Knoxville in 1888. The home was listed in the National Register of Historic Places in 1979. (Right, BC; below, CU.)

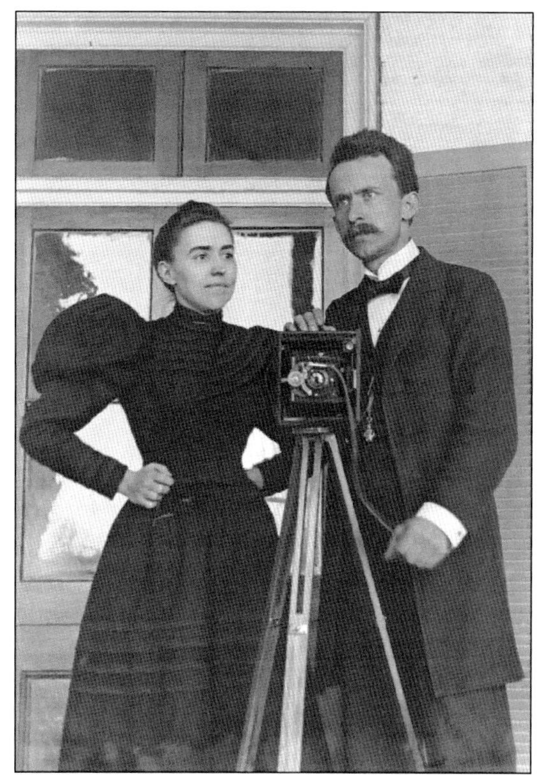

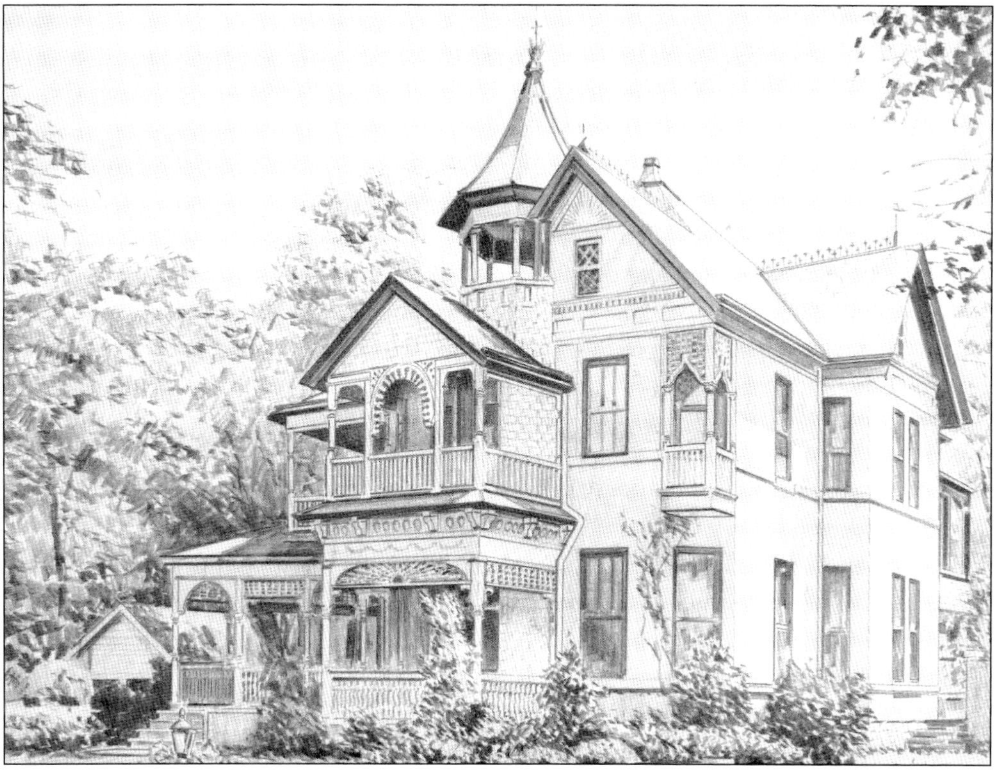

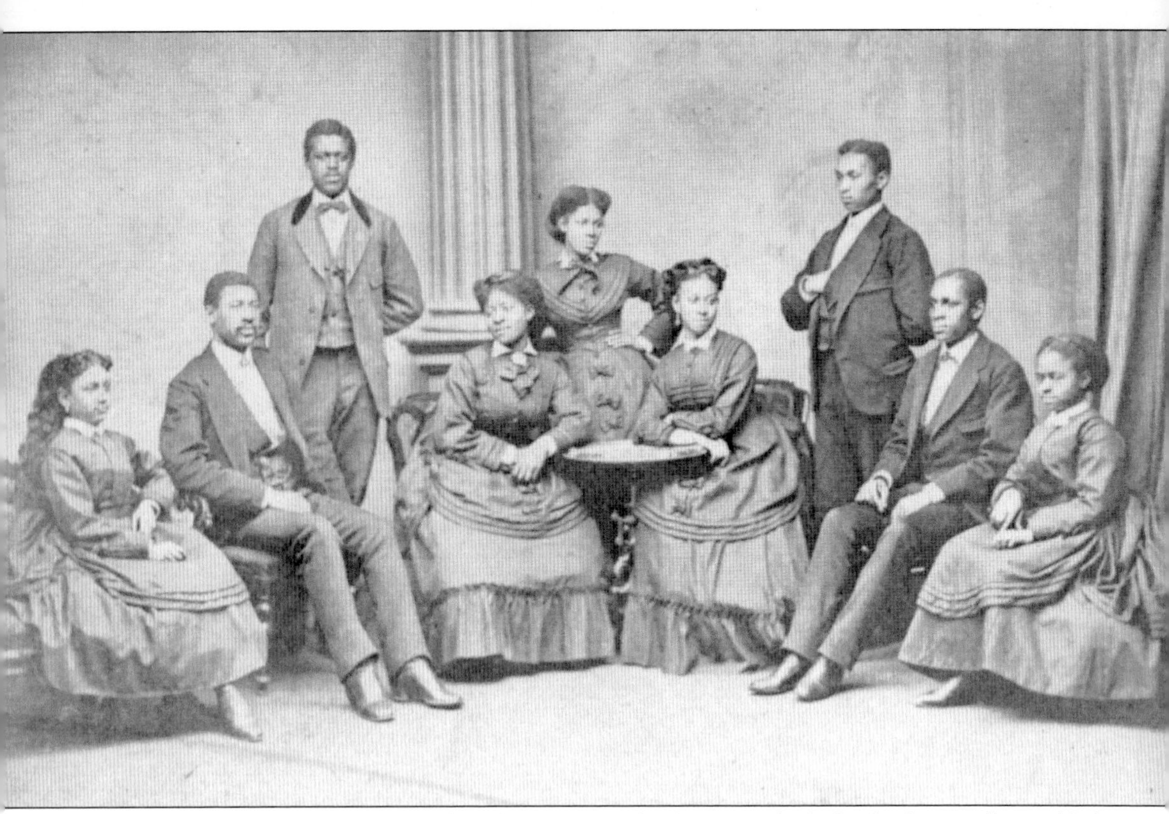

The original Fisk Jubilee Singers formed in 1871 as a fundraising vehicle for the financially troubled Fisk University, which had begun five years earlier at the end of the Civil War to educate freed African Americans. George L. White organized the nine original members (from left to right): Minnie Tate, Greene Evans, Isaac Dickerson, Jennie Jackson, Maggie Porter, Ella Sheppard, Thomas Rutling, Benjamin Holmes, and Eliza Walker. The a cappella group left Nashville on October 6, 1871, for an 18-month tour of eastern cities. They are credited with introducing the Negro spiritual to the world. With two additional members, the group toured Great Britain and Europe, performing for Queen Victoria in 1873. Members Maggie Porter and Thomas Rutling were born in Lebanon in 1853 and Wilson County in 1854, respectively. (LC.)

Two

Education

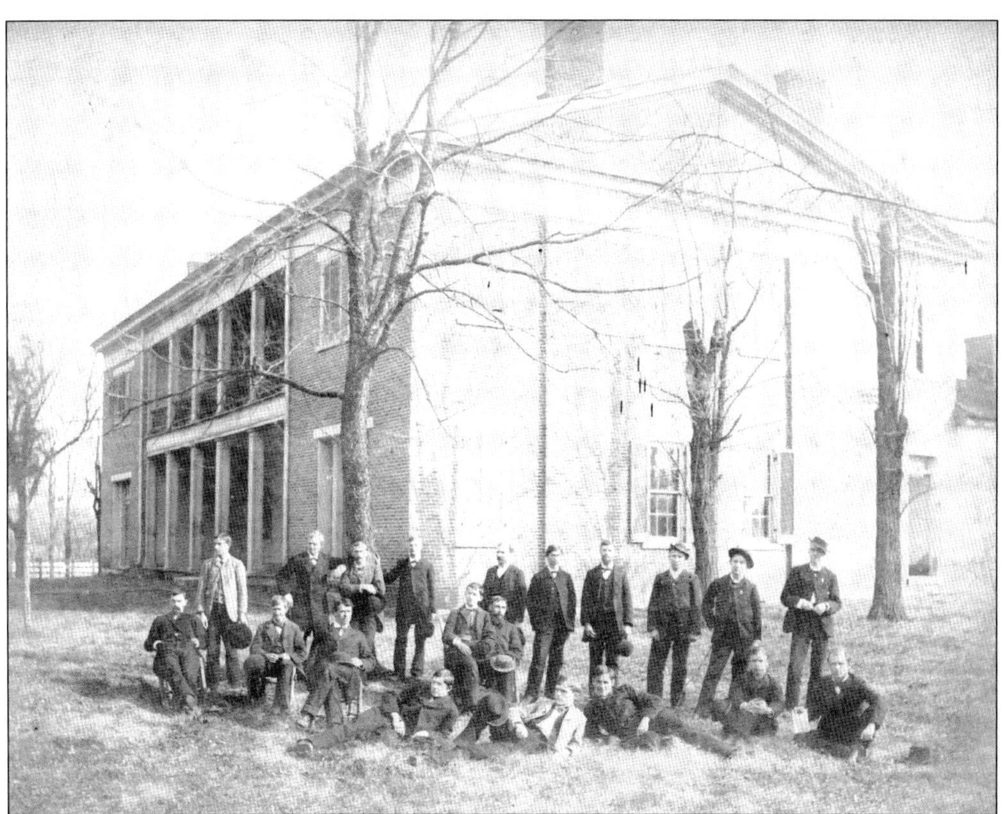

Cumberland University had not celebrated its 20th anniversary when the Civil War began in 1861. The law school closed in April, and the College of Arts followed in February 1862. They were both closed for the duration of the conflict. When the school reopened in 1865, it abandoned its original campus. In 1873, Corona Hall on West Main Street, seen here, became home to the College of Arts, which stayed there until 1896. Fire destroyed this structure in 1903. (CU.)

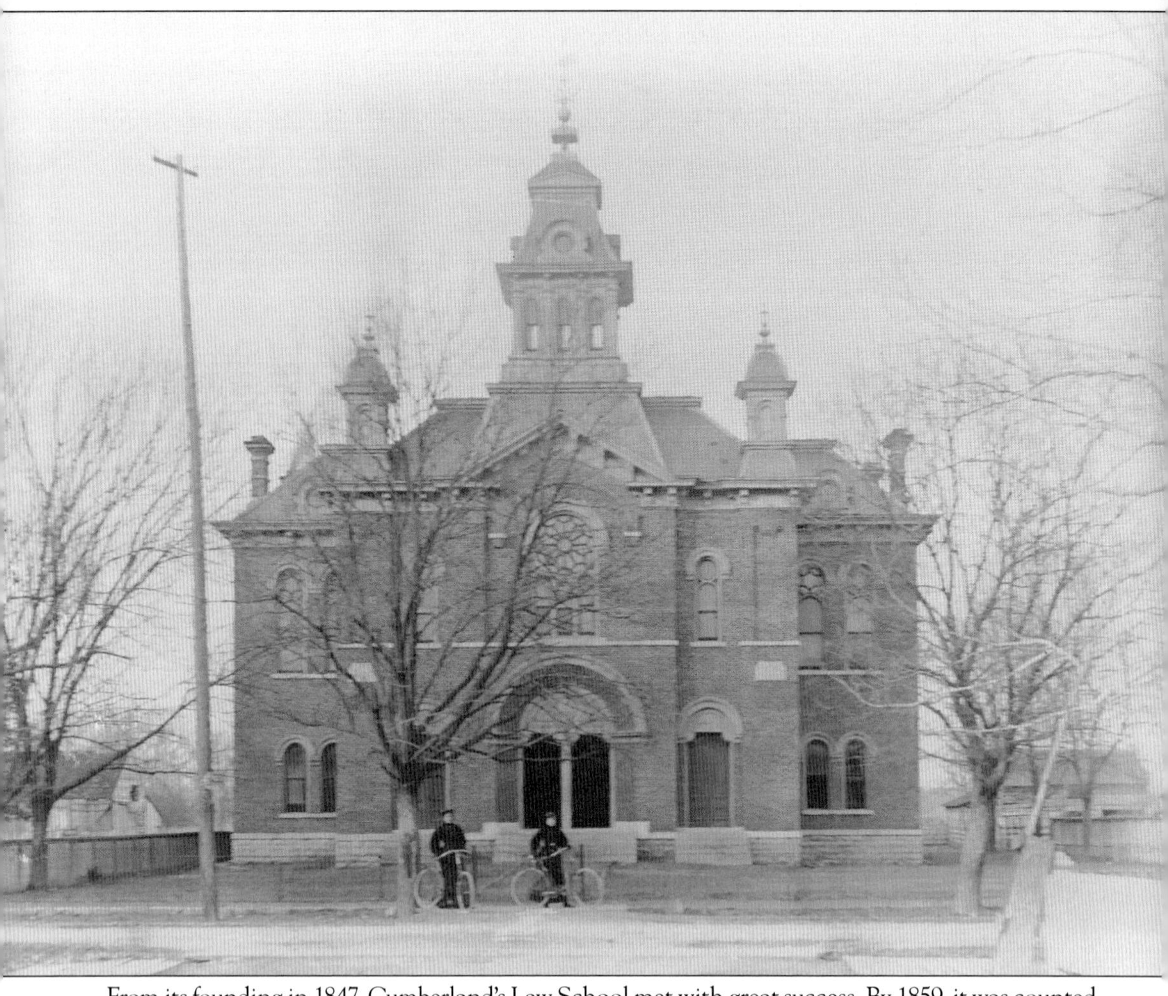

From its founding in 1847, Cumberland's Law School met with great success. By 1859, it was counted with Harvard and the University of Virginia as one of the nation's three largest law schools. Following the destruction of the original university building, the law school, which reopened in 1865, lacked a permanent home. From 1873 to 1878, classes were taught in Corona Hall. In 1877, Robert L. Caruthers gifted a lot just west of his home on West Main Street and $10,000 to Cumberland University in order to build a structure to house the law school. With additional contributions of $25,000, Caruthers Hall was built and placed in use in 1878. Known as the "Law Barn," it sat opposite the South Greenwood Street terminus into West Main Street until it was razed in 1962, the year after the law school's sale to Samford University of Birmingham, Alabama. (BC.)

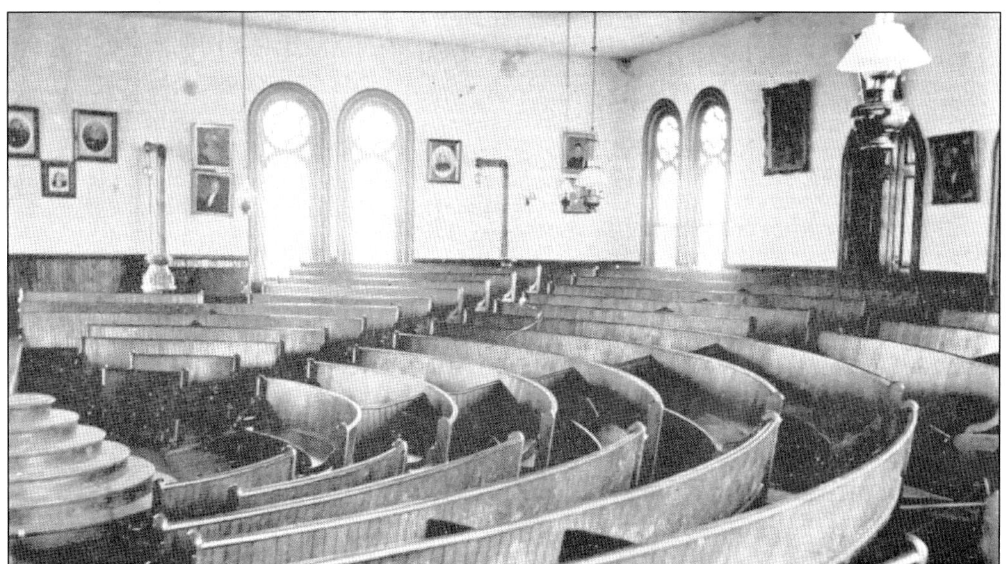

A large auditorium occupied the second floor of Caruthers Hall, where portraits of university leaders were prominently displayed for the public's view. This space, seen here, was conceived both for university exercises and community use and could seat an audience of 1,100. The original woodstoves and hanging kerosene lamps are seen in this early photograph. (CU.)

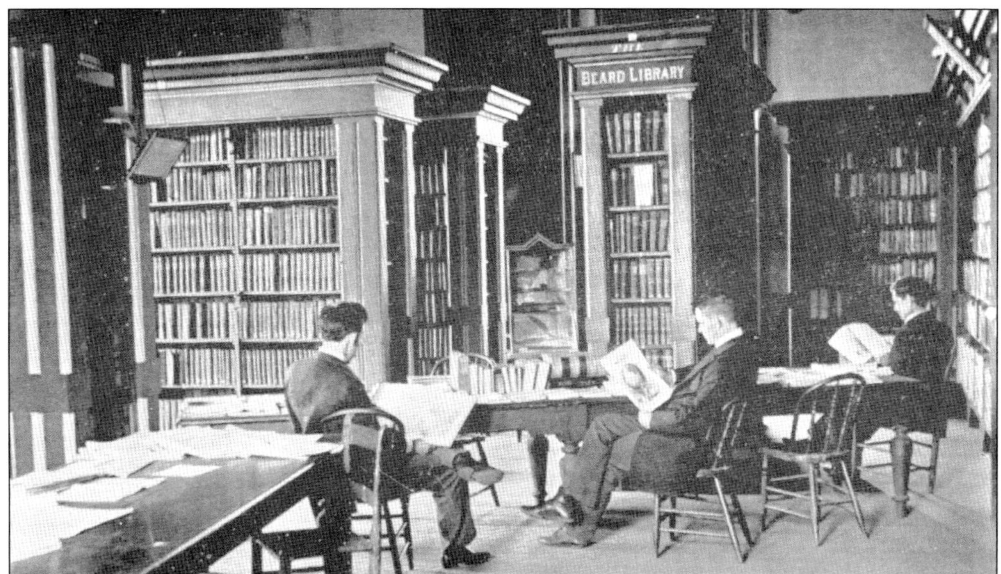

With the completion of Caruthers Hall, all departments of Cumberland University's libraries became centrally located in the building. This library space served the entire university until 1896, when, with the completion of Memorial Hall, the Caruthers Hall library became devoted exclusively to the school's law library. This 1895 photograph is from *The Phoenix*, Cumberland University's yearbook. (BC.)

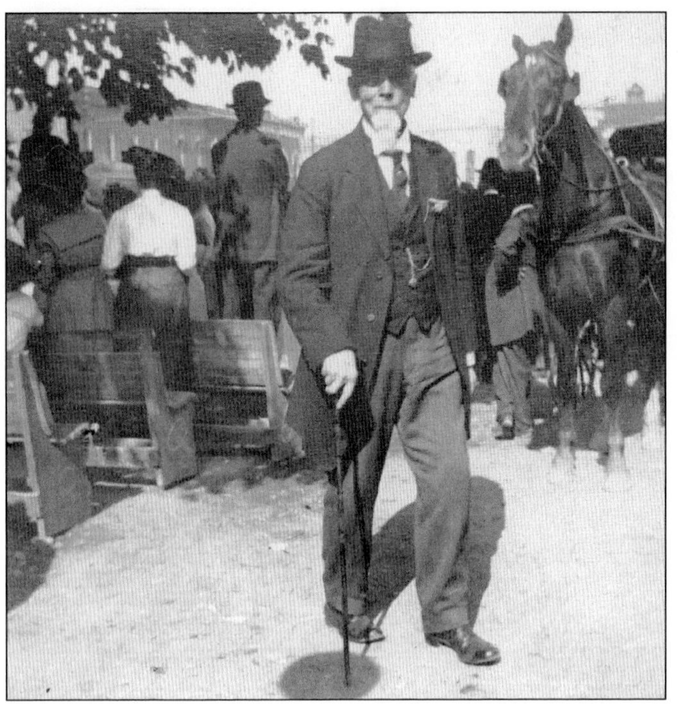

Nathan Green Jr. is seen here around 1900 at an event on Lebanon's Public Square. In addition to his duties at Cumberland University, Green frequently wrote newspaper articles under the pseudonym "Over Forty." A collection of these articles was published by Green in *Sparks from a Backlog* in 1891, which followed his first effort, *The Tall Man of Winton*, a fictionalization of his father's life. (CU.)

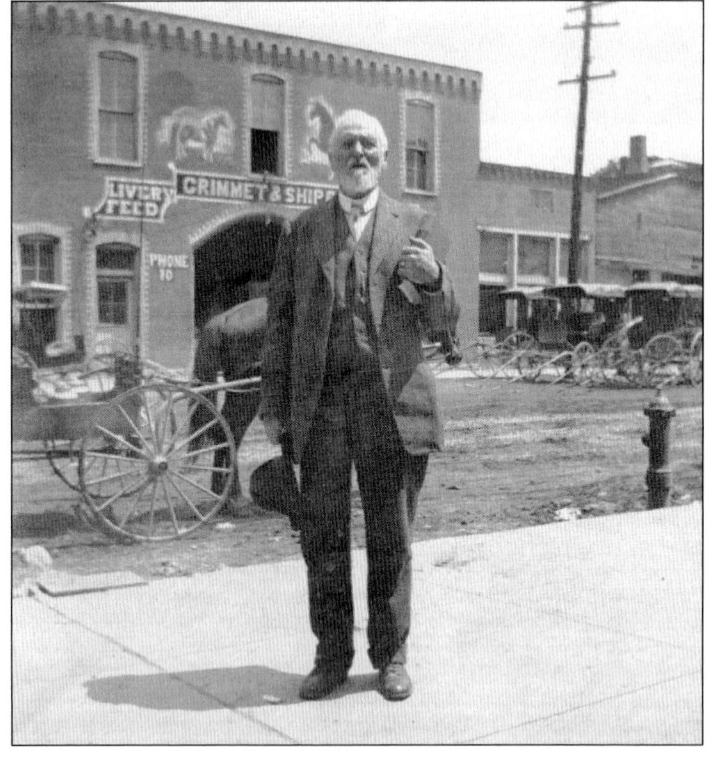

Andrew B. Martin (1836–1920) graduated from Cumberland's law school in 1858 and went on to be a successful attorney. In 1878, he became a professor of law at Cumberland, a position he held until 1920. He enlarged, annotated, and revised Caruthers's *History of a Law Suit* and also served as president of Cumberland's board of trustees from 1882 until his death. (CU.)

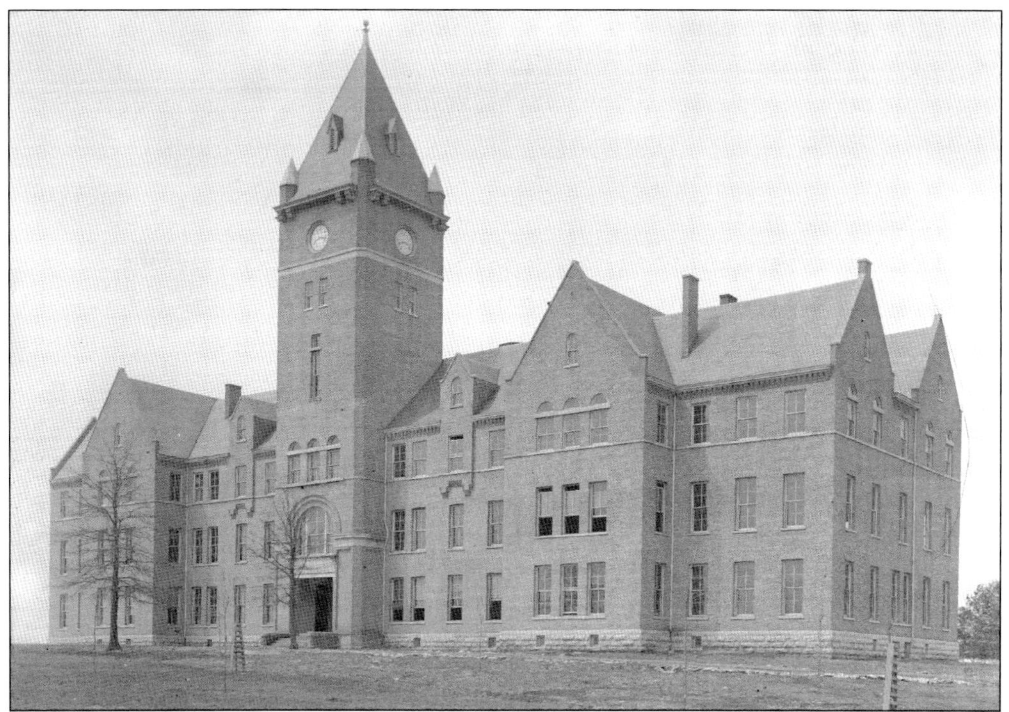

The cornerstone for Cumberland University's Memorial Hall was laid in 1892 near the center of a 55-acre campus on the southwestern border of Lebanon. Construction continued until September 1896, when classes were first held in the new structure and this photograph was taken. The College of Arts occupied the first floor, and the Theological School met on the second. Several years passed before the third floor was finished. (CU.)

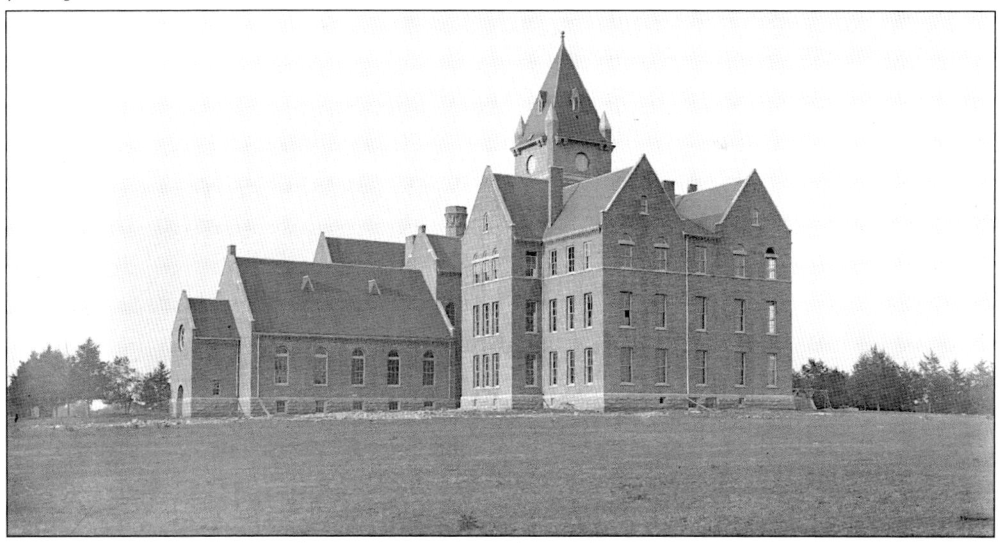

The plans for Memorial Hall were the product of Dr. John Iredell Dillard Hinds (1847–1921), a professor of chemistry, and Nashville architect W.C. Smith. It included a chapel that projected from the west elevation, the interior of which was not finished until 1903. When completed, the space boasted an elegant, painted Art Nouveau ceiling, but poor acoustics led to its conversion to gymnasium space. In 1939, it was restored to its original purpose. (CU.)

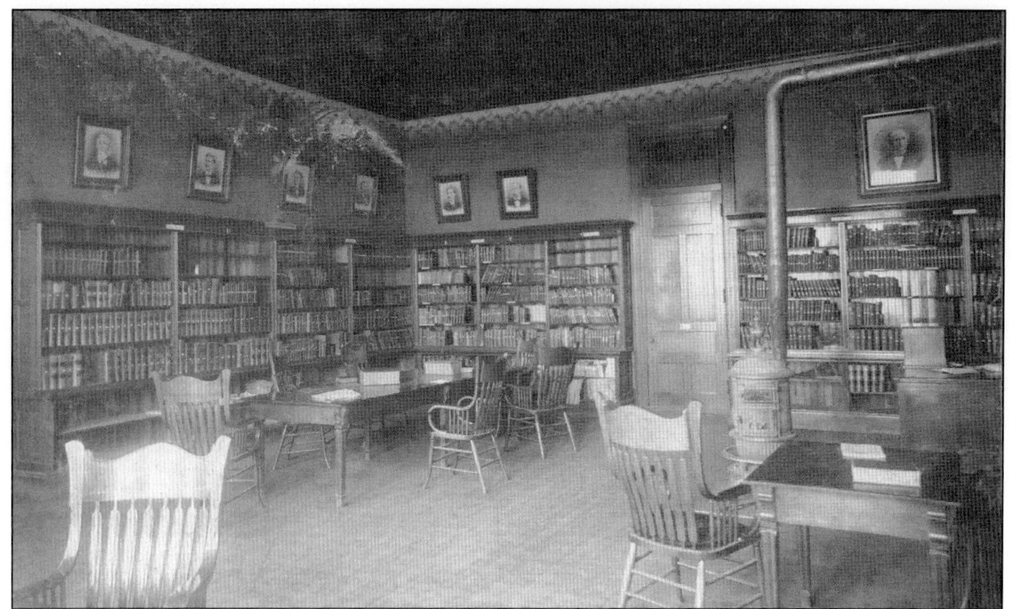

The Theological School maintained its separate library on the second floor of Memorial Hall, which was named the Hale Library for Mrs. E.J. Hale of Morristown, Tennessee, who contributed $1,000 for its original furniture and equipment. It would hold 3,000 volumes by 1906. Woodstoves like the one seen here served as the only source of heat for the building when it was first occupied. (CU.)

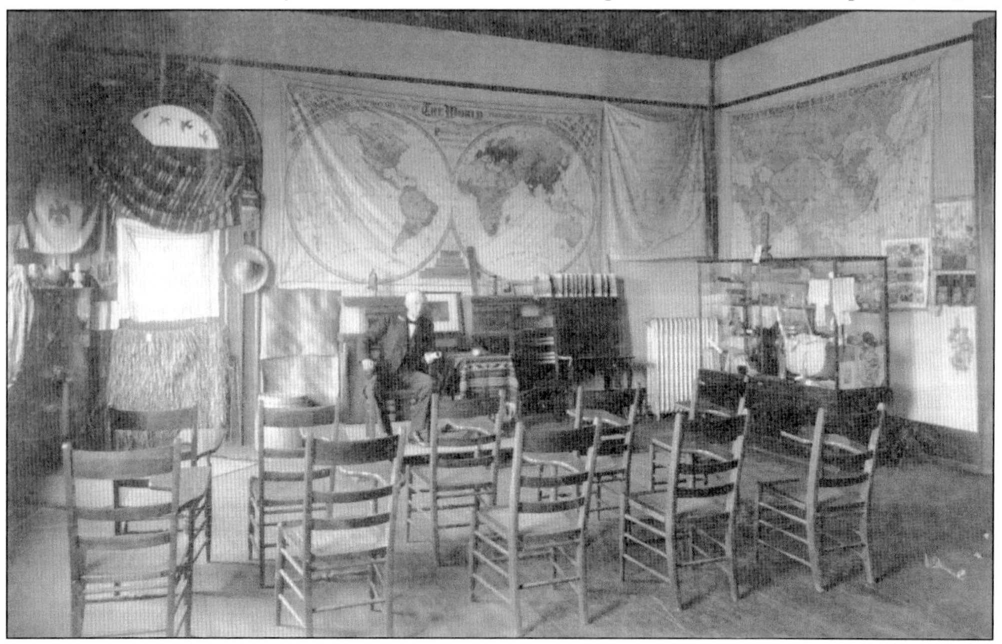

Cumberland University's theological department existed from 1854 until 1910, when it closed following a Tennessee Supreme Court decision invalidating the union of the Cumberland Presbyterian Church with the Presbyterian Church USA. Previous to that, space located on the north end of the third floor of Memorial Hall was devoted to the display of cultural relics from foreign missions. The Mission Museum included artifacts from China, Japan, India, Mexico, and Samoa. (CU.)

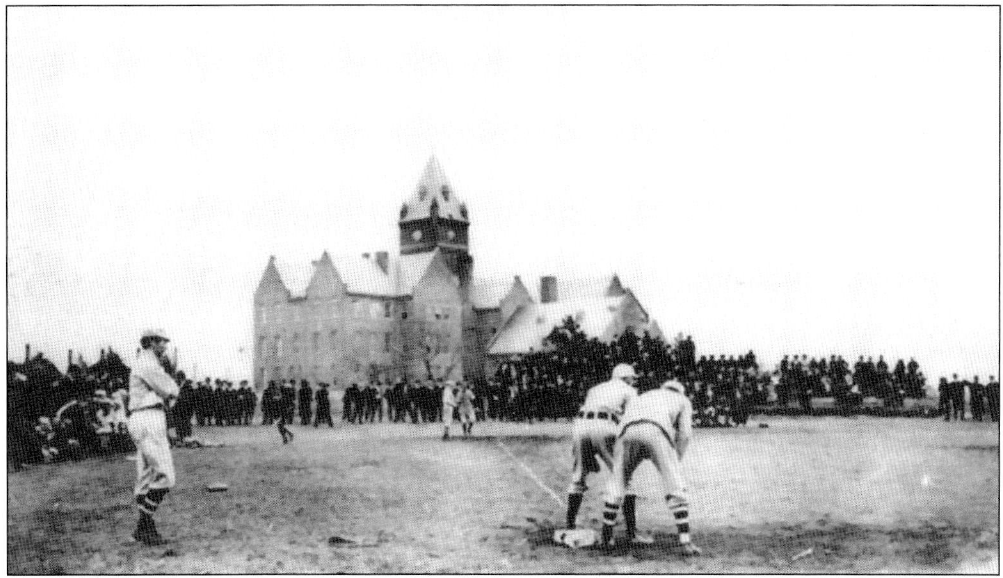

Cumberland began participating in intercollegiate athletics in 1889. The northwest corner of the campus served as the site of athletic events from 1894 until 1922 and featured a baseball diamond as well as a football gridiron. Professional baseball teams often stopped for a game on the way north from spring training. Cumberland's 1902 baseball team was undefeated save for two contests lost to the Milwaukee Brewers. (CU.)

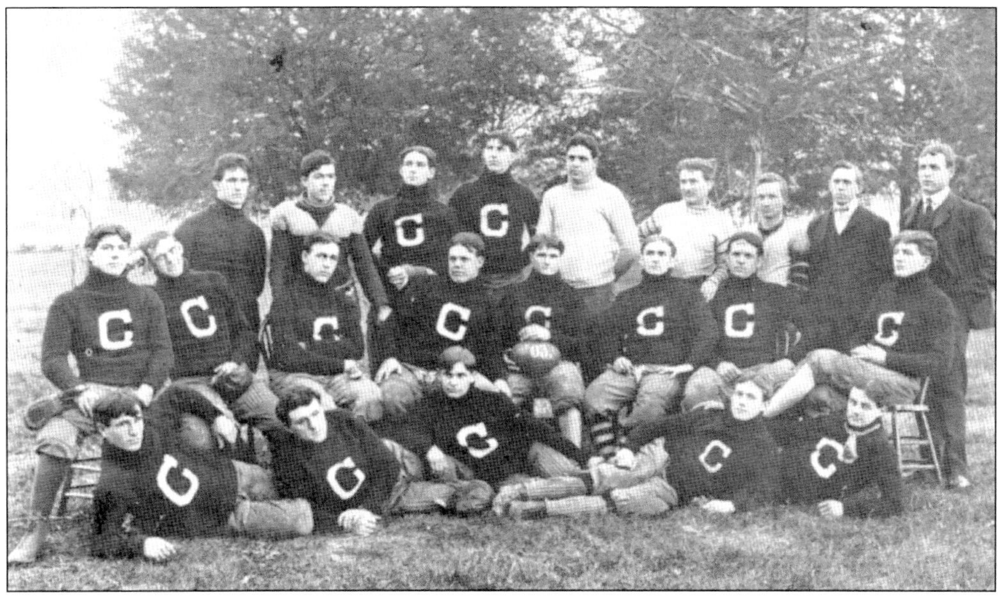

The 1903 football squad (pictured) outscored their opponents 308-17, after which the team played Clemson to a tie in the first invitational postseason championship game in the South. More famously, in 1916, Cumberland was outscored 222-0 by Georgia Tech, coached by John Heisman. At a spirited 1956 reunion held in Atlanta, a former Tech player quipped, "This rematch is fixed. How do they expect 22 engineers to out-talk six lawyers?" (CU.)

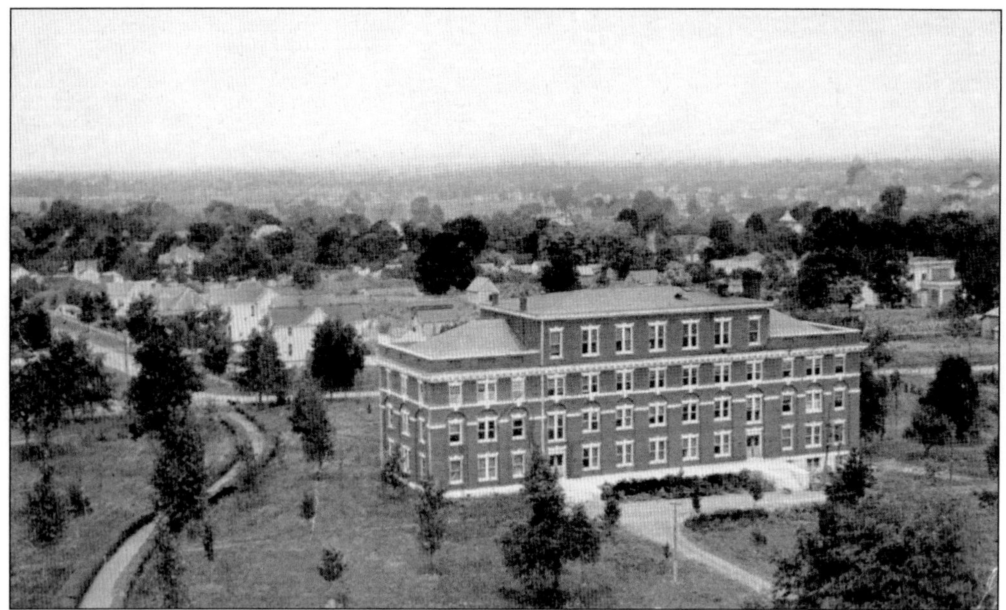

In 1903, the university erected its first significant structure since Memorial Hall, a men's dormitory. The impressive four-story structure was located on campus and constructed parallel to West Spring Street. This dormitory space offered the first opportunity for students to reside on campus since the destruction of the original university building, which included living space in addition to its classrooms. (RWPCCU.)

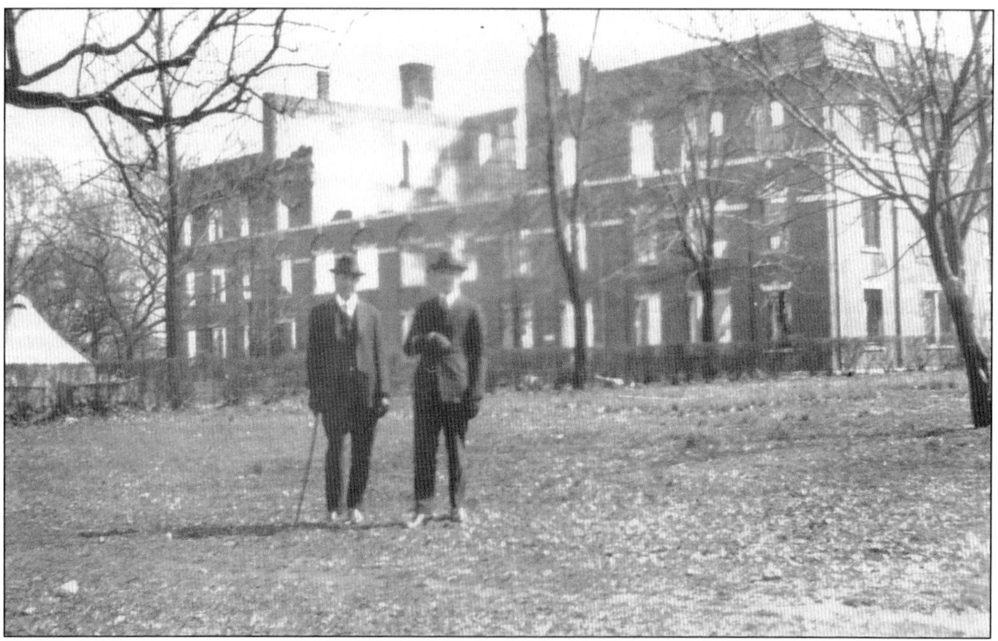

Fire swept through the men's dormitory in 1925, leaving only the outer walls largely intact. The building was quickly rebuilt, this time with the fourth floor extending the full length of the structure. In 1951, this second dormitory was named for Winstead Paine Bone Sr. (1861–1942), the university's sixth president, who authored *A History of Cumberland University* in 1935. Fire consumed the building again in 1957. (CLMHC.)

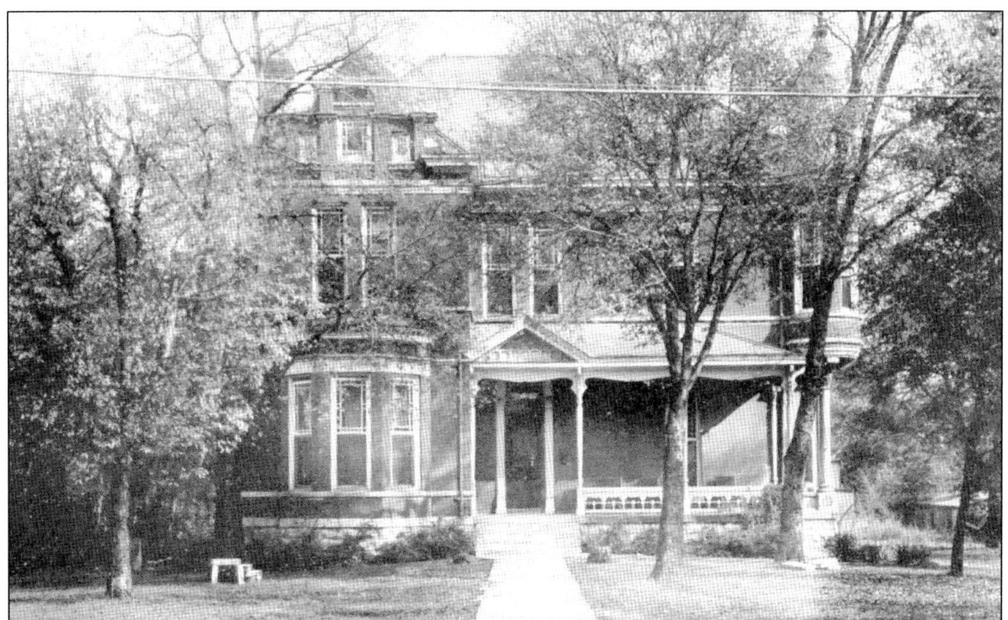

This large brick dwelling stood on the north side of West Main Street east of Hatton Avenue. It was built in the 1890s by John Iredell Dillard Hinds (1847–1921), the university's professor of chemistry and biology from 1873 to 1899. The school became coeducational in 1897. In 1932, when this photograph appeared in the university's 90th-anniversary edition of *The Phoenix*, the house was being used as a women's dormitory. (CU.)

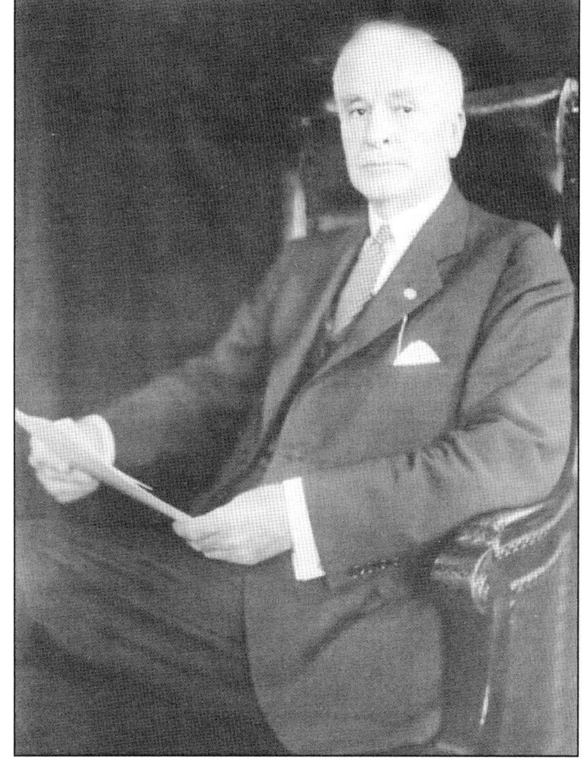

Cordell Hull (1871–1955) is probably Cumberland's most famous graduate, having received his law degree in 1891. He was elected to 11 terms in the US House of Representatives and also served as a US senator from Tennessee. From 1933 to 1944, he held the office of secretary of state. Hull was instrumental in the creation of the United Nations and was honored with a Nobel Peace Prize in 1945. (CU.)

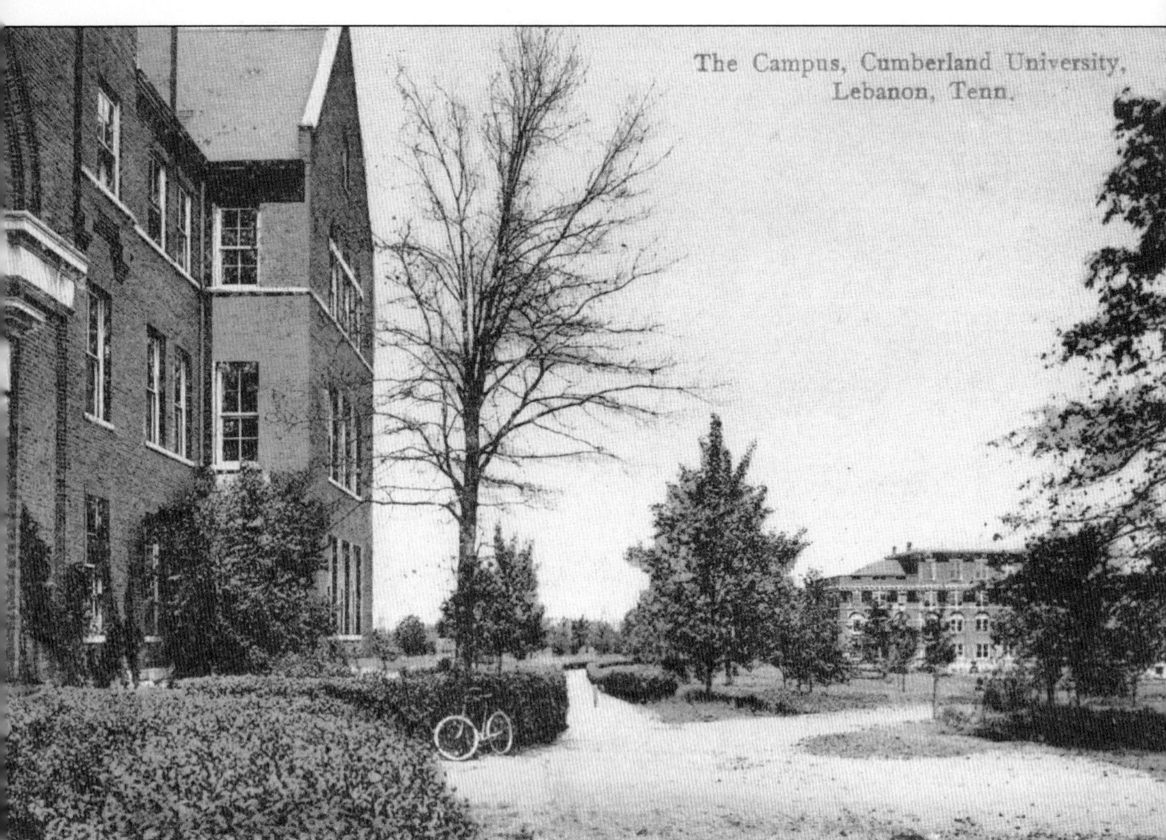

Counted among Cumberland University's many graduates are US Supreme Court justices Howell E. Jackson and Horace Lurton. Other notable alumni include James Lafayette Bomar, president of Rotary International; Thomas P. Gore, US senator; more than 80 congressmen, including Albert Gore Sr.; 13 governors, including Frank G. Clement; three ambassadors, including Edward Albright, US ambassador to Finland; many local, state, and federal judges, including Charles Dickson Clark; and 50 college professors, including the "Father of Political Science," John Burgess. After 1944, the school was no longer associated with the Presbyterian Church. A brief ownership by the Tennessee Baptist Convention ended in 1956. From then until 1982, the school continued as a two-year college, returning to university status in 1983. (RWPCCU.)

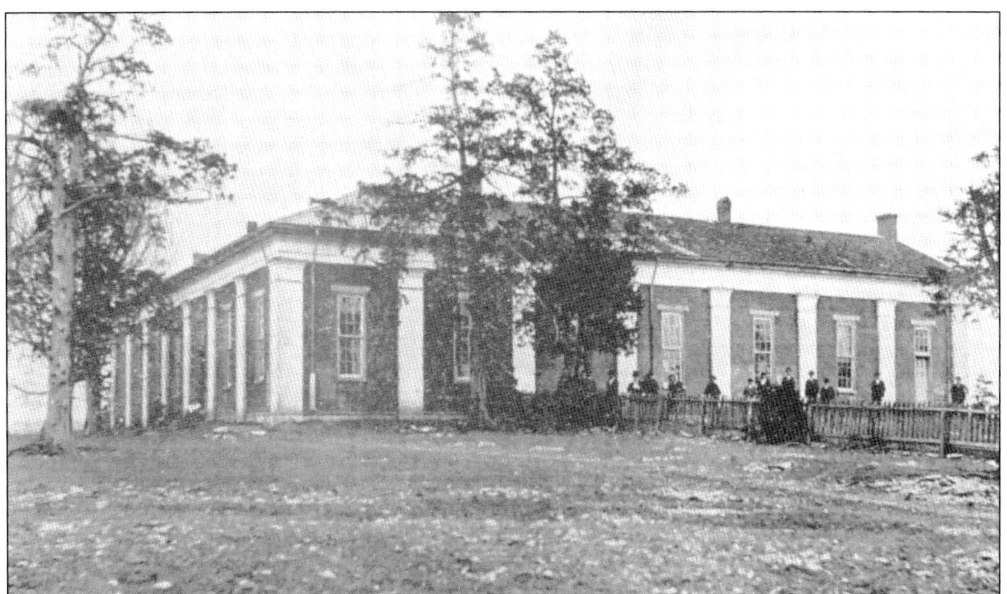

Campbell Academy was established in 1806 eight miles west of town. It relocated to the northeast corner of North Cumberland and Hill Streets in January 1828, where it operated as a preparatory school for boys. Pictured above is the brick building, 50 feet by 30 feet. Although new, the accommodations were not luxurious. Professor H.S. Kennedy commented that "the school boys brought their drinking water from the town spring." From 1842 to 1846, Campbell Academy's board of trustees also had control of the Abbe Institute, a nearby female school. The academy operated for 96 years, merging in 1854 with Cumberland University to serve as that institution's preparatory school until 1902. The photograph below shows the school building with the addition of a cupola. (Above, CU; below, courtesy of Ken Thomson.)

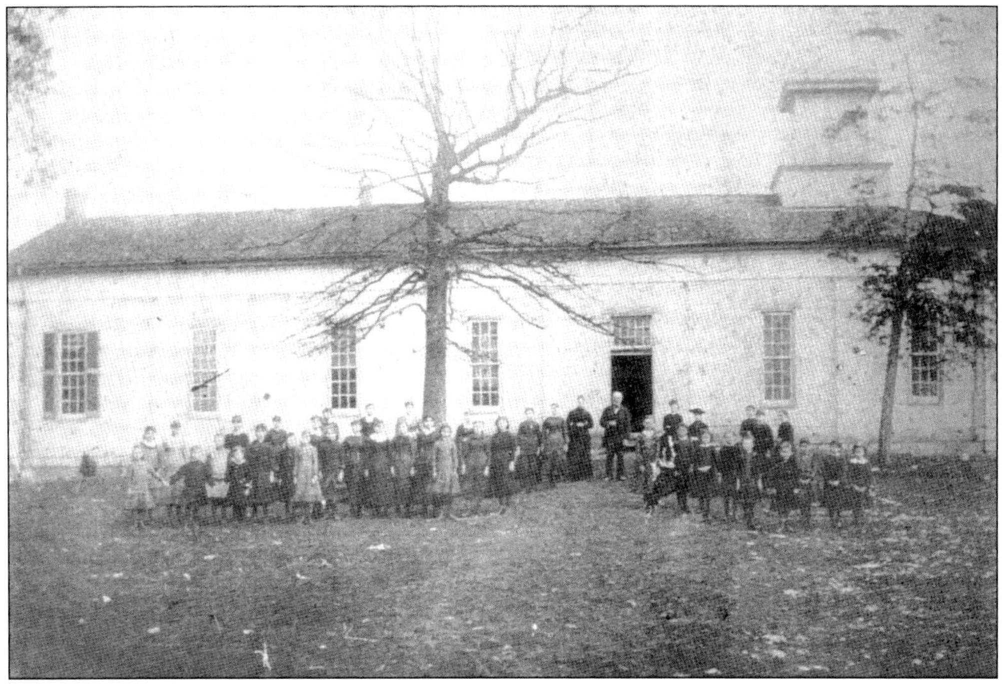

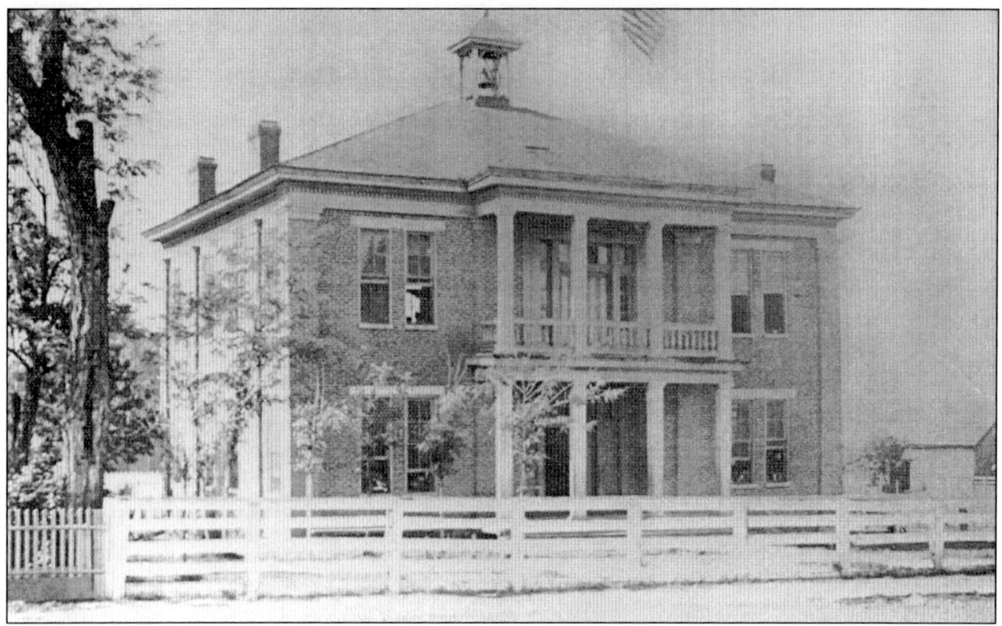

The Baptist Seminary opened on the south side of East Main Street in 1859, in the 300 block, just east of Cherry Street. The school had a curriculum for female students. This structure became the home of the Lebanon Public School in 1873, and continued at this location until a new structure was completed in 1903. (CLMHC.)

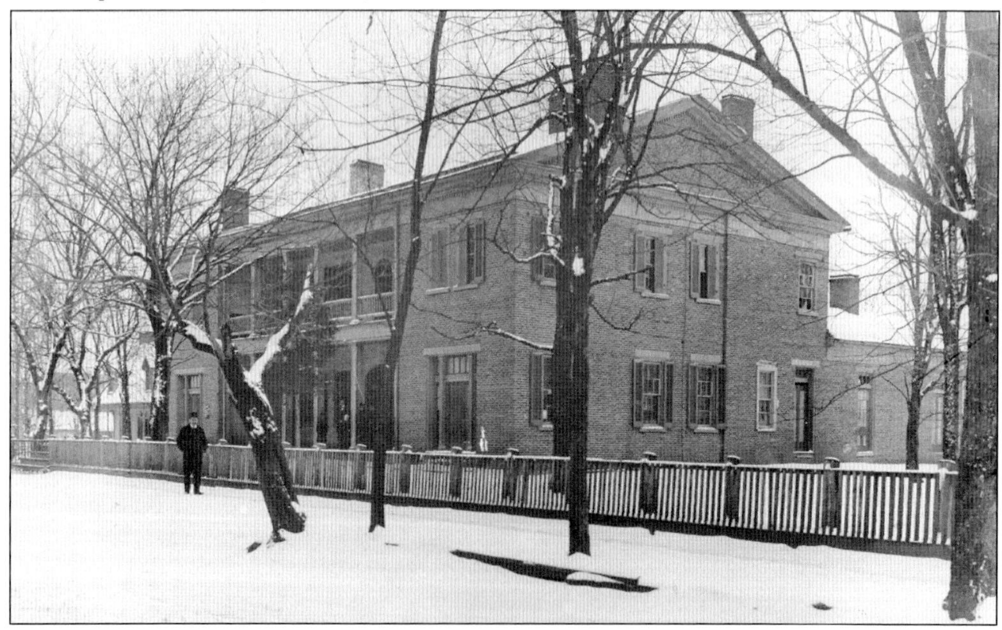

Corona Institute, a female college, was founded in 1866 by David Campbell Kelley. Housed in an impressive home on West Main Street, in the 200 block on the south side of the street, its original center section was built in 1820. A new owner in 1830 added the two wings. The institute continued until the site was purchased by Robert L. Caruthers in 1873 and given to Cumberland University for the use of the law school. After Caruthers Hall was built in 1878, Corona Hall continued to be used for classroom instruction until 1896, when it became a boardinghouse for students. (CU.)

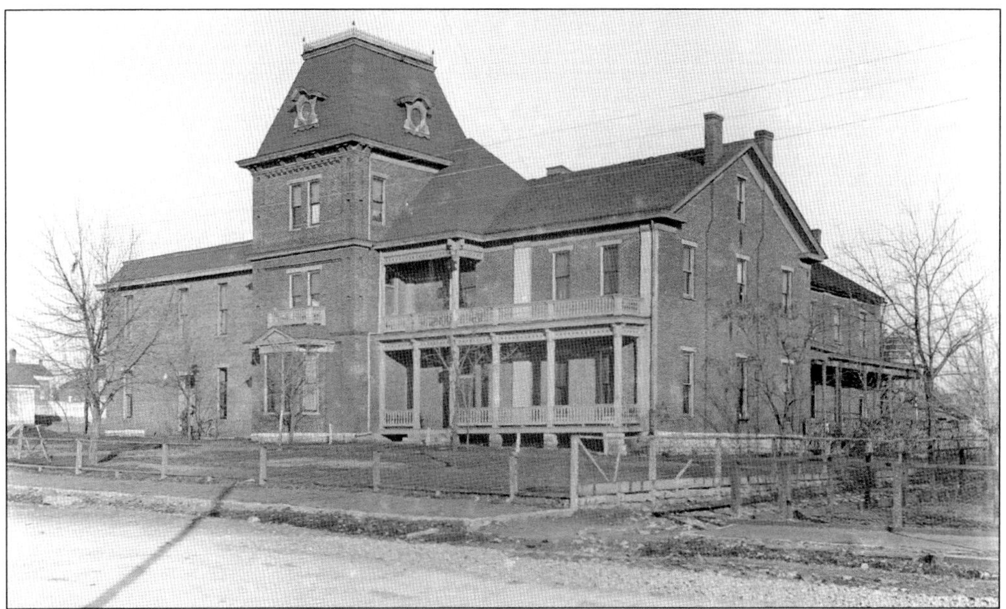

Lebanon College for Young Ladies was cofounded in 1886 by E.E. Weir and Benjamin Foster. The brick and stone structure was located on the east side of North Cumberland Street, the present site of the Valley View Shopping Center. The college educated students from 15 states, who boarded and attended with day students. Students earned a four-year degree upon graduation. From 1894 to 1897, it was the Cumberland University Annex. Female students had equal benefits as the young men enrolled at the university, with the same studies offered and some of the same teachers, but the ladies took their classes and lived in the Annex building. In this fashion, the university could offer an equal education but avoid becoming coeducational. The image below shows students with their books in front of the college in the 1890s. A fire in 1909 destroyed the building and ended the school. (Both, CU.)

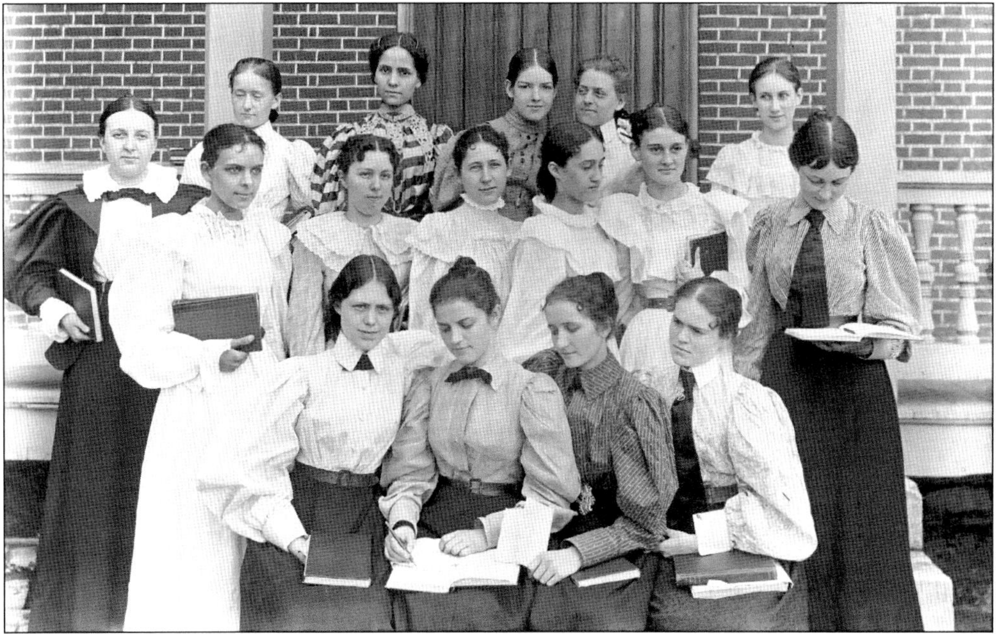

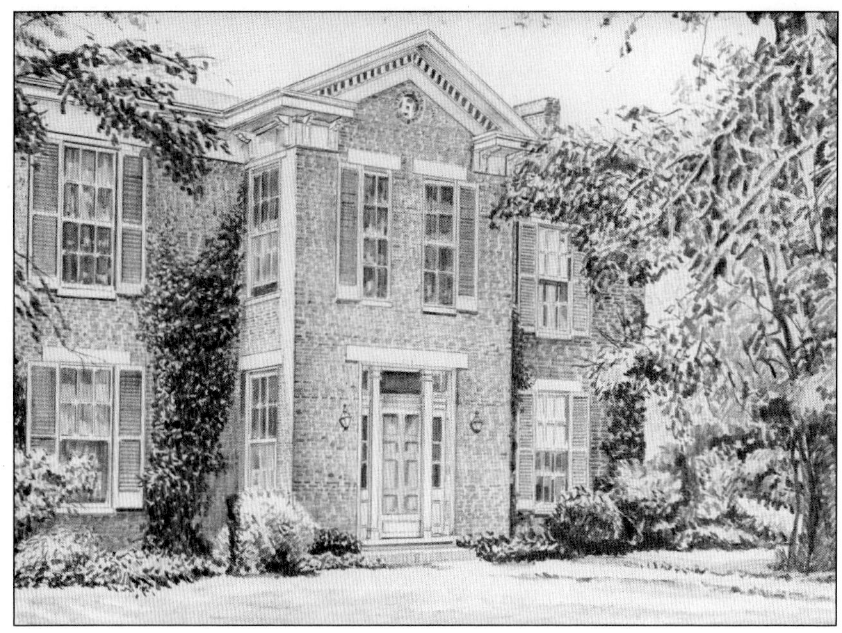

Margaret Fite Harsh opened an elementary school in her home on West Main Street, seen above, in 1891. Classes from first through sixth grade were taught. The two-story Federal-style house was built about 1870 by Margaret's father, Dr. James L. Fite, a local physician. After Harsh, a widow, remarried in 1917, she moved to Florida, and Virginia Wooten continued the school until 1920. The W.H. Fessenden family purchased the home in 1928. Their daughter Sallie Barry Fessenden directed in her will that the house be used as a museum. Today, it is operated by the History Associates of Wilson County as the Wilson County Museum. Below, students of the school pose for a class photograph in 1917. From left to right are (first row) Mary ? and Madeline Humphreys; (second row) two unidentified, Nancy Belle Campbell, Virginia Adams, and Julia Humphreys; (third row) unidentified. (Above, courtesy of CLMHC; below, courtesy of Edward L. Thackston.)

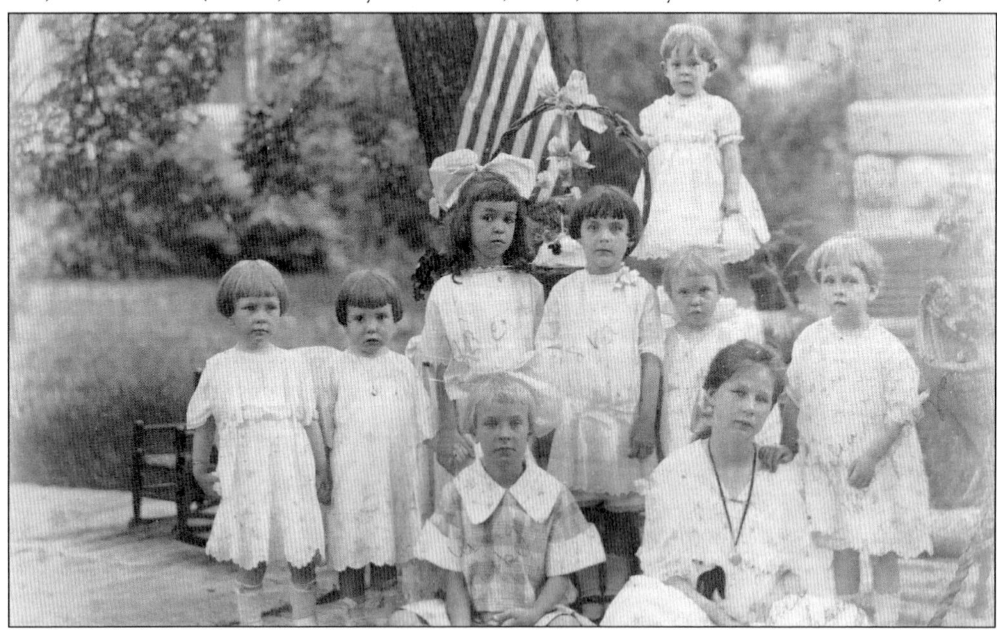

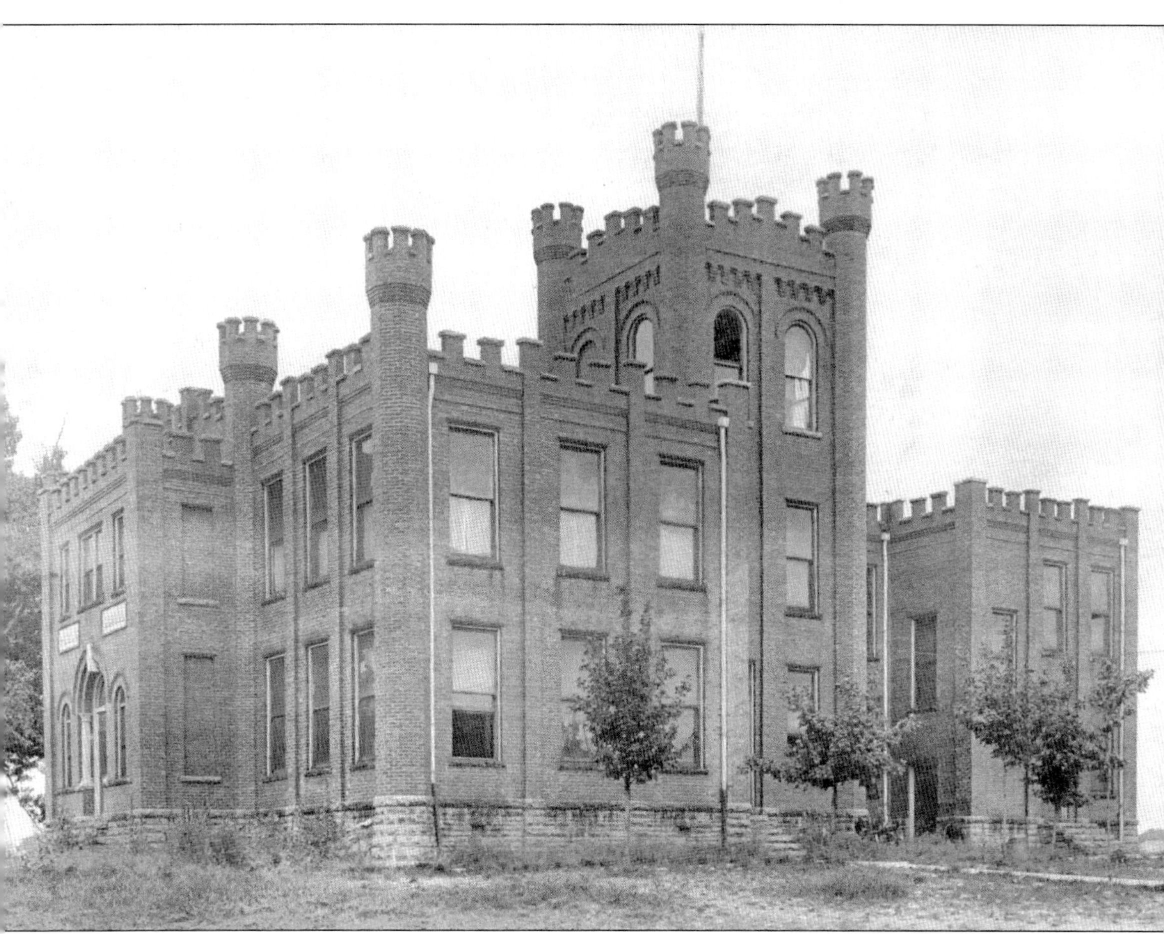

In 1902, Cumberland University's board of trustees transferred to the town of Lebanon the grounds and building of Campbell Academy. The structure proved to be too small and antiquated. A new building was planned, and the Lebanon Public School began classes at the site in 1903. The Public School housed just the elementary grades, one through eight. The building, seen here, was enlarged in 1908 and consumed by fire in 1911. A new school building was constructed in 1912 on the old foundation and with the same floor plan. In 1918, students began attending classes for a four-year high school in the building, along with the elementary school. By 1923, the building had become overcrowded. A new building was needed, but complicating the process was the fact that the land and building were owned by the Lebanon Tenth District Schools, and the high school was operated by Wilson County. (CLMHC.)

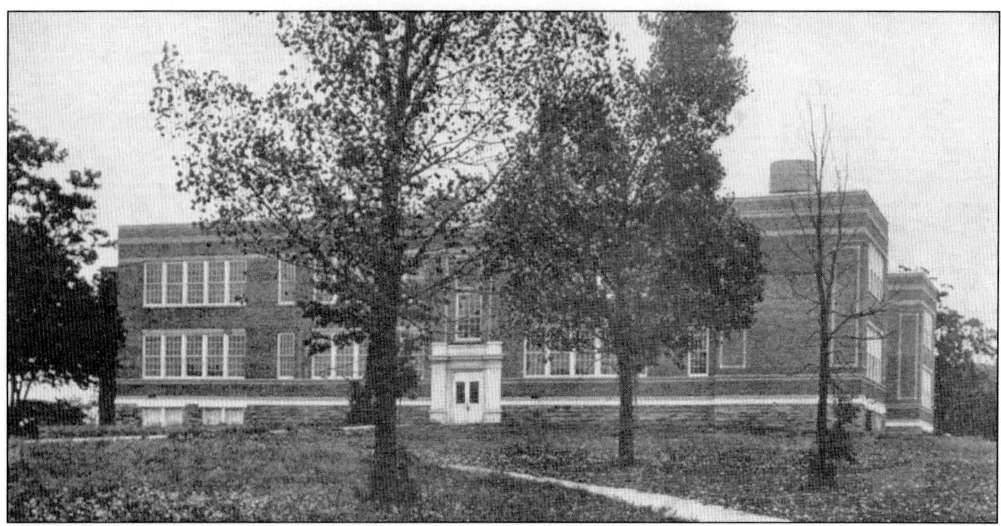

The building seen here was the product of a community campaign for a new school. A Progressive League formed to rally the community for a new school. An opposing Protector's League organized with an anti–new school platform. In 1923, the vote for a new school prevailed. The grounds and building would remain the property of the Tenth District, but the high school would have a section of the building. Classes began in the new structure in October 1924. In March 1936, the school building was destroyed by fire. (CLMHC.)

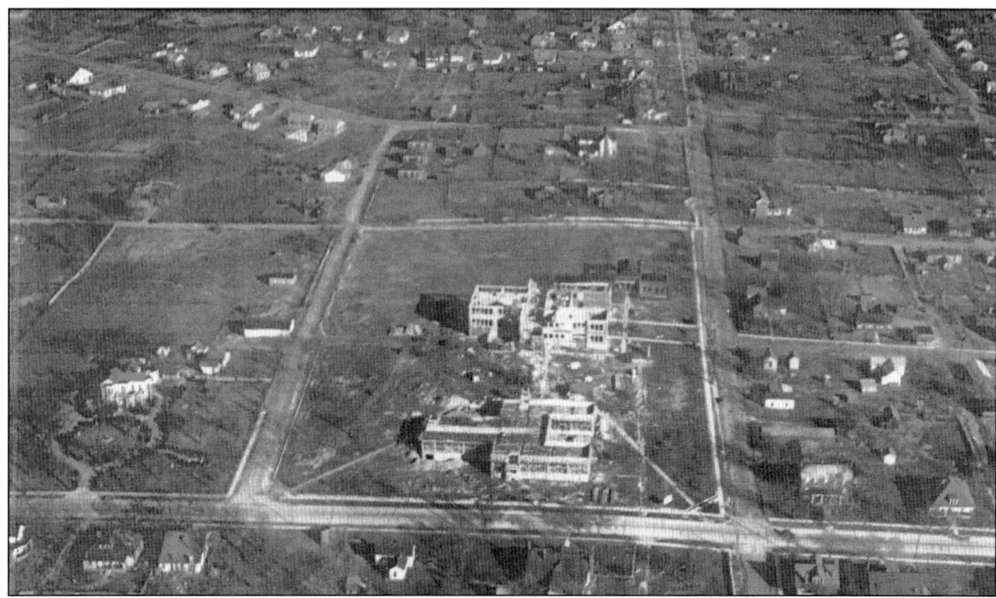

During the next round of construction, completed in 1937, the Tenth District allowed the county to build a separate high school on the property of the Public School. The new campus, shown during construction, contained the new Lebanon High School, the Lebanon Gymnasium, and the Lebanon Elementary School, later named Highland Heights Elementary School. When the high school moved to new quarters in 1955, its former building became the Tenth District's junior high school, for seventh and eighth grades. This building still stands and is occupied by the Wilson County Sheriff's Department today. (CLMHC.)

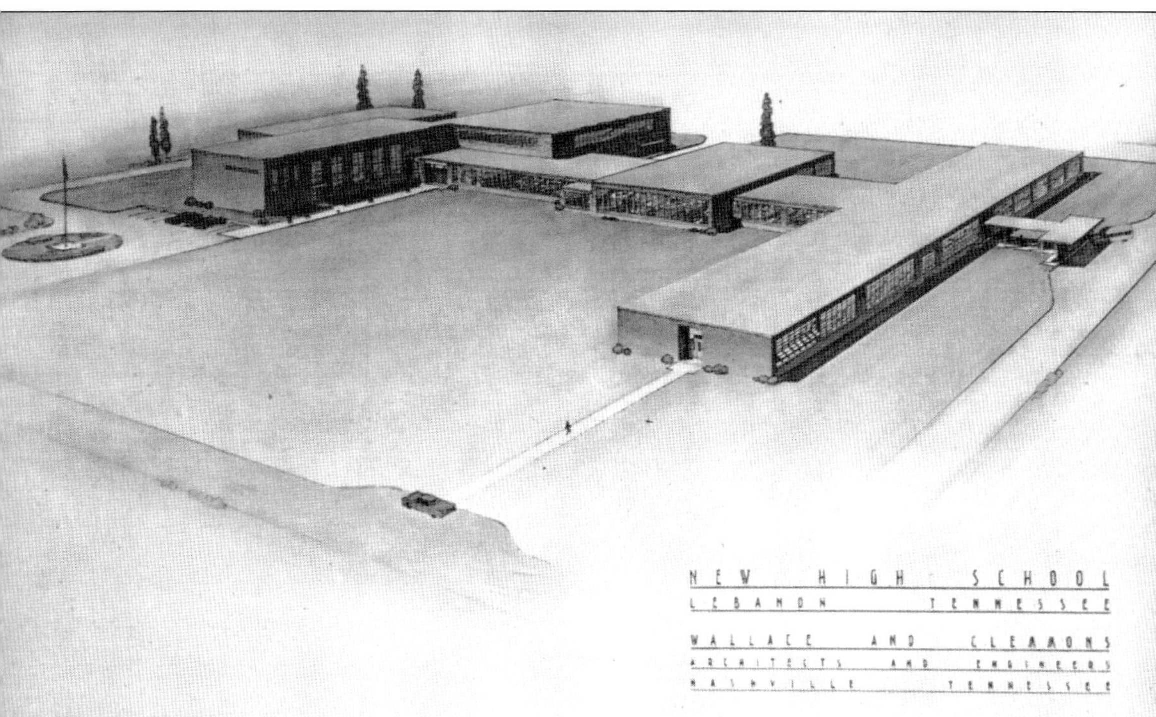

By 1954, a new location for the high school had been selected on East Spring Street. The school would for the first time move off of land owned by the Tenth District School System. The cost of construction was $610,000. Classes for the new Lebanon High School began in the fall of 1955. Over the years, additions were made to the building, and a football field was added in 1965. Classes were last held in this building in June 2013. The school's colors, blue and white, were chosen in the early days. They represented fidelity, light, and purity. *Les Diables Bleu*, the nickname of the famed French 2nd Infantry of World War I, was selected as the mascot. During the war, units of the French Blue Devils toured the country to raise money for the war effort. Thus, the school's mascot was chosen for military and patriotic reasons. (Courtesy of Carolyn Jackson.)

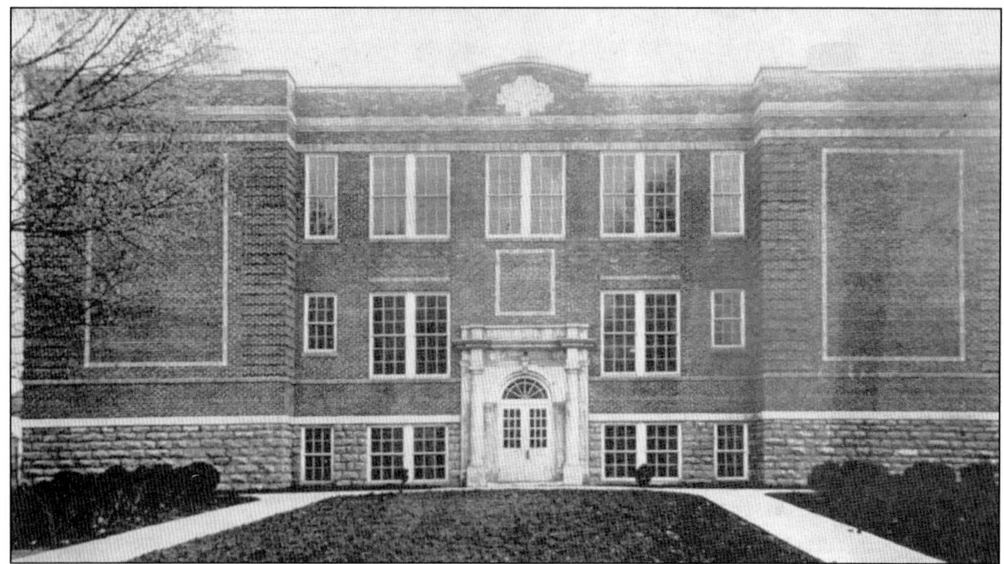

One of the Tenth District School System's early schools, the McClain School was completed in 1923 on West Main Street. It was built on the site of the old McClain place, the former home of Dr. Cossitt in 1842. This school was used until June 1984 and razed in 1995. Pictured below is Mrs. Victor Miller's 1957 second-grade class in front of the school. From left to right are (first row) David Eskew, Butch Blair, Bruce ?, Ronnie Williams, Charlie Bennet, and unidentified; (second row) Suann ?, Lydia ?, Shirley ?, unidentified , Jimmy Green, unidentified, Kathy Brown, David Allen, Martha Ballesy, William Brown and Lynn Eastes; (third row) Bill Shannon, Jimmy Frost, Jimmy Floyd, Kendall Porter, Joe Ligon, Patricia Rye, Janice Hibbit, Glen Andrews, Jane Alsup, and Linda Fay Bennet. Mrs. Miller is standing in the back. (Above, courtesy of Edward L. Thackston; below, CLMHC.)

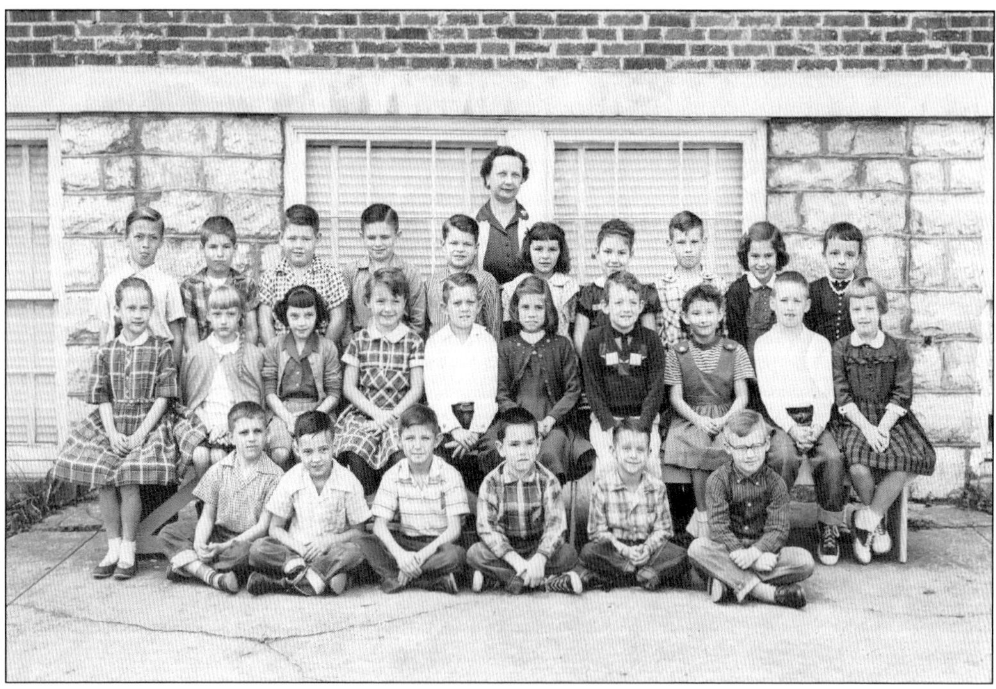

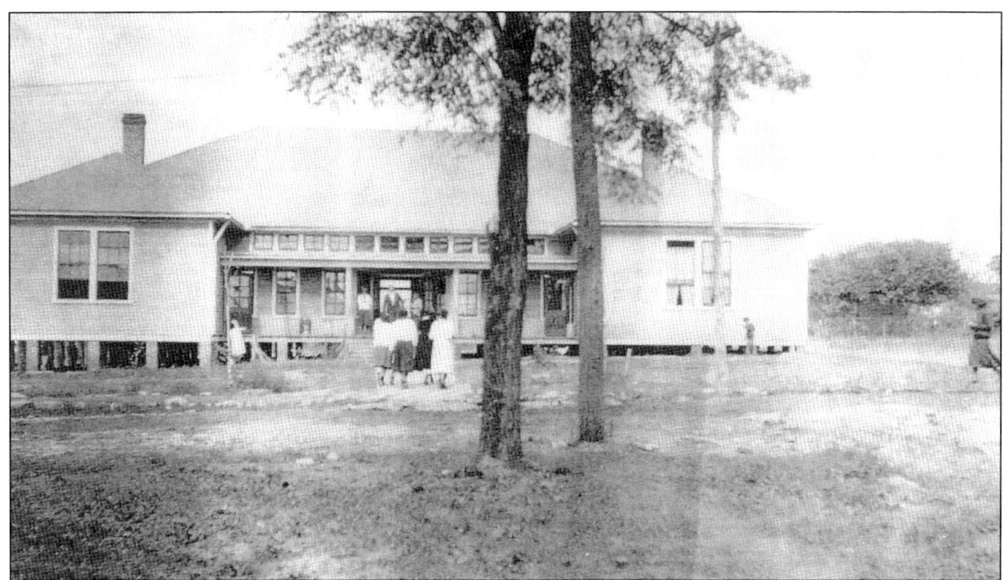

The first school in Lebanon for the African American community was built on East Market Street in the late 1800s. This structure, seen above, was destroyed and rebuilt with assistance from the Rosenwald Fund, founded by Booker T. Washington and Julius Rosenwald, the CEO of Sears, Roebuck & Co. Money from the fund was used to build schools in underserved communities. Public funds and contributions from the African American community were both required. In the photograph below, Mrs. Hattie Bryant's third-grade class at Market Street Elementary School poses for a group picture in 1944. (Both courtesy of the Wilson County Civic League.)

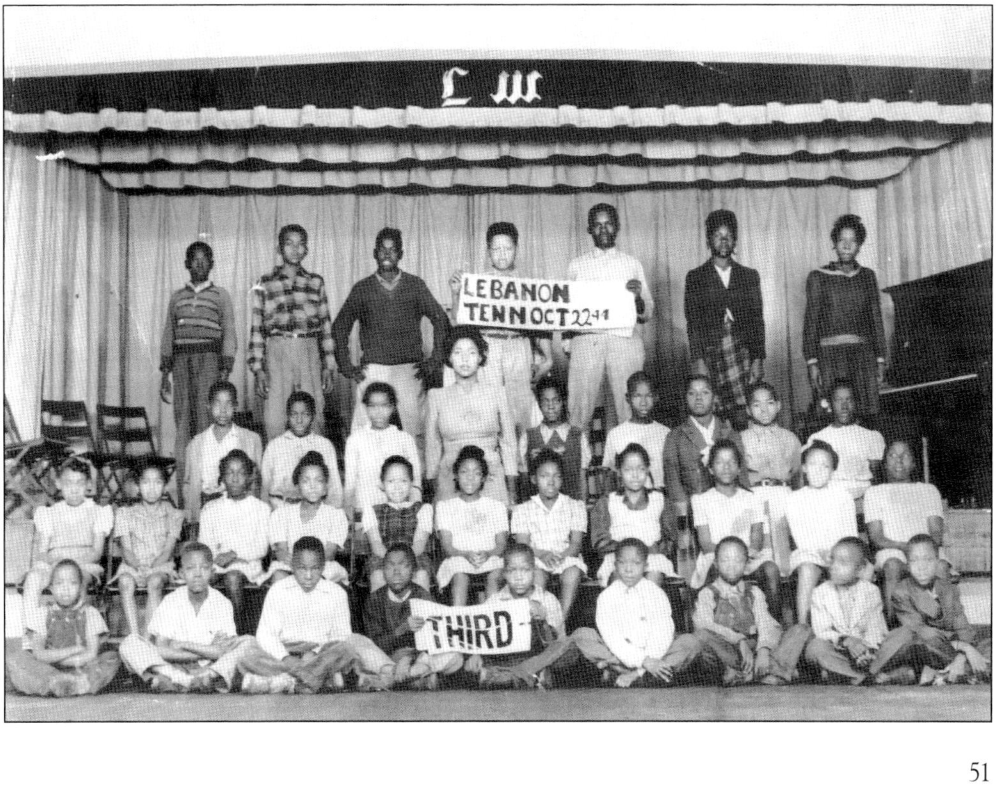

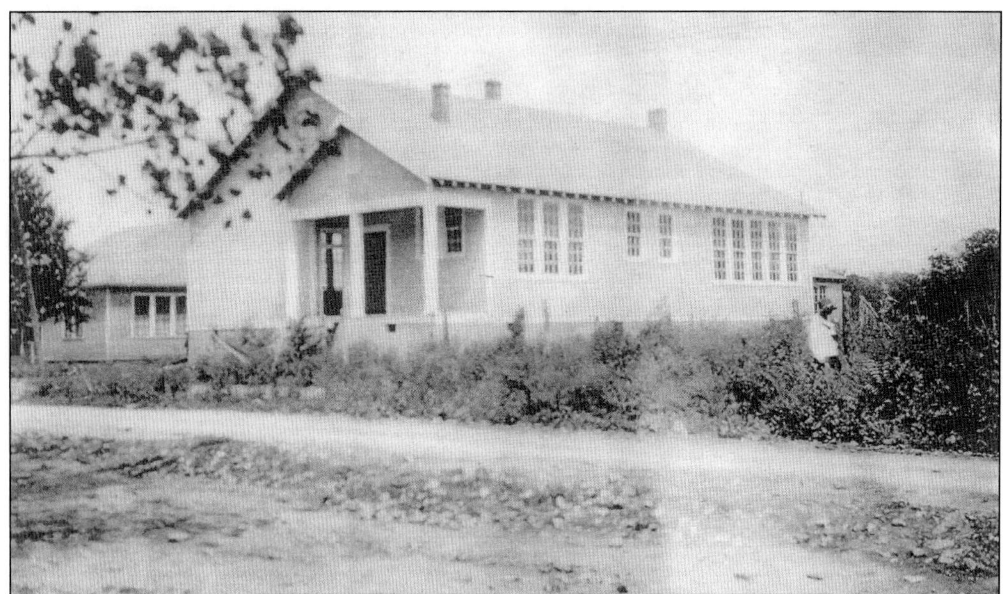

The Market Street School housed elementary grades until the addition of classes for a four-year high school in 1920. In 1927, another frame building was constructed to provide more room, seen above. This housed the Wilson County Training School, as the high school was then known. In 1950, a new building was constructed for the high school, seen below. Classes continued here until 1969, when the integration of the public schools saw all students attend Lebanon High School. (Both courtesy of the Wilson County Civic League.)

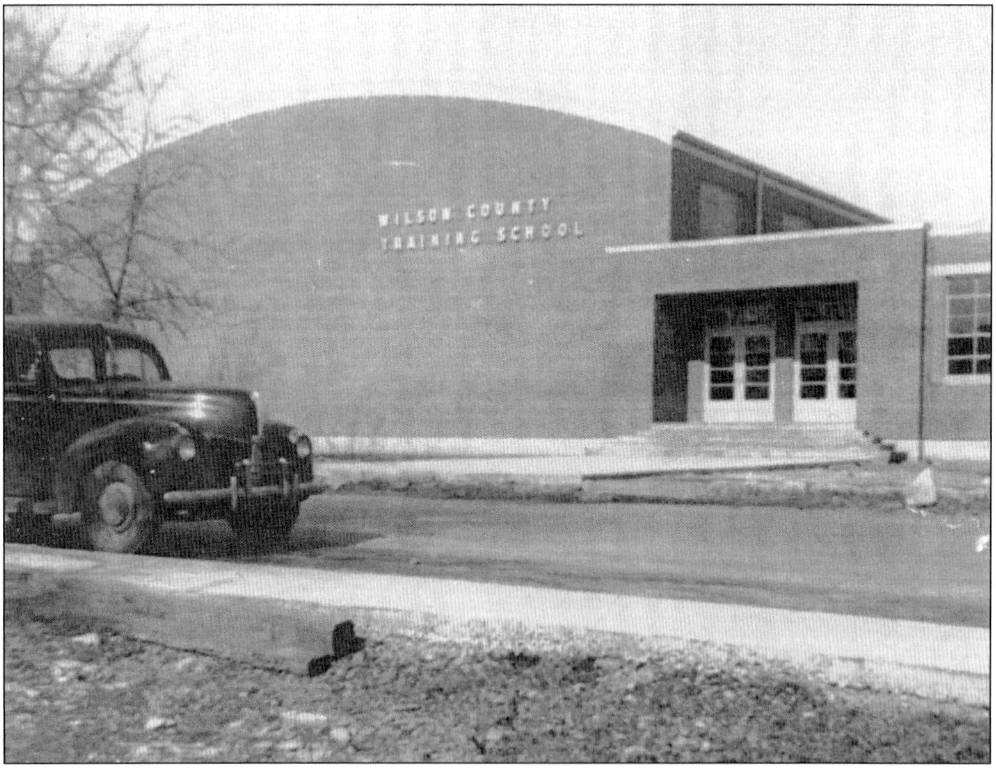

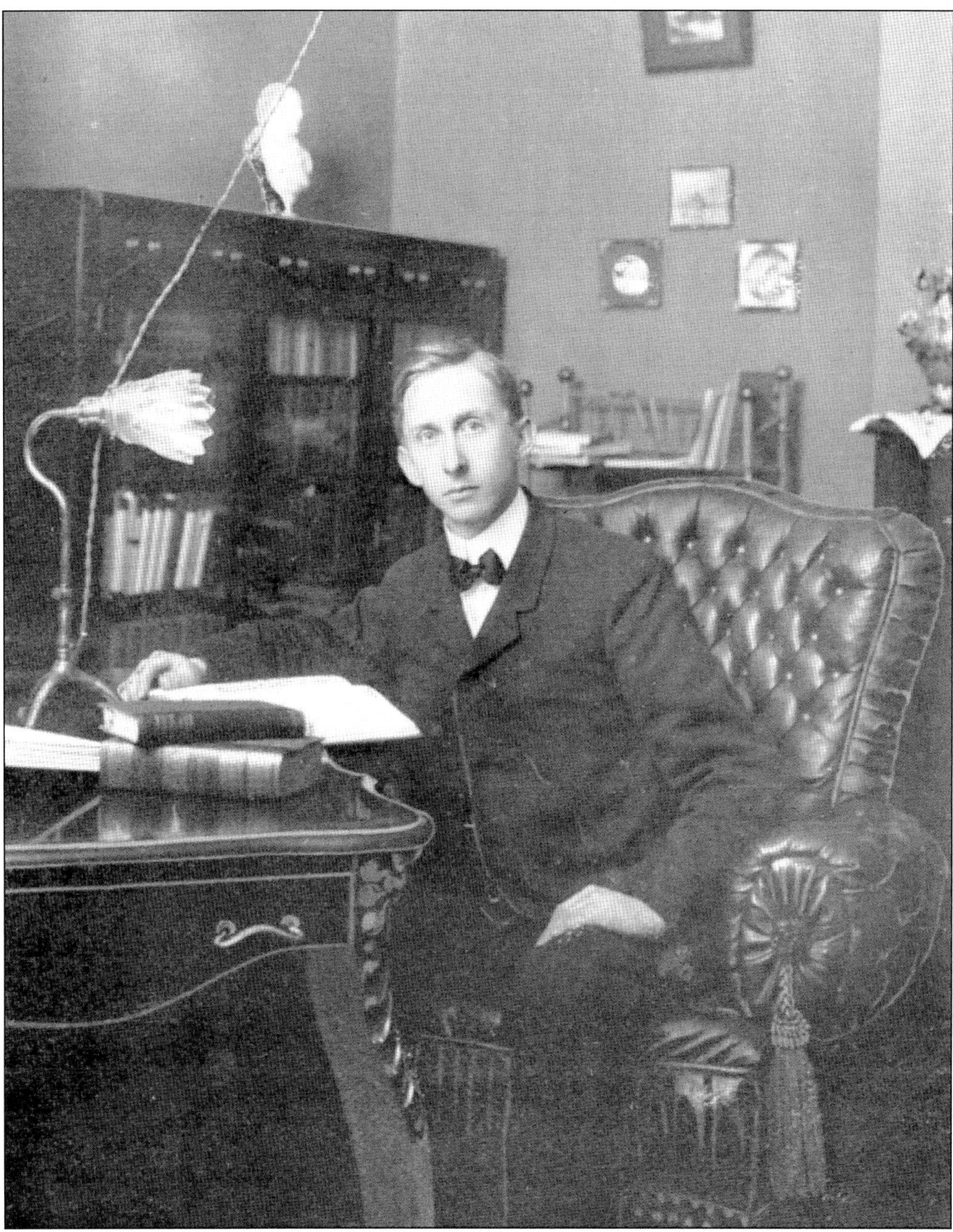

David E. Mitchell, seen here, and I.W.P. Buchanan established the Castle Heights School in 1901. Mitchell had just been named president of Cumberland University, where Buchanan was professor of mathematics. With the closing of Campbell Academy, a private boys' preparatory school, there was a concern in the town about this gap in readiness for students coming to the university. Their idea was to create an environment unlike any other school. Students who did not live in town were required to board at Castle Heights. A school catalogue explained the technique: "So far as possible teachers are to be *in loco parentis*; and that no substitute could be allowed for home influences save the healthful and guarded atmosphere of the school." The school opened in September 1902 with 94 boarding students and 59 day students. (CU.)

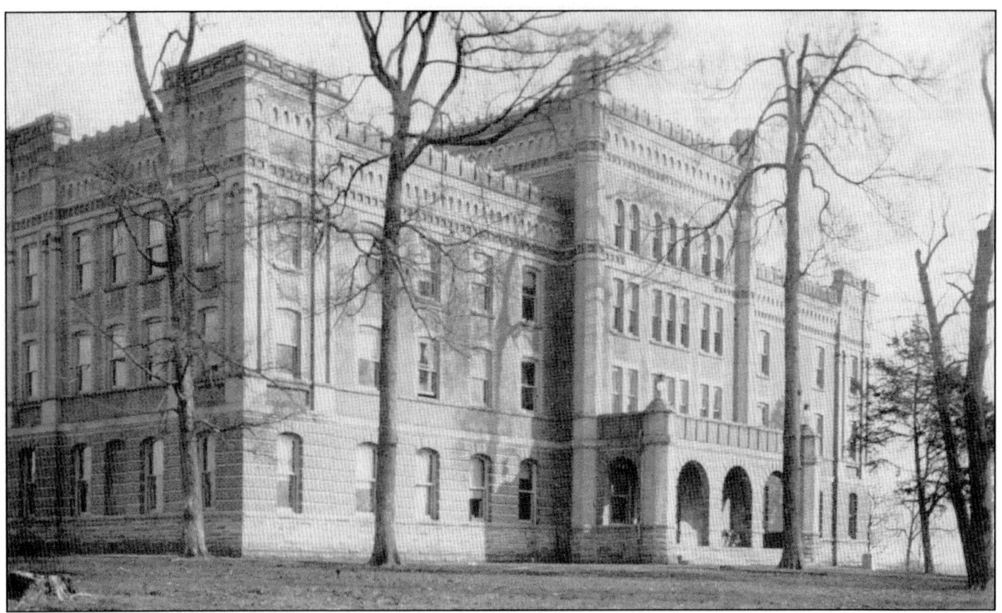

The Castle Heights School Main Building, or "Old Main," was situated one mile from the Public Square on West Main Street. The building (above) is 150 feet long, 60 feet deep, and 60 feet high. The front section of the building, on the first floor, housed a chapel, a study hall with room for 200 students, the associate headmaster's room, the public parlor, a reading room, and the library. Recitation rooms, laboratories, showers, lockers, and rooms for younger boys were located on the second floor. The third and fourth floors were the location of the dormitories for the boys age 15 and older. In the back of the Main Building (below) were the kitchen and dining room, basement space for bicycles, and a gymnasium on the second floor. In 1996, the City of Lebanon purchased the building and completed a thorough renovation for use as the city hall. (Both, CHMA.)

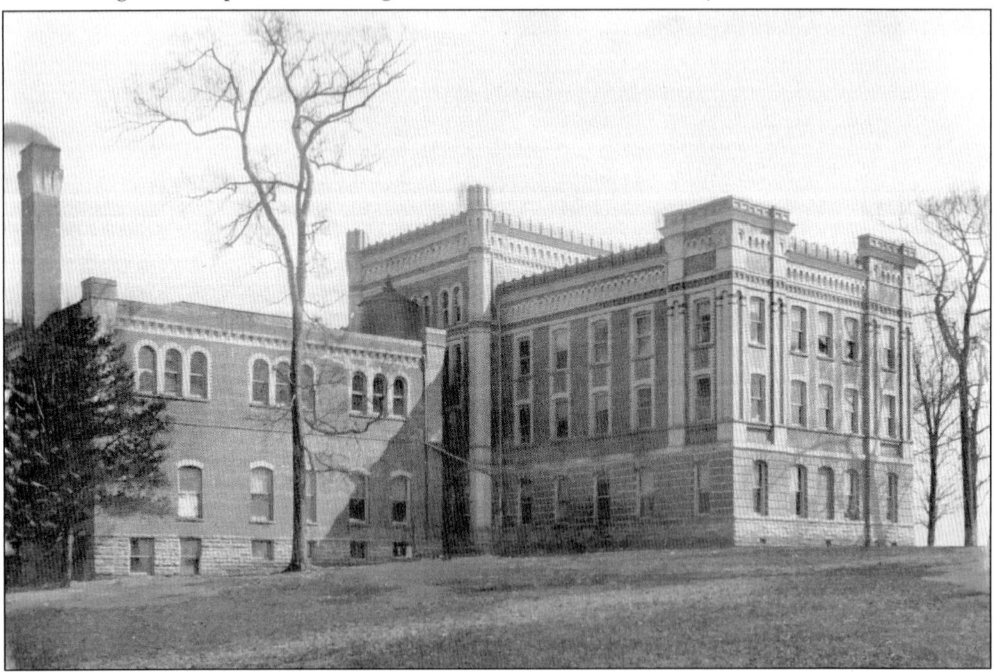

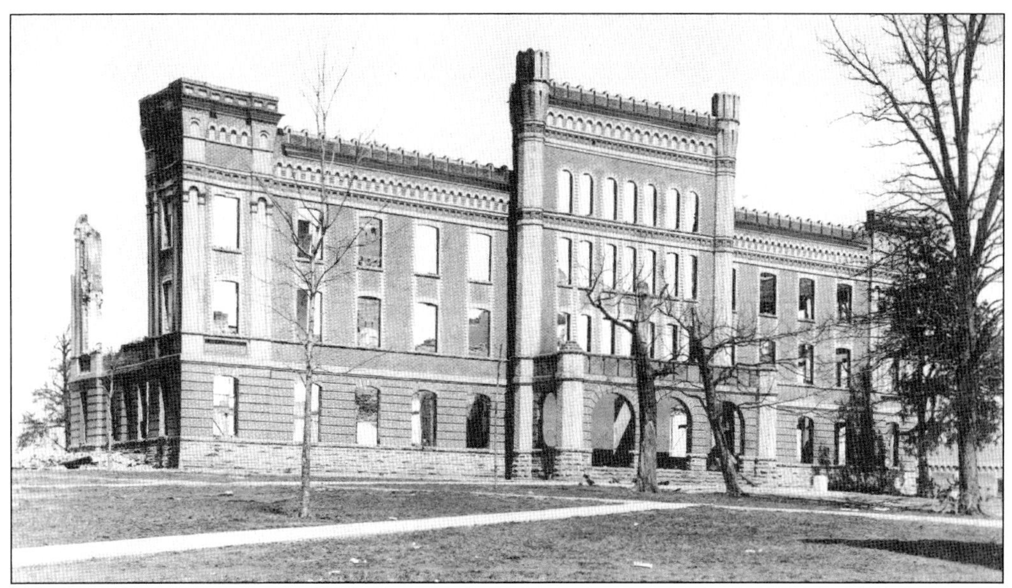

In February 1915, the Main Building was engulfed in flames. The interior was partially gutted, and the outside walls were unstable. The foundation, however, was still strong. The school was quickly rebuilt. Ironically, in an early description of the school's attributes, fire protection for the building is described as: "Plugs for hose on every floor, having a connection with a seven thousand gallon tank on the roof and with the steam pump itself in case of need." Soon after the rededication of the Main Building, fire again ravaged the structure in 1916. The Castle Heights Main Building was then again rebuilt on the same foundation. This building and the remaining structures on the campus grounds were listed in the National Register of Historic Places in 1996. (Above, CLMHC; below, CHMA.)

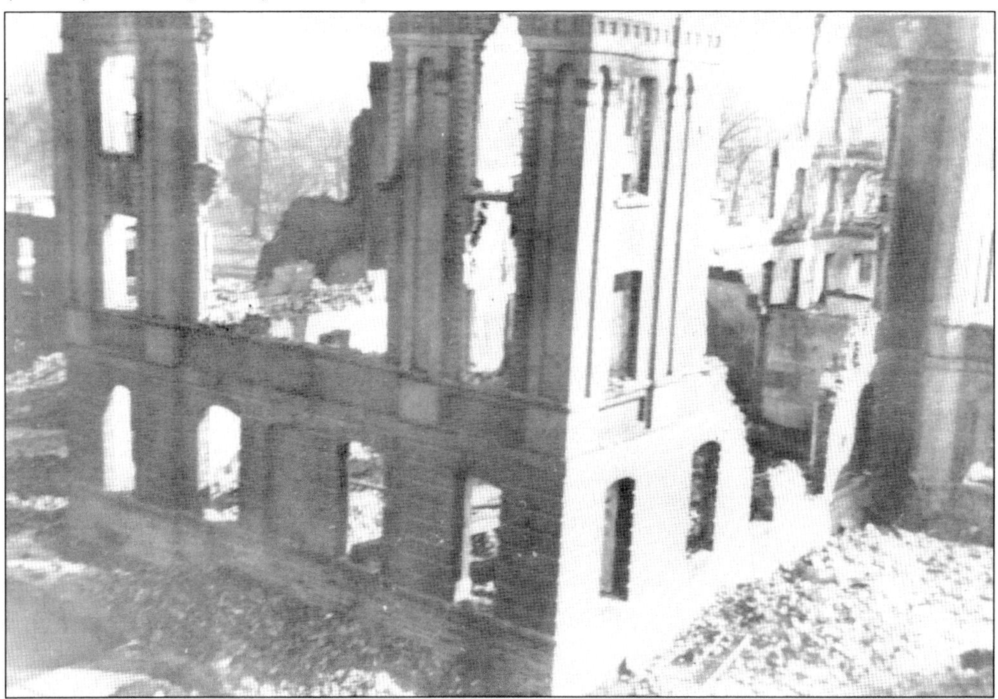

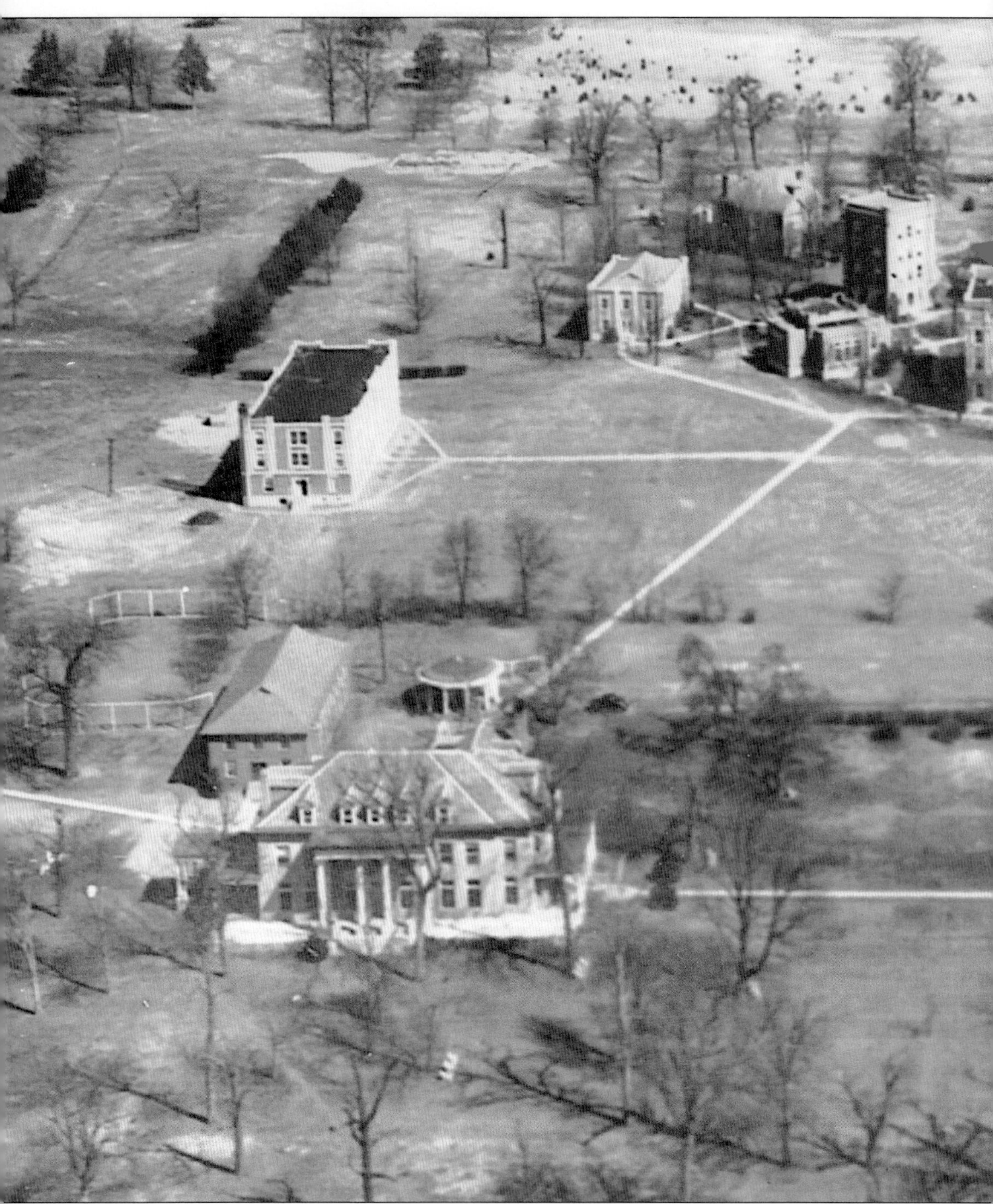

This aerial view shows the full facilities of the Castle Heights School in the 1930s. By this time, the school had experienced several changes. Laban Lacey Rice became co-headmaster with Buchanan in 1903. Rice purchased a one-third interest in the school in April 1904. In 1913, Rice bought out his partners and assumed full control. The old Divinity Hall and the Kirkpatrick house, across West Main Street, were purchased in 1916 for use as Annexes A and B. World events influenced

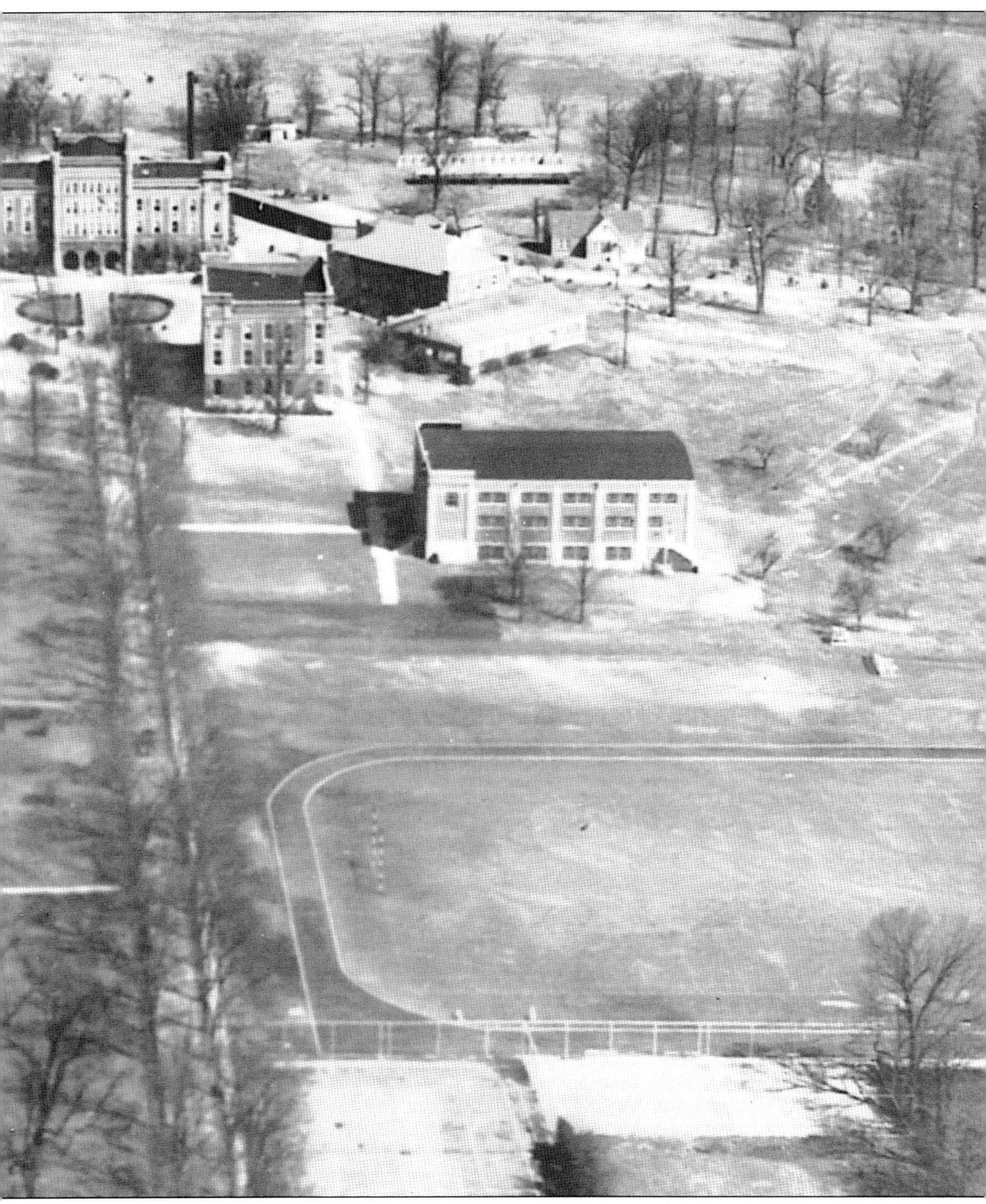

the decision to change the school to the Castle Heights Military Academy in 1917. Rice sold the academy in 1921 to Clark Mathis and Howard Jackson. By 1925, the school was reorganized with a plan from the Lebanon Chamber of Commerce. This action was of little avail; on April 16, 1928, the whole school campus was sold at auction to Benarr Macfadden, a millionaire publisher, and a new era of prosperity began for Castle Heights Military Academy. (CHMA.)

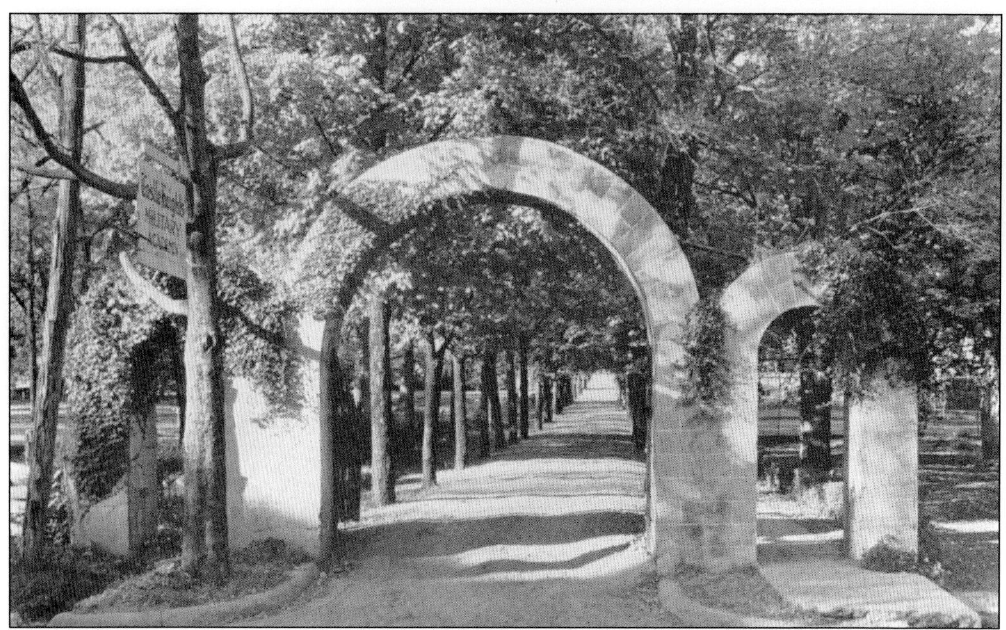

The original arched entrance to Castle Heights School from West Main Street was a familiar sight. It is seen above in 1930. The lane to the campus was lined with beautiful trees. In later years, the entrance was a wrought-iron sign arched over a two-lane entrance. Shown below is an addition to the campus in 1941, the Benarr Macfadden Auditorium. Alvin C. York, a Congressional Medal of Honor recipient, and Gov. Prentice Cooper attended the ceremonial laying of the cornerstone. The auditorium, when completed, could seat 1,400 people and also housed office and classroom space. This was but one of many buildings added to the school during the Macfadden years. Shown in its better days in the postcard view below, the auditorium sat vacant for years after the close of the school. It was demolished in 2010. (Above, CHMA; below, RWPCCU.)

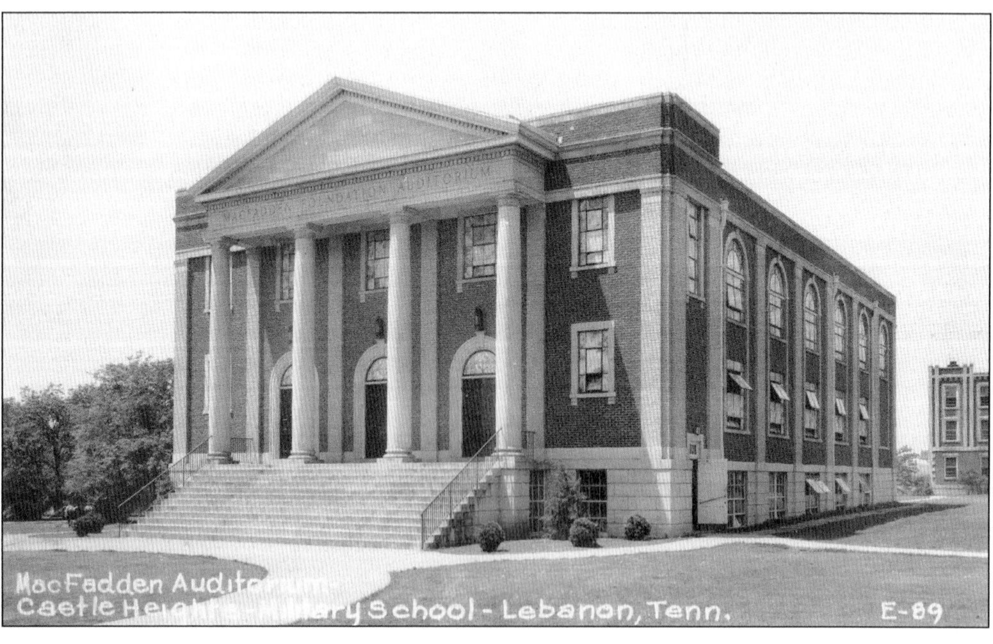

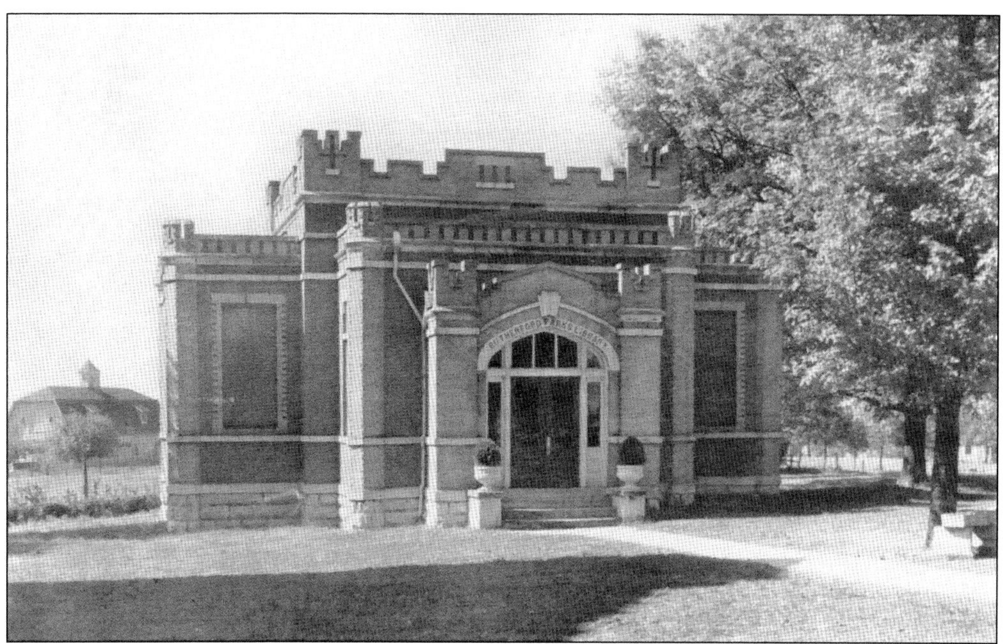

The Rutherford B. Parks Library was built in 1912, funded with a donation from Parks, who was from Dallas and was still a student at the time. The structure was state-of-the-art, with plenty of room for a growing student body. The building's center roof was glass and shaped in a pyramid to allow light through onto a stained-glass ceiling inside. The library contained room for quiet study and had many volumes of books, as seen below. Students were provided a copy of the pamphlet *Learning How to Study*, authored by the headmaster. Skills emphasized were concentration and memorization. Although the curriculum changed over the years, some of the various courses offered included zoology, mechanical drawing, plane trigonometry, Latin and modern foreign languages, and ancient history. The Rutherford Parks Library building still stands and is now owned by the Castle Heights Alumni Association. (Both, CHMA.)

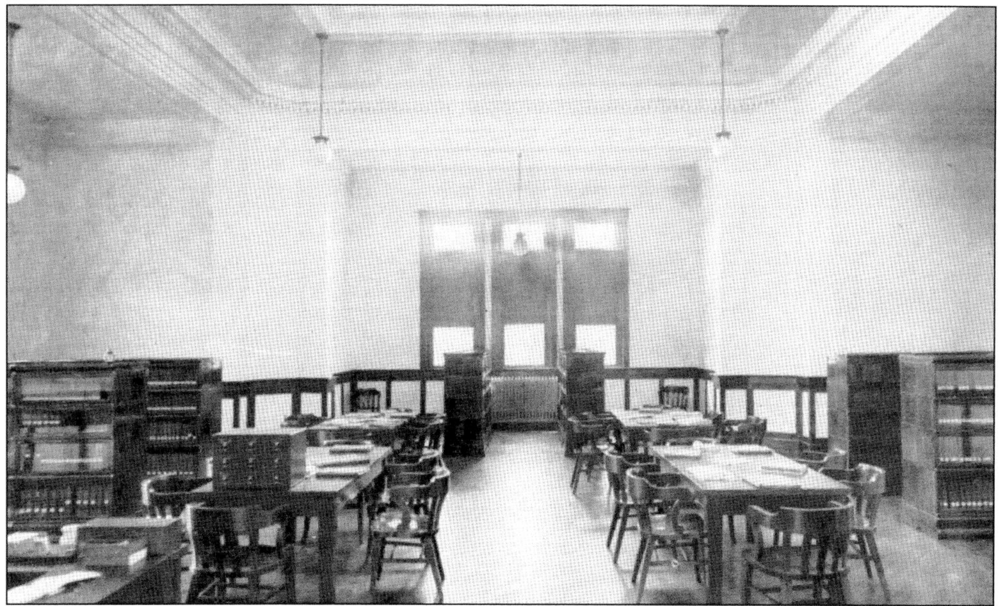

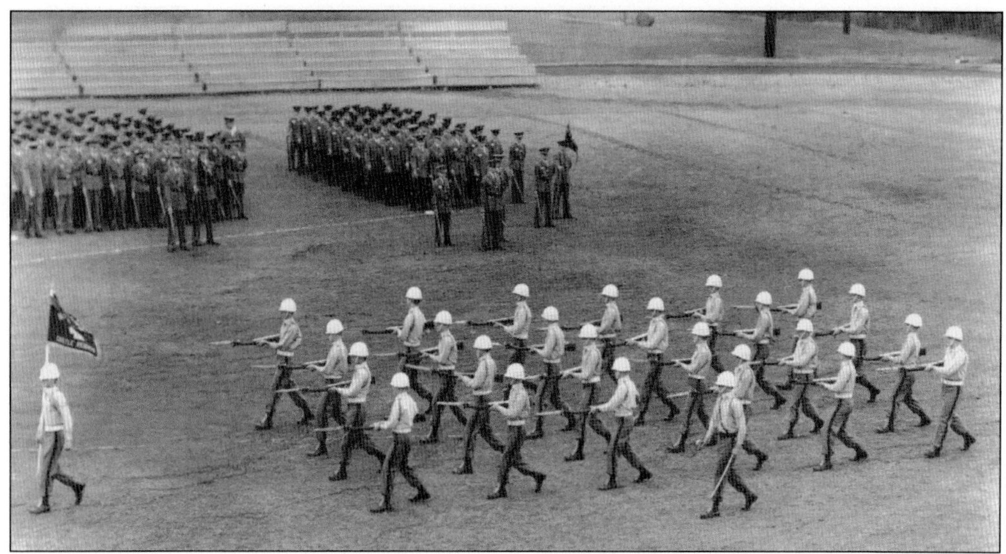

Castle Heights Military Academy was recognized by the US government as a military school, class M1. It also had a senior-unit Reserve Officers' Training Corps (ROTC) recognized by the State of Tennessee. The purpose of ROTC training was to assist in the development of the student's sense of responsibility and self-discipline. The photograph above shows the cadet drill team from around 1960 performing during a Sunday parade. Life at the school was not always so serious. Pictured below is librarian Maj. C.H. Hurd in the midst of the annual Christmas party in 1952. Other activities during leisure time on campus included a recreation room, known as the "Dug Out," which offered billiard tables, as well as the swimming pool, movies in the auditorium, and dances. (Both, CHMA.)

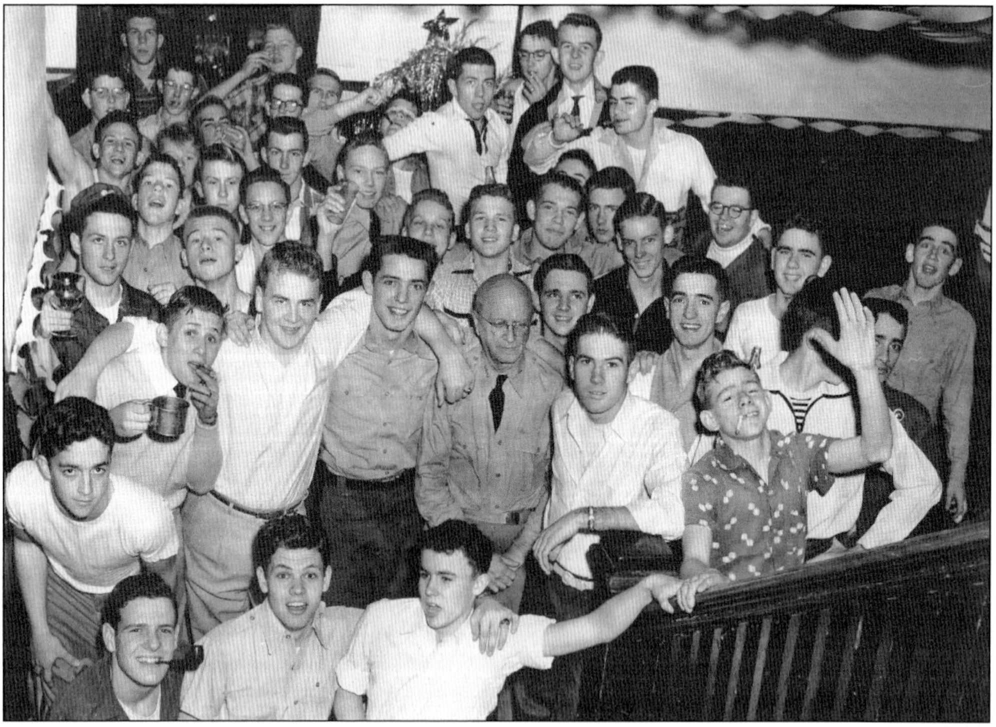

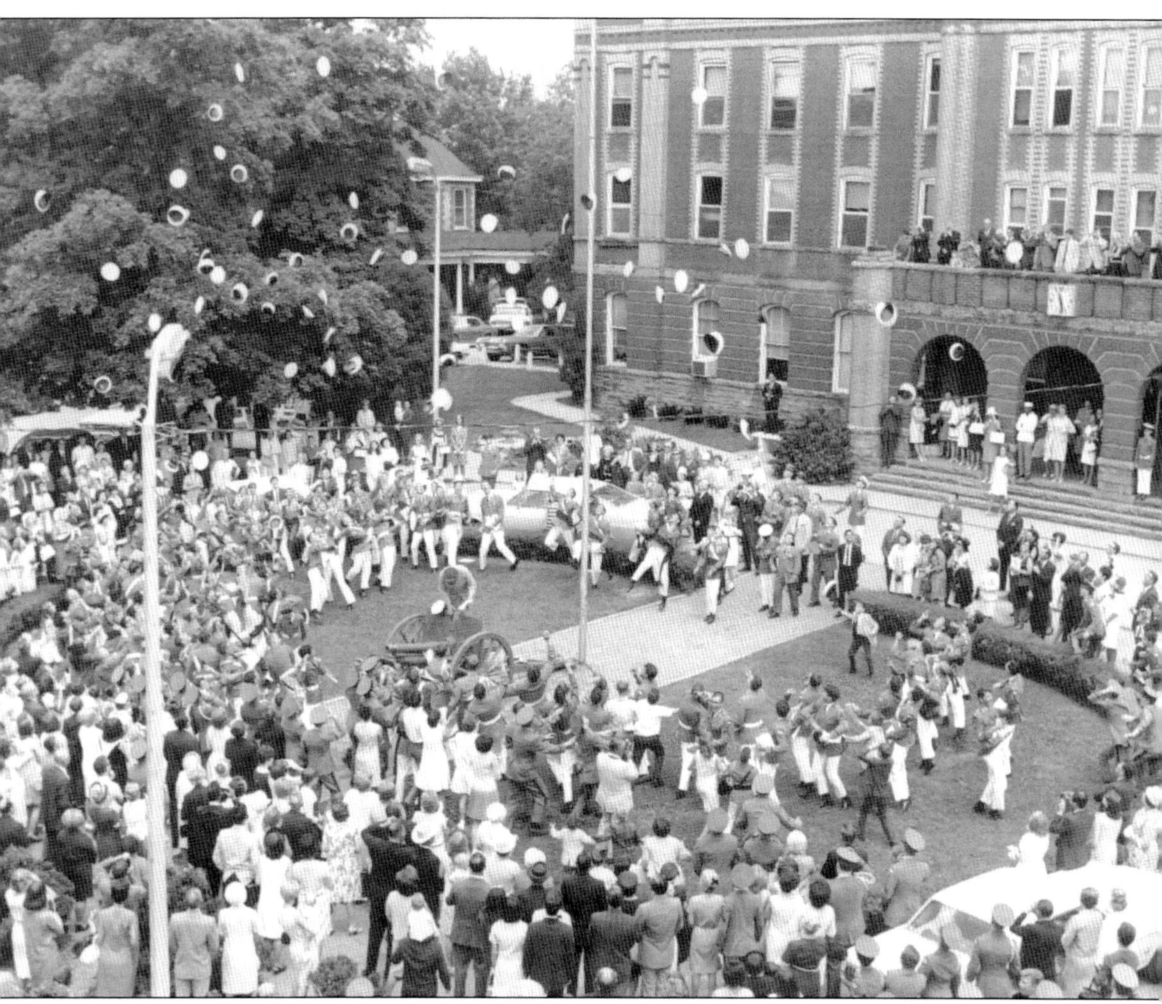

CHMA seniors assemble around the circle in front of Old Main one last time for graduation ceremonies in 1967. Following tradition, the hymn "God of our Fathers" was sung during the graduation ceremony as well as a recitation of the alma mater: "On the city's western border / Reared against the sky / Proudly stands our Alma Mater / As the years go by / Forward ever be our watchword / Conquer and prevail / Hail to thee, our Alma Mater / Castle Heights, all hail!" Castle Heights School's first graduating class, in 1903, matriculated three students, all from Tennessee. By 1937, enrollment had reached 400 students. Although the school experienced highs and lows in enrollment through the years, 1964 was the beginning of a decrease that would never improve. Several factors, including the availability of more private schools and an anti–Vietnam War sentiment, were to blame. (CHMA.)

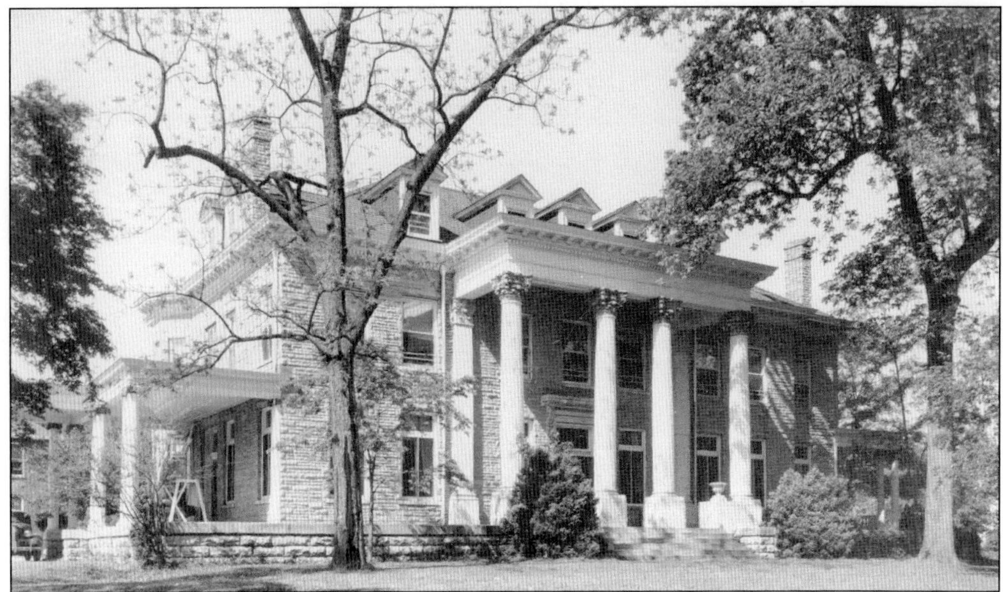

David E. Mitchell's home and surrounding property on West Main Street was purchased by Castle Heights Military Academy in 1936. The impressive structure was to house the Junior School, formed in 1930. Originally, the Junior School taught boys in grades three through eight, including boarding and day students. By 1961, the school accepted students as early as first grade. (RWPCCU.)

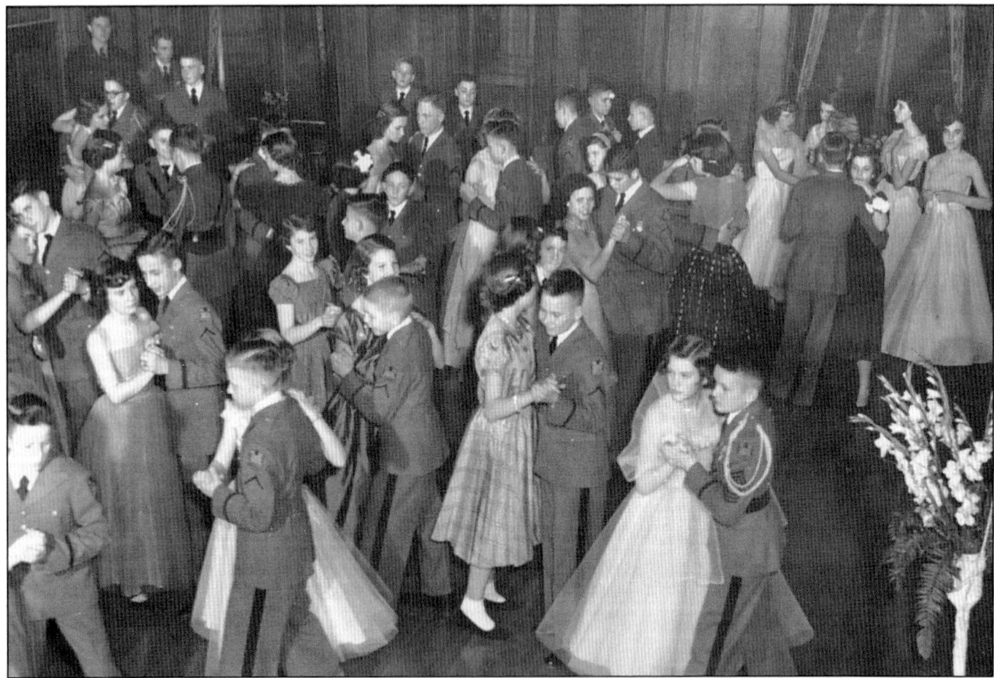

The Castle Heights philosophy was to create well-rounded young men. This included not only academics but social skills as well. The Junior School, along with the upper cadets, had the opportunity for weekly dance lessons. These skills were put to use at the four formal dances and several informal dances held each year. The director of social activities, Mary Fahey, arranged the activities, as well as the dance partners, who came from Lebanon and surrounding towns. (CHMA.)

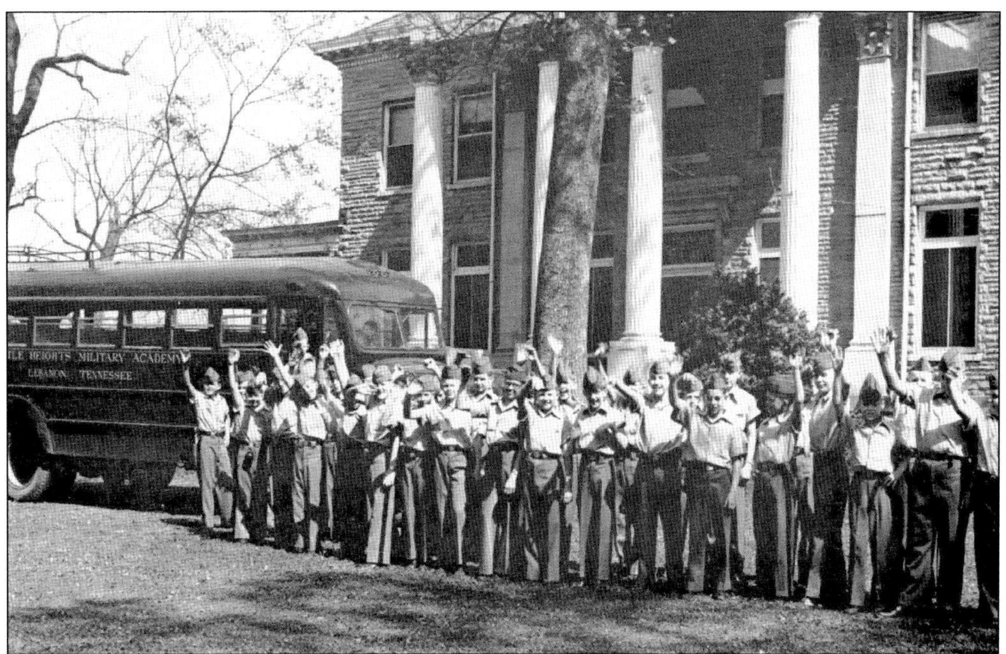

Outings for the boys enrolled at the Junior School took advantage of the campus's close location to surrounding attractions. Visits to nearby sites such as the Hermitage, the Parthenon, and Mammoth Cave were regularly scheduled. On-site activities including possum hunts, hikes, and swimming were highlighted in the 1961 school catalog. Another aspect of the Junior School was the Glee Club. The group photograph below shows a young Duane Allman (first row, far left). Duane and brother Gregg Allman were students in the Junior School from 1955 to 1957 and the Senior School from 1961 to 1964. They went on to form the legendary Allman Brothers Band. (Both, CHMA.)

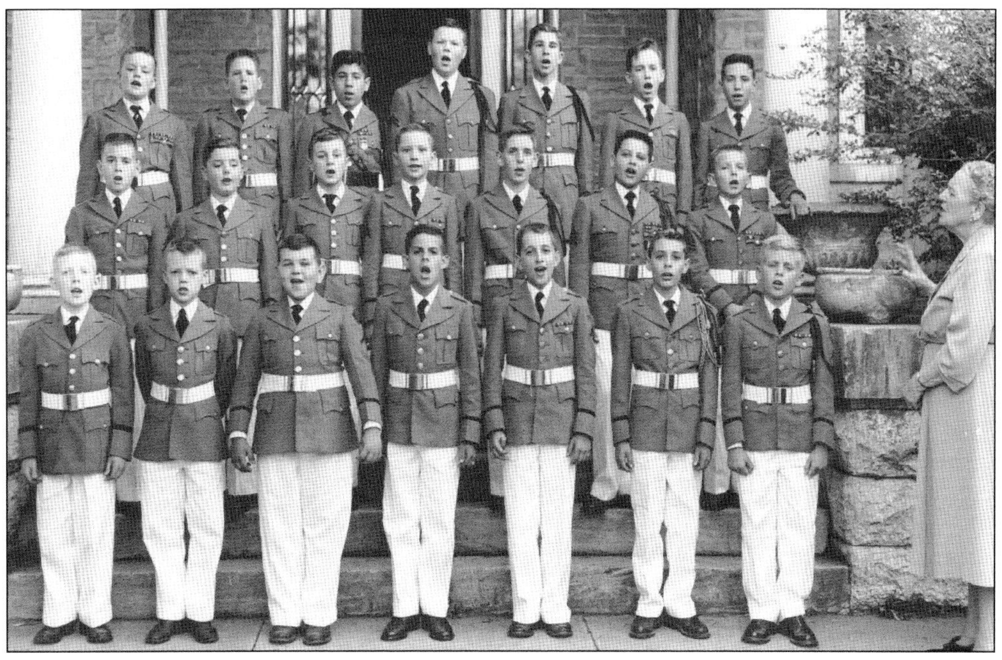

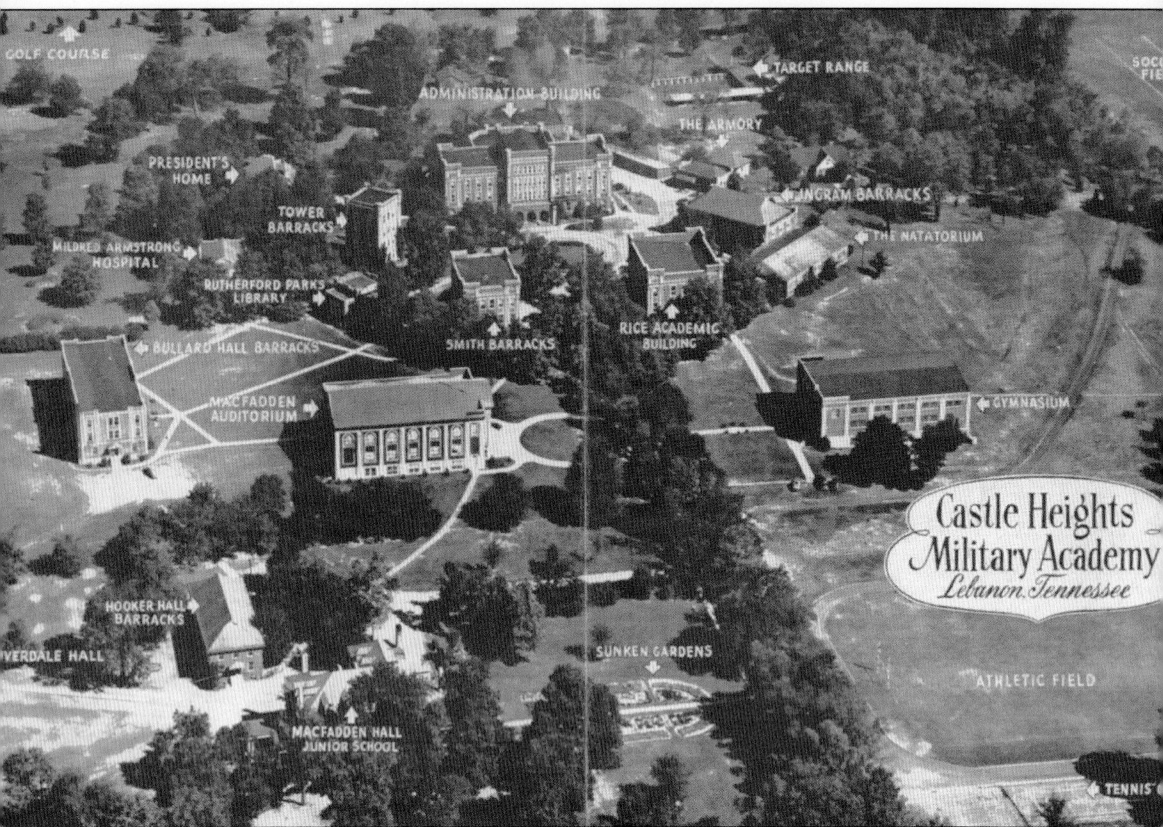

Castle Heights Military Academy closed its doors forever on August 13, 1986. For 84 years, the school had shaped boys and, beginning in 1973, girls, but it was not able to carry on, hindered by a lack of enrollment and adequate financing. The passing was not without monumental efforts to keep the school open. In 1974, Lebanon businessmen Col. J.B. Leftwich, Carl Wallace, and Roy Wauford formed a nonprofit, the Castle Heights Foundation, and purchased CHMA from the Macfadden Foundation. The academy's precarious situation was temporarily leveled. By 1983, Dan Evins took over as chairman of the foundation and initiated a passionate campaign to improve the school's future. Some progress was made, but not enough to save it. An auction was held immediately following the school's end. Planned for just one day, it turned into a two-week wake, with memorabilia, books, furniture, and even the pots and pans from the kitchen on the auction block. Proceeds were used to pay off debts, and the remainder was placed into a Cumberland University scholarship fund. (CHMA.)

Three

Lebanon from 1900 to World War II

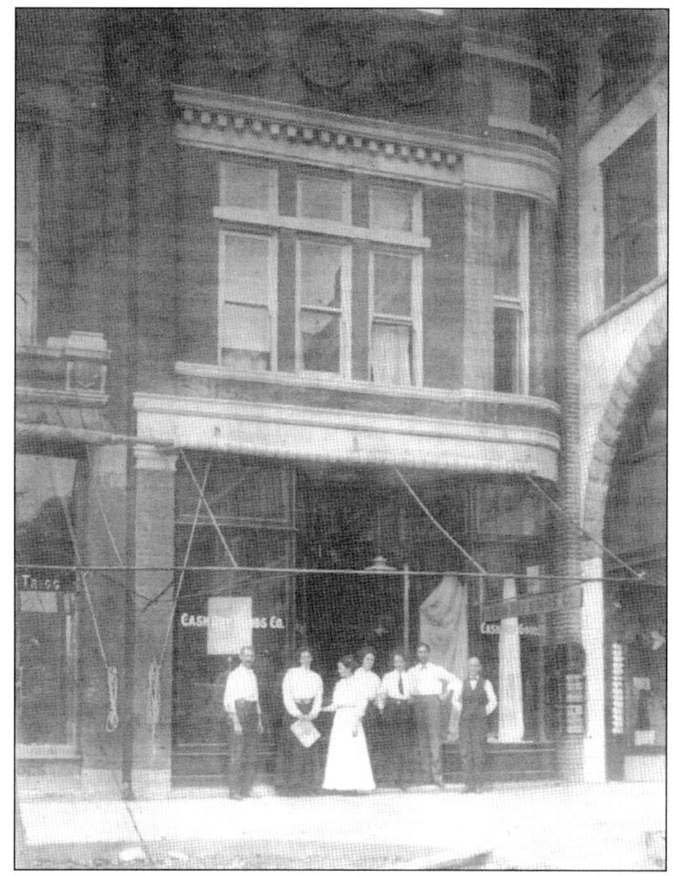

Shown here is the newly built Arcade Building, to the right of Cash Dry Goods on the southeast corner of the Square in 1909. The new Arcade Building replaced J.T. McClain's building, destroyed by fire on January 31, 1909. The Arcade was a first for Lebanon. On February 25, 1909, the *Lebanon Democrat* described the new venture as "at least five stores fronting west on an arcade extending north and south from the corner of the square." (CLMHC.)

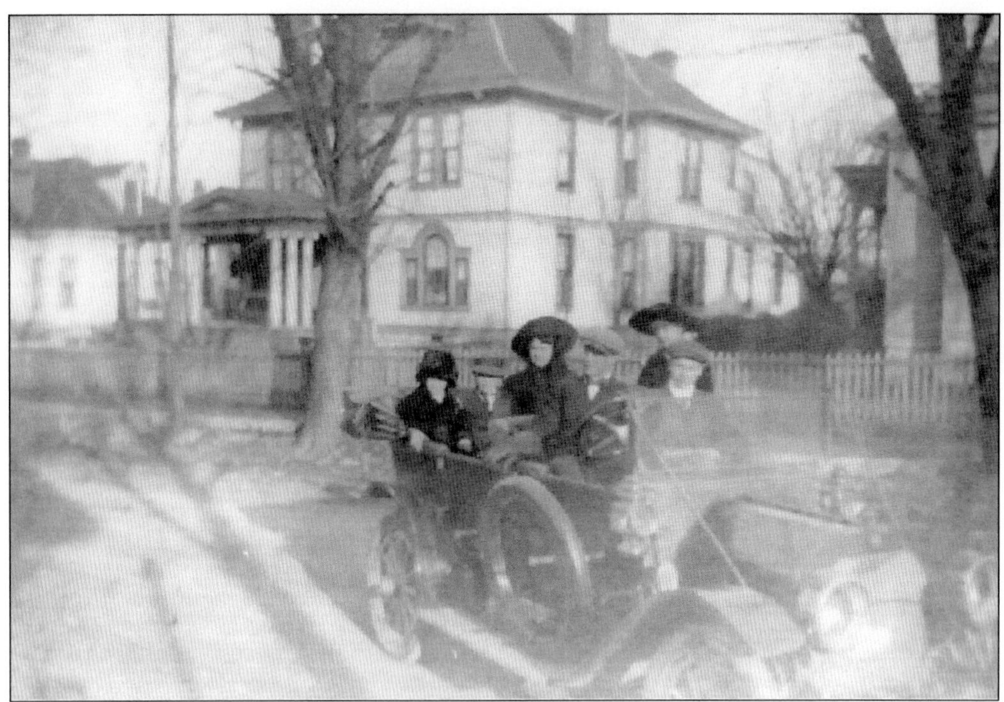

Edgar Green started a retail grocery business in 1887. By 1904, he had moved into the old grain and feed store on the south side of East Main Street's 100 block. Green and his wife, Louise, bought a lot at 208 South College Street in 1906. Soon after, the family home was built, as seen above. Enjoying a ride in their Studebaker, one of Lebanon's first cars, are, from left to right, (front seat) Edgar Green and Kirk West; (backseat) Eleanor Green and Louise West Green. Standing is Louise Green. By 1908, Edgar Green had partnered with Harry Freeman to run a hardware and grocery store, Freeman & Green, located on North College Street. Below, standing in front of the store are, from left to right, unidentified, Harry Freeman, and Edgar Green. (Both, CLMHC.)

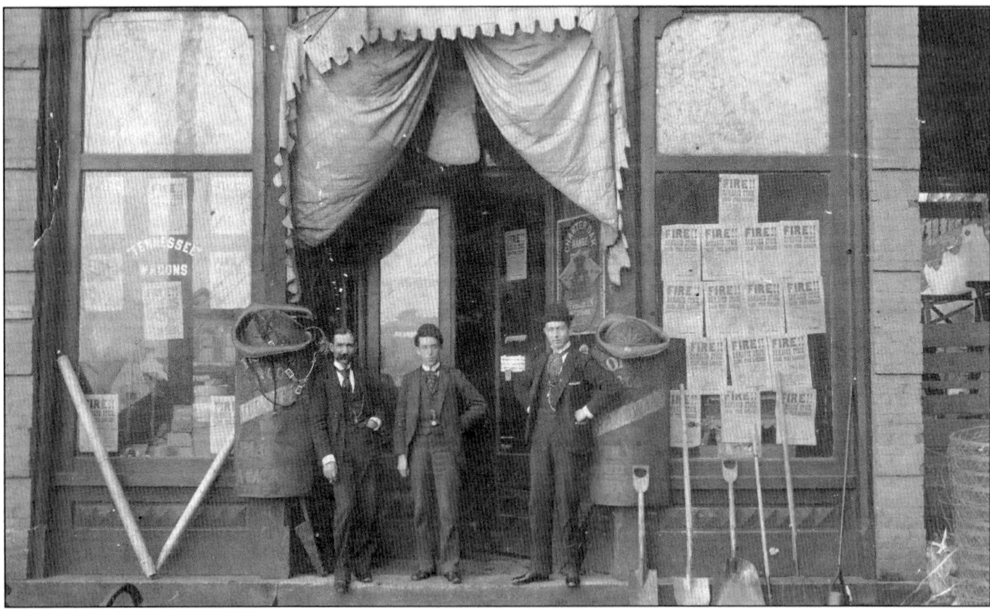

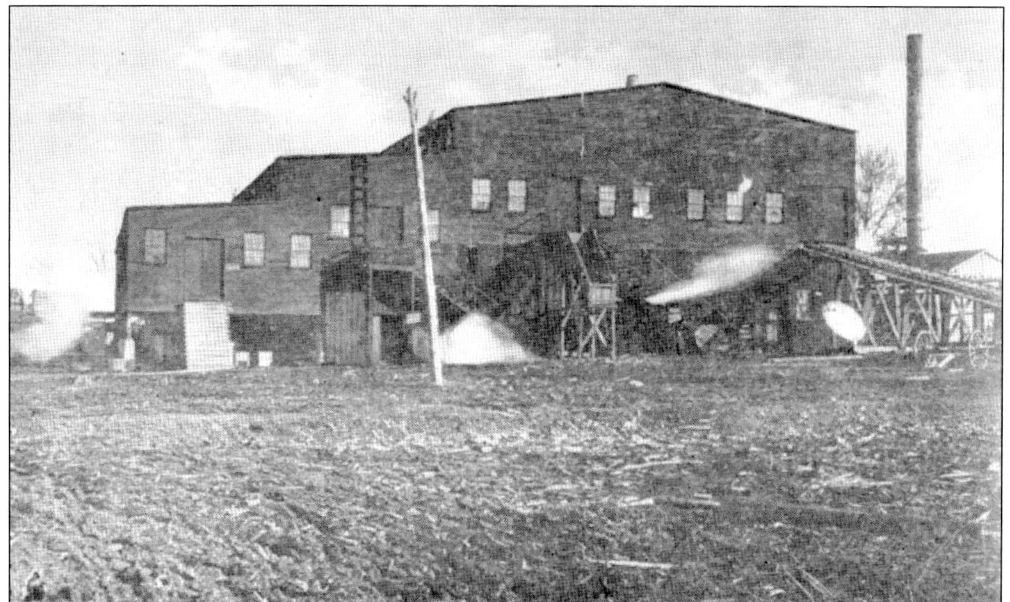

Industry in Lebanon was booming in 1908. That year saw the establishment of the Gulf Red Cedar City Pencil Factory, seen in a postcard image above. The factory was located near the NC&StL depot on present-day Gulf Street. Another new concern in town was the Cedarcroft Sanitarium, formed in 1905 and first located on the northwest side of the Square on North Cumberland Street. A fire on this side of the Square in 1908 caused a move to a new location on West Main Street, the site of the former Robert Hatton home place. This structure is shown below on a 1909 postcard. By 1910, new ownership changed the name to the Cumberland Sanitarium. A fire in 1915 destroyed all but one wing of the building. This remnant still stands today on the northeast corner of North Hatton Avenue and West Main Street. (Above, courtesy of Thomas Partlow; below, RWPCCU.)

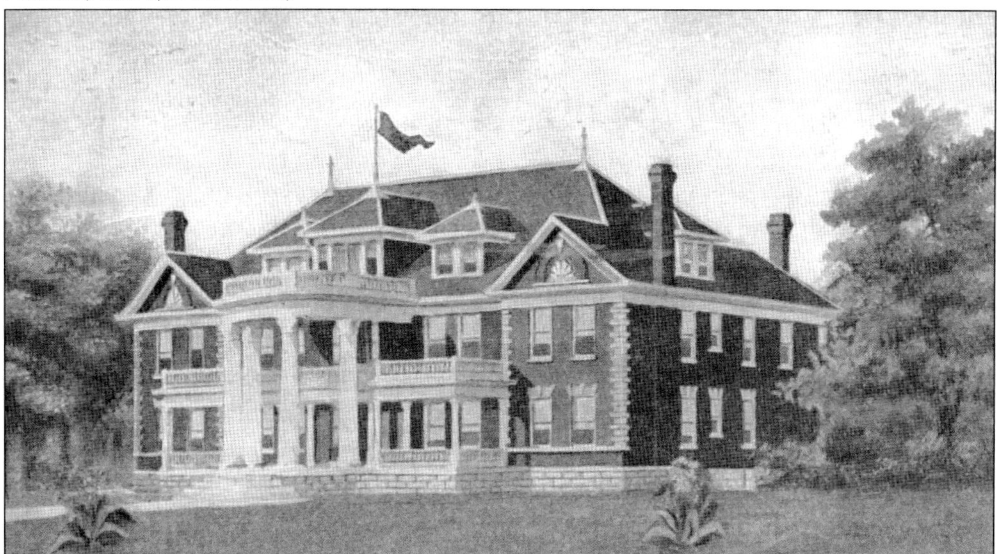

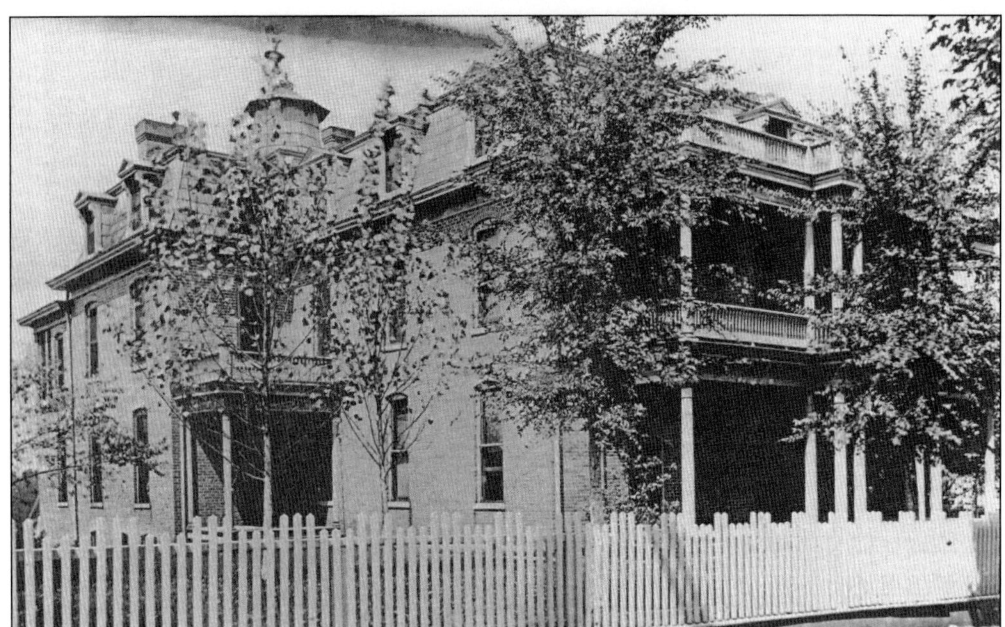

Dr. Howard K. Edgerton purchased a lot on the west side of South College Street in 1896. By 1897, the Edgerton Infirmary had been constructed. Author Ellen Taylor Schlink confirms this date in volume two of her book *"This Is The Place": A History Of Lebanon, Tennessee, 1780–1972*, with information from Edgerton's daughter in a letter dated 1971. Through the years, ownership and names changed many times. As mentioned earlier, the Cedarcroft Sanitarium had a change of ownership in 1910, and the new owners purchased the Edgerton Infirmary in May and continued on in this building under the name Cedarcroft until 1914. The property sold in 1915 to the McFarland Infirmary, in 1917 to the Lebanon Hospital Inc., and then to an individual in late 1917. From 1932 to 1967, it was the site of the Martha Gaston Hospital. The front and rear of the building are shown in these photographs. (Both courtesy of T.A. Bryan.)

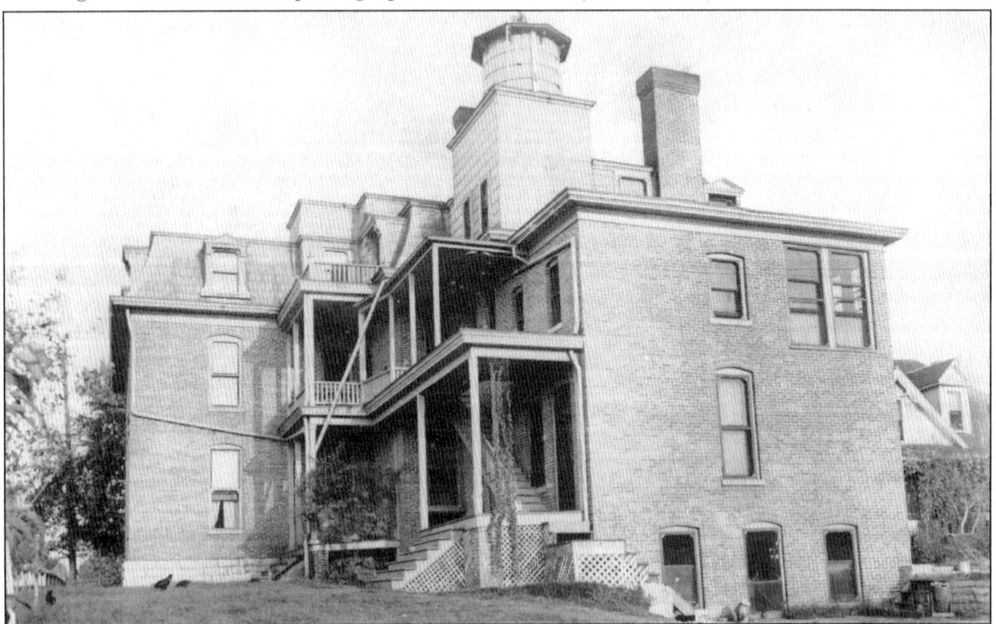

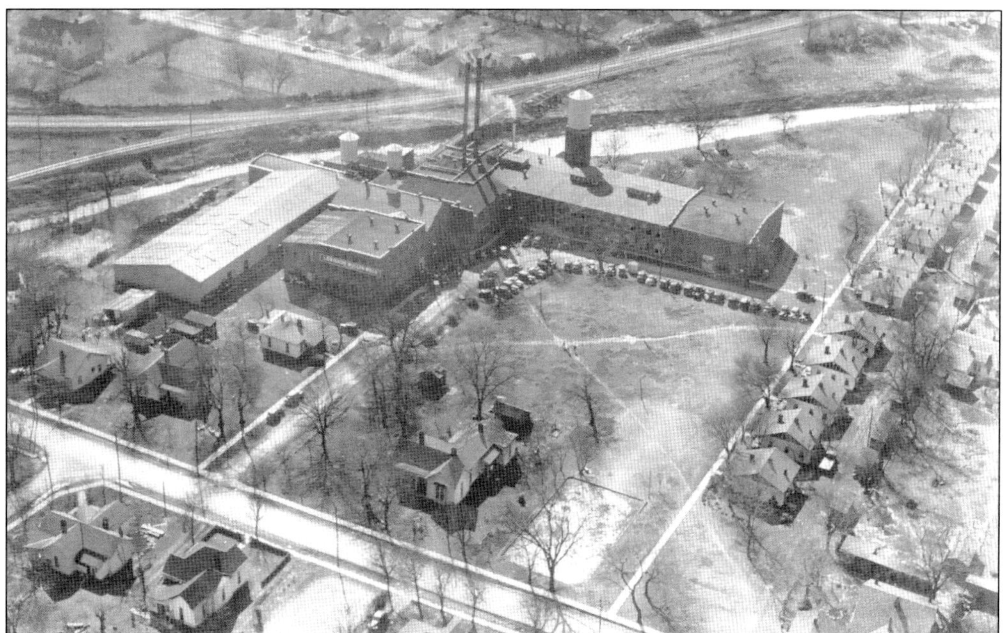

At the turn of the 20th century, Wilson County produced large quantities of wool. The lack of nearby markets and a growing need for employment prompted a local group of businessmen to take action. In December 1908, the Lebanon Woolen Mills Corporation formed. Howard K. Edgerton was the president of the board of directors. A year after incorporation, the first blankets were produced by the mill's 40 employees. The Lebanon Woolen Mills continued operations until 1998. Above is an aerial view from the late 1930s. Below, Agnes Wilson poses on the railroad tracks on the west side of the Lebanon Woolen Mills in 1930. (Both, CLMHC.)

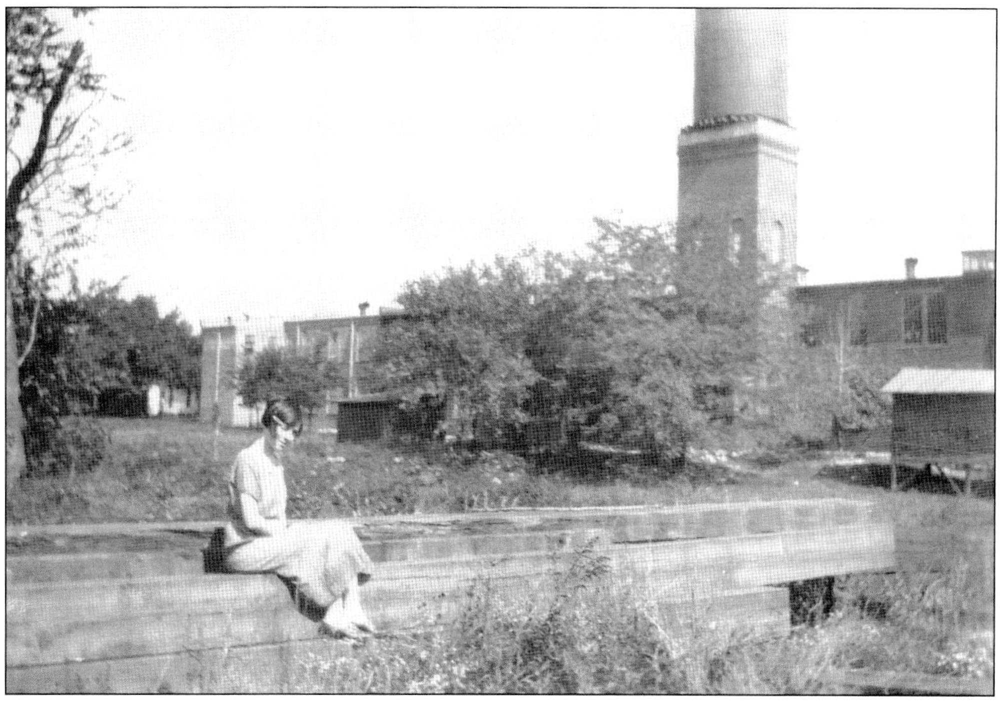

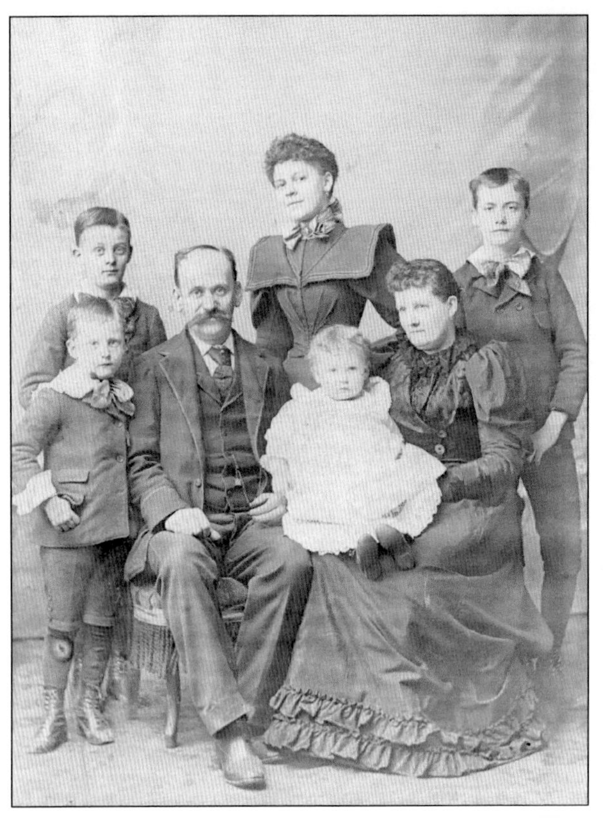

Joseph Scheuerman crated all his bakery equipment in 1905 for shipment to Nashville from Georgia. A mistake by the railroad freight agent landed the equipment in Lebanon. Pleased with the looks of the town, Scheuerman decided to stay and open the City Bakery. Joseph and his wife, Carrie, are seen at left with five of their eight children in an earlier photograph made in Columbus, Georgia. After operating the bakery for five years at 102 North Cumberland Street (the building no longer stands), Scheuerman opened the Bottling Works Company, bottling and selling ciders, soda, and ginger ale. Will Scheuerman joined his father in this venture. In 1912, the Scheuermans created the Perfection Ice Cream Plant, becoming the first local manufacturers of ice cream. The delivery wagon for these businesses is seen below. (Both, CLMHC.)

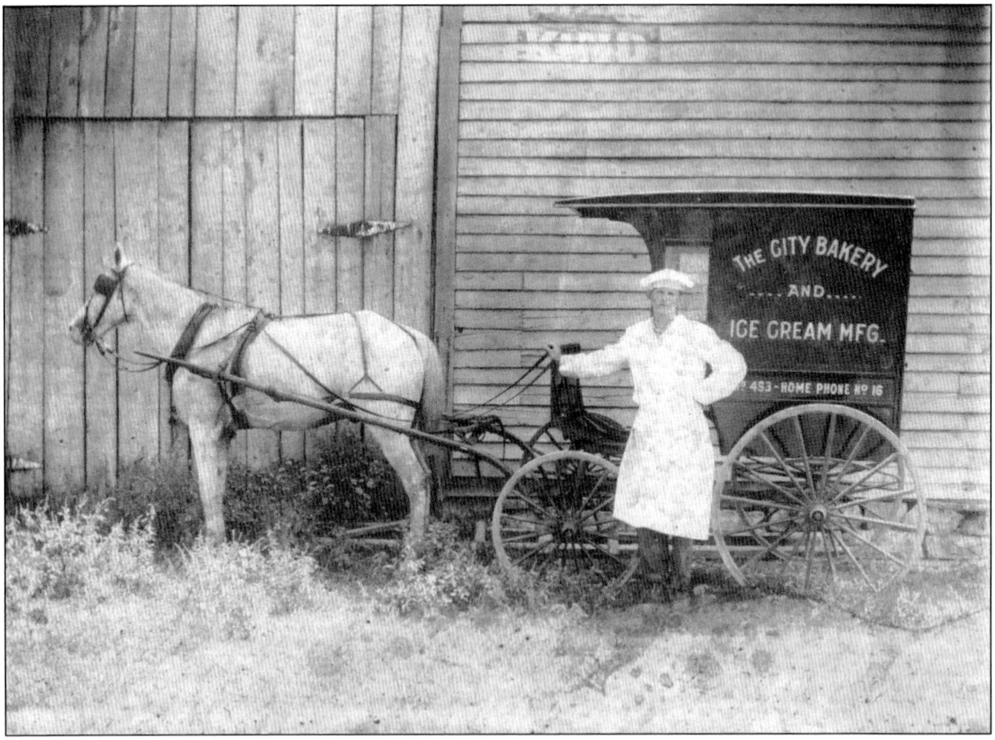

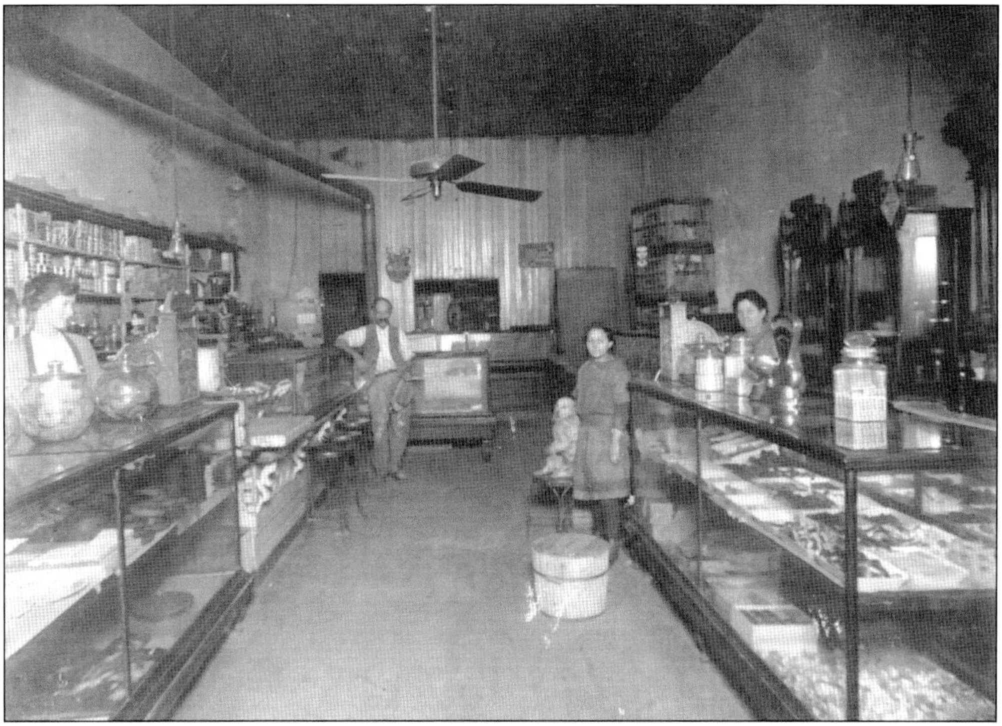

Other ventures followed: an ice plant in 1925, supplied with a 200-foot well, and in 1930, Perfection Dairy, with door-to-door delivery of milk. These five businesses were run by the Scheuerman family, seen above inside the City Bakery in the early years of the business. By 1934, a butter department was added to the dairy, and the bottling plant was reorganized in 1940 to bottle orange and chocolate milk drinks. In the early 1930s, the bakery became the Old Glory Baking Company and continued until 1950. The bakery and ice cream plant are seen at right in their early years on North Cumberland Street. All of the Scheuerman plants were located on the west side of North Cumberland, a block off the Square. (Both, CLMHC.)

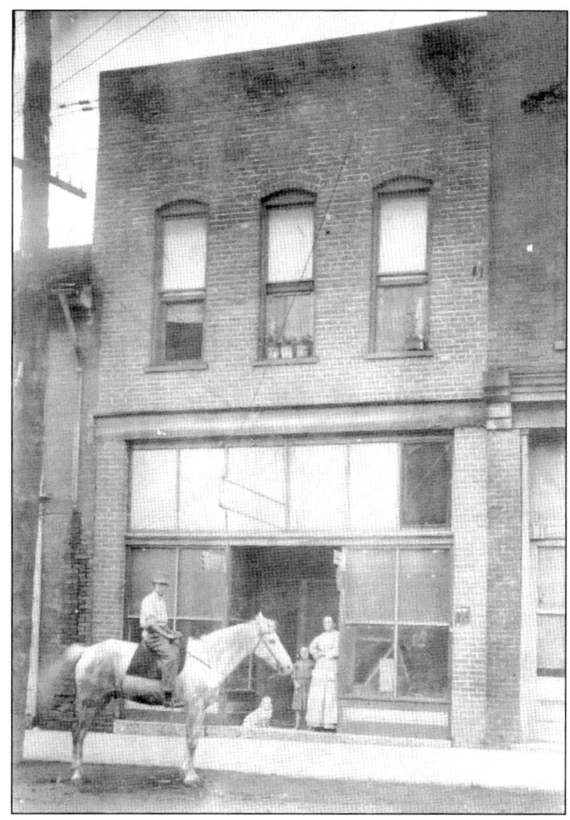

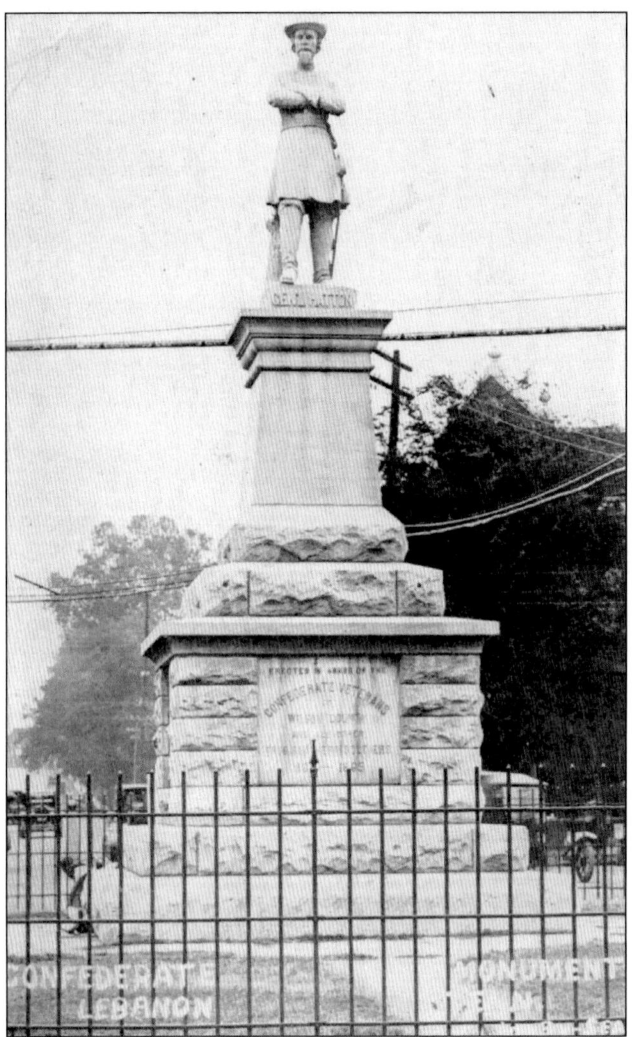

A monument to Gen. Robert Hatton was placed in the center of the Public Square on May 20, 1912. It is seen at left, and the dedication ceremony for it is seen below. Hatton, killed at the Battle of Seven Pines in 1862, was a well-respected attorney and statesman. A believer in a unified nation, he gave an impassioned speech at the Lebanon courthouse on April 1, 1861, on the efforts of compromise and a moderate course of action. According to James V. Drake's *Life of Robert Hatton*, later that night, a crowd gathered on the lawn of Hatton's home on West Main Street, "beating tin pans and whooping savagely," disapproving of his earlier speech. Afterwards, Hatton was burned in effigy. After President Lincoln's call for volunteers to fight against the Southern states, Hatton sided with Tennessee in its vote for secession and formed a Confederate unit, the Lebanon Blues. (Left, RWPCCU; below, CLMHC.)

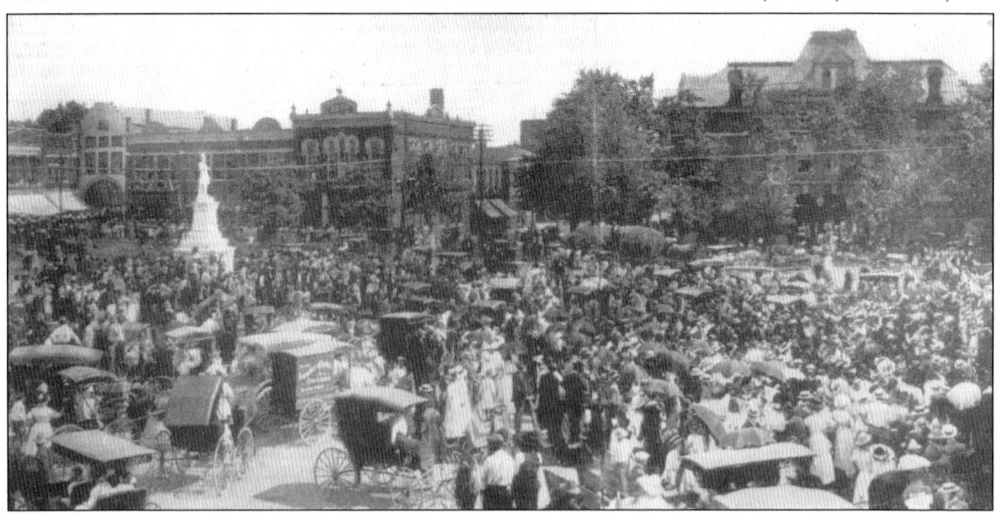

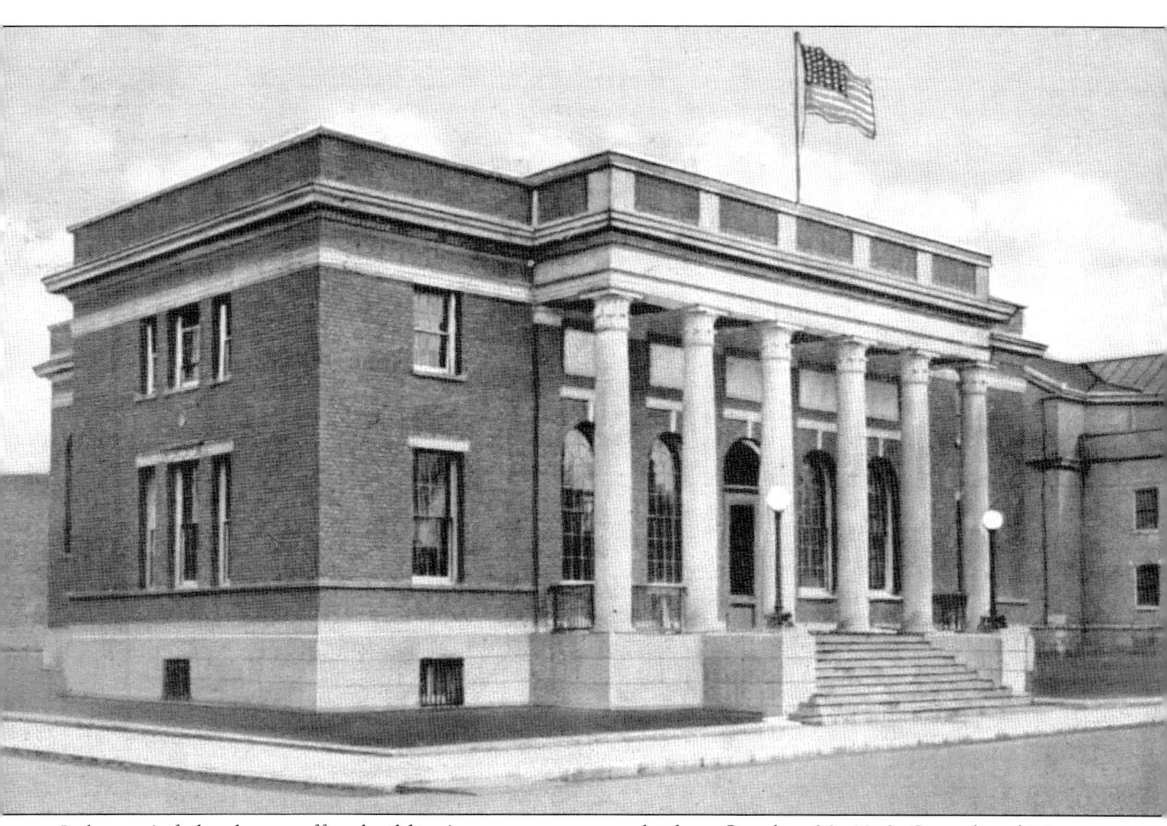

Lebanon's federal post office building's cornerstone was laid on October 30, 1913. Completed 18 months later in April 1915, the new post office signified Lebanon's growing population and business community. By 1908, the town's receipts had grown enough to qualify for free delivery of mail. Sidewalks were placed and houses were numbered in anticipation of mail delivery. Sen. Cordell Hull secured the funding through Congress; $50,000 was appropriated for the construction. The Federal Architects Office was in charge of the design. Oscar Wenderoth held the title of chief architect at the time. The interior was furnished with classical motifs and materials. Pink and gray East Tennessee marble was chosen for the floors and wainscoting. The post office would stay in this building until 1963, when new, modern quarters were built on East Gay Street. The federal post office building was listed in the National Register of Historic Places in 1998. (RWPCCU.)

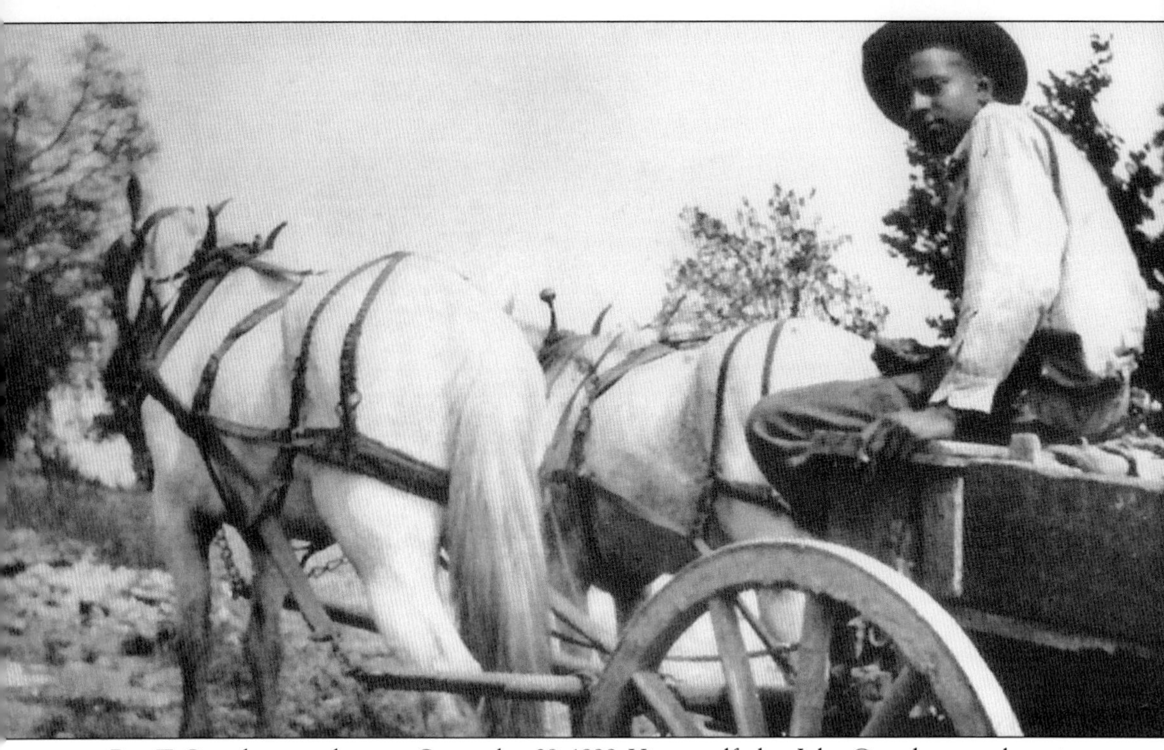

Ben T. Caruthers was born on September 29, 1899. His grandfather John Caruthers was born into slavery at the Robert L. Caruthers home in Lebanon. Pictured at an early age, Ben Caruthers went into business with Sam Hellum to open the Hellum and Caruthers Funeral Home in 1919. By 1928, he had formed the Wilson County Funeral Home; in 1940, he bought out his partners and formed the Caruthers Funeral Home. Caruthers, along with his wife, Bessie, also founded the Greenwood Cemetery on West Adams Avenue in 1933. In his older years, he formed a partnership with Leslie Allen and J.C. Hellum Jr. Other early businesses run by African Americans in the community were Reuben Hale's restaurant on the north side of the Public Square, in the early 1900s, and Jim Harris's butcher shop on the west side of the Square. Dr. Jones and Dr. Turner were both Lebanon doctors. Jones was in Lebanon from 1911 to 1930, and Turner came here as early as 1907 and practiced out of his house on East Market Street. (Courtesy of David Brooks.)

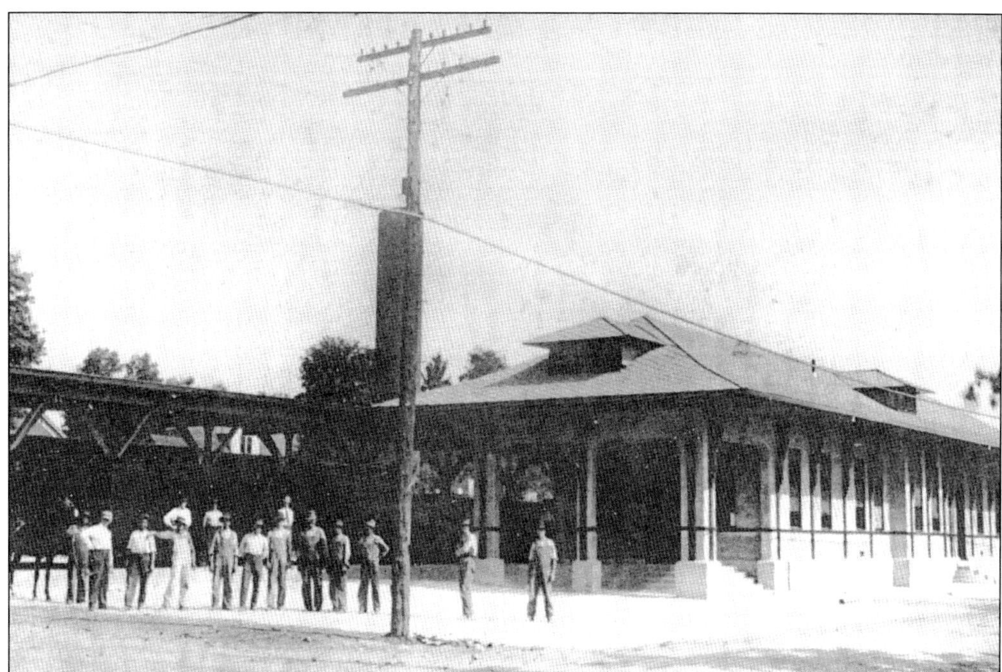

The NC&StL Railway abandoned its depot at the southern edge of town in 1916 after the completion of a new depot on the corner of South Cumberland and East Gay Streets, seen above during construction. Its competitor, the Tennessee Central Railroad, completed a depot on South Maple Street in 1902, seen below. The location of the Tennessee Central depot was close to large industries in this area. These can be seen on the east side of the depot in the same photograph. South Maple Street in 1902 was crowded with several industrial sites. Both depot buildings survive; the South Maple Street depot is part of the Nashville Eastern Railroad, and the NC&StL depot is occupied by Shenandoah Mills. (Both, CLMHC.)

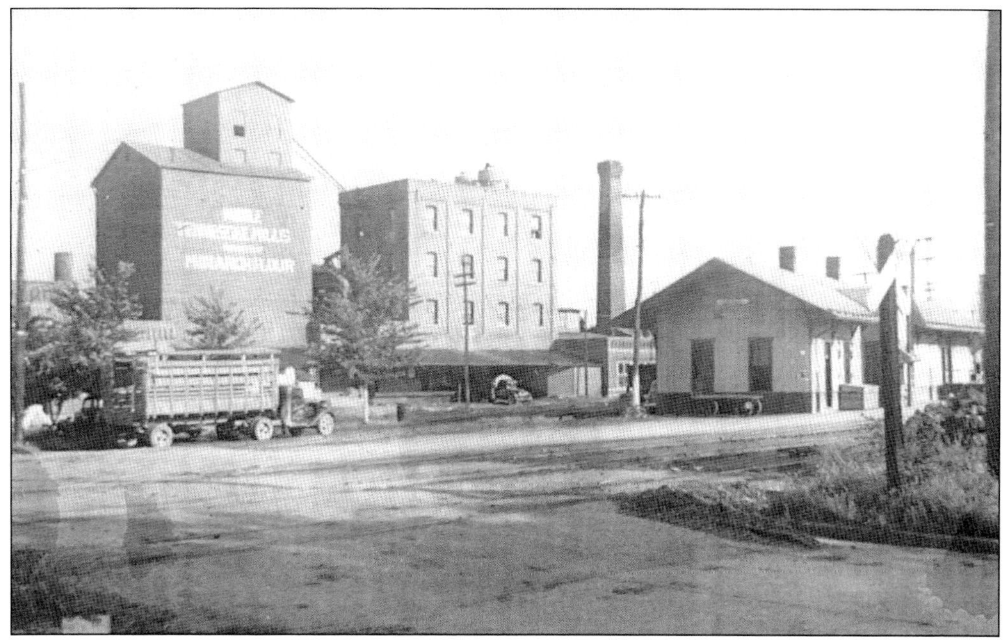

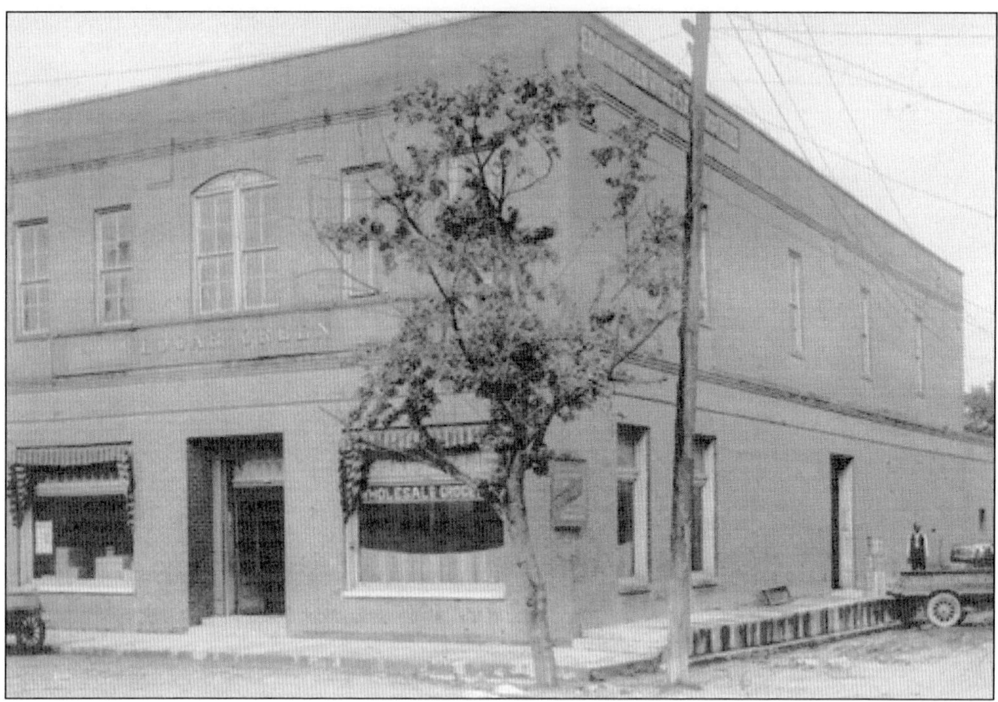

Edgar Green moved his business from North College Street to the southwest corner of South Cumberland and Gay Streets (above) in 1915. Green purchased adjoining property to the south in 1916. The business was a wholesale grocery serving clients in the county and several other states. Standing inside the business below are, from left to right, Edgar Green, Charlie Johnson, "Major," Kitty Raines, and William Green. Edgar Green was a member of the Lebanon Business Men's Association, an organization similar to a present-day chamber of commerce. The group was concerned with promoting businesses but also lobbied for civic improvements to enhance quality of life and the local business environment. (Both, CLMHC.)

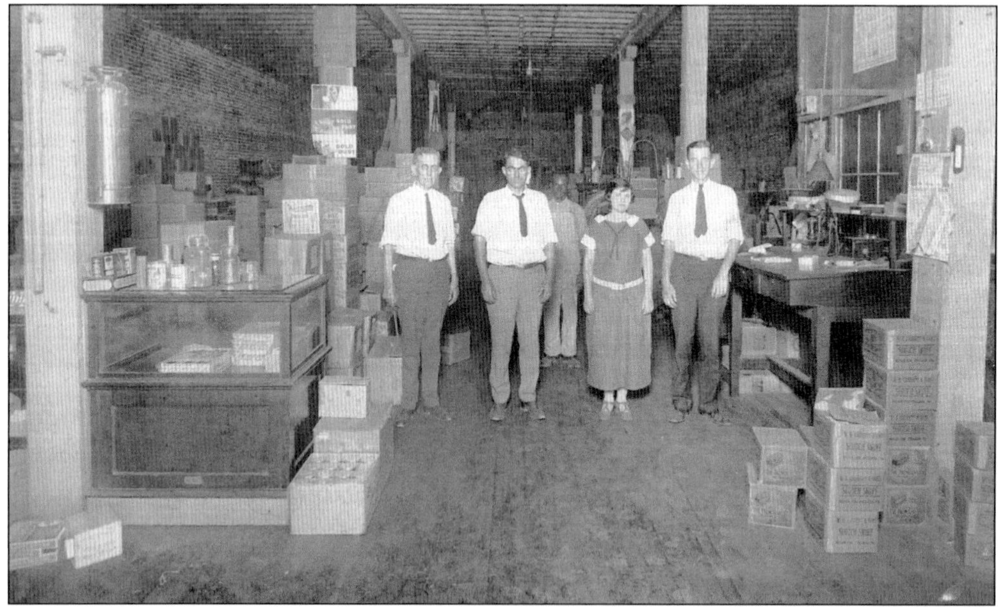

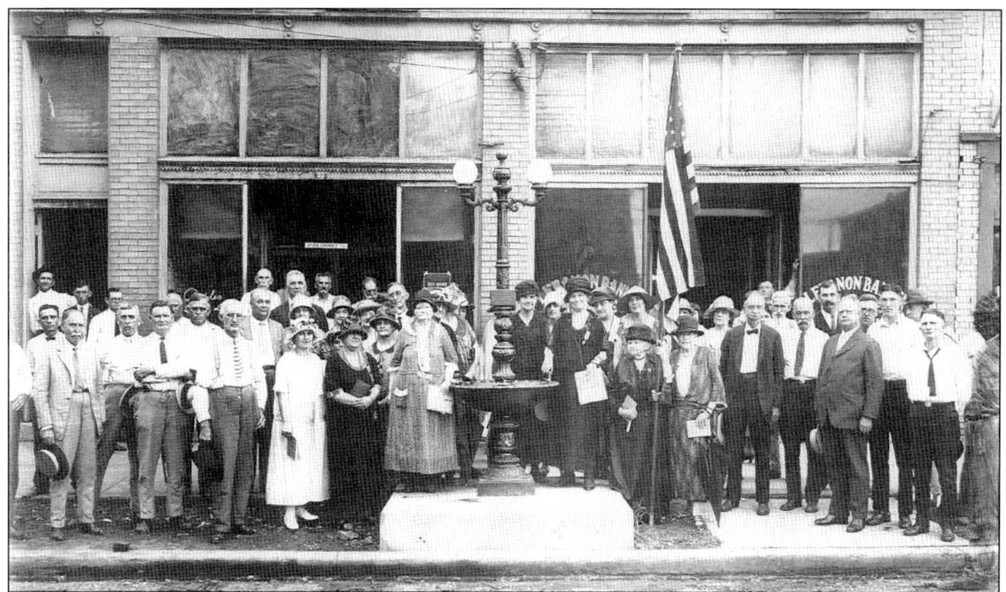

The National Society Daughters of the American Revolution, Margaret Gaston Chapter, memorialized the town spring with a bronze drinking fountain on September 25, 1924. The foundation was placed over the spring on the sidewalk in front of the northeast corner of the Square (these buildings no longer stand). Members of the chapter and the community participating in the unveiling and dedication were Mrs. Andrew B. Martin (regent), Ethel Bouton Baird, Edward Baird, Alice Bone Gilreath, A.A. Adams, and Temple Martin. (CLMHC.)

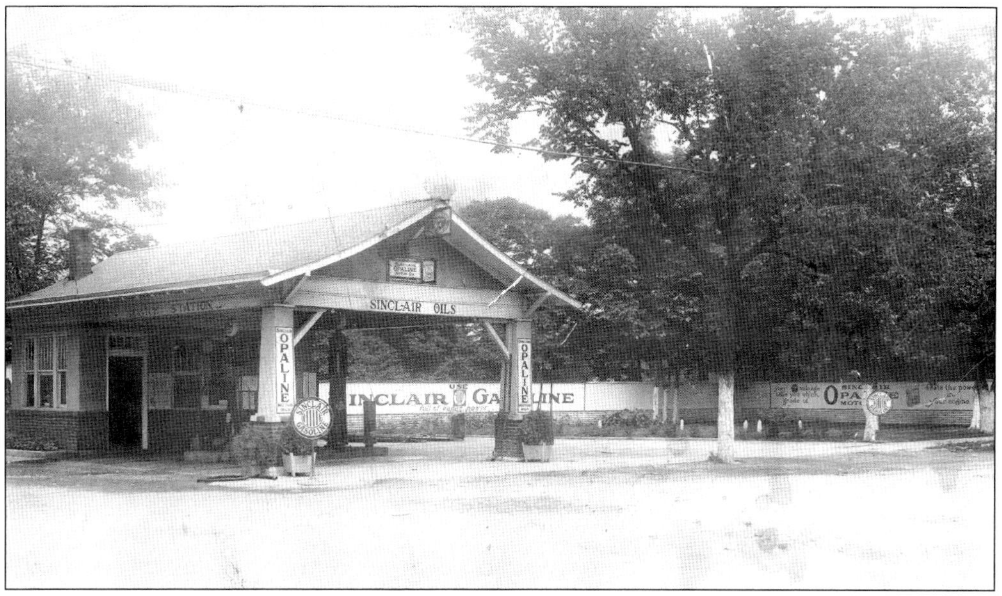

The Diamond Oil Company opened the People's Service Station on the corner of North Cumberland and West Market Streets on November 10, 1920. The station was a first for Lebanon. W.C. Clay was the manager. It later added a modern car laundry. By 1924, there were at least 2,500 cars of all makes in the county, including 650 Fords with an average price of $543 and 25 larger cars worth an average of $1,500 each. Popular demand for cars kept the service station running. (Courtesy of Partlow Funeral Home.)

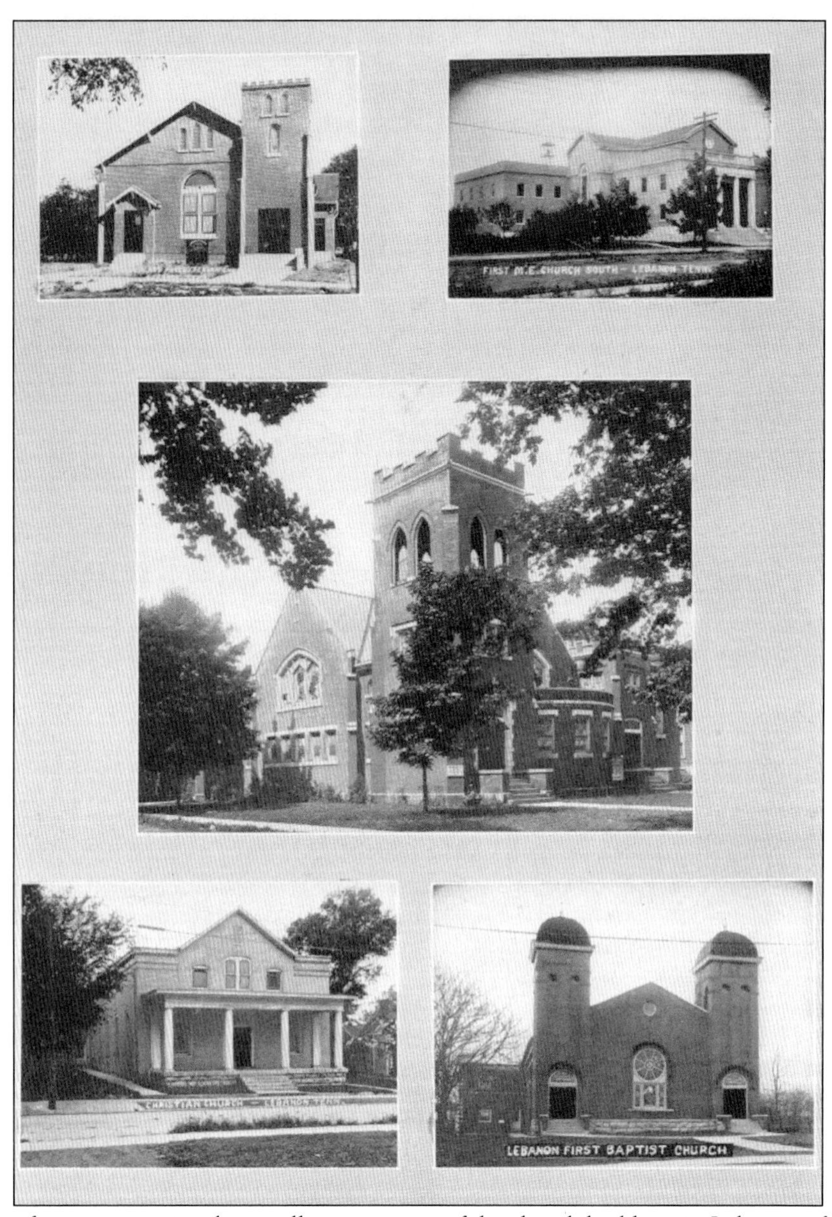

This page from a promotional piece illustrates some of the church buildings in Lebanon after 1922. They are, clockwise from upper left, Cumberland Presbyterian Church, 201 North Cumberland Street, a new building on the same site as the older one damaged by a tornado in 1917; First Methodist Church, East Main Street, the second church building on this site, which replaced the 1856 church building in 1914; First Presbyterian Church, 304 West Main Street, a new church and building, the cornerstone for which was laid in 1911 (an addition in 1960 gave the church its present-day footprint); First Baptist Church, 227 East Main Street, the original building for which was remodeled in 1912 and razed in 1950 for a new church building; and Lebanon Christian Church, 134 South College Street, later named College Street Church of Christ (a 1921 remodeling of the original redbrick church building added eight rooms and enlarged the auditorium). Not pictured but from this same era is the Mt. Zion Baptist Church, on Cedar Street, built in 1913 in a style similar to the First Baptist Church building. (CU.)

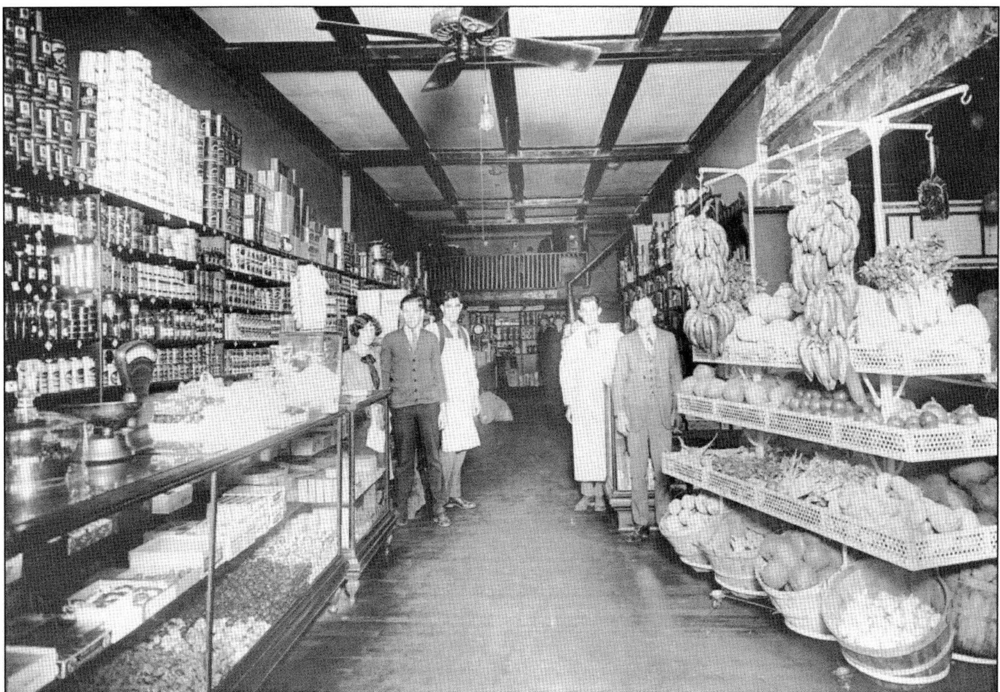

The name Eskew's Grocery meant fresh produce and meats for Lebanon and Wilson County. The original grocery store was located on the west side of the Public Square in 1912. The Eskew and Clemmons family stocked the store with fresh items from their nearby farm. Hogs were fattened, and seasonal fruits and vegetables were grown there for the store. Pictured above in their store are, from left to right, Anna Belle Clemmons, Morris Bryan, Perry Price, unidentified, and Hubert Clemmons Sr. In 1942, the store moved to new quarters on the corner of West Main Street and South Hatton Avenue. The sign from this location is shown below. Eskew's opened a companion store, known as Little Eskew's, on the corner of West Main Street and South Tarver Avenue. (Above, courtesy of Hubert Clemmons; below, CLMHC.)

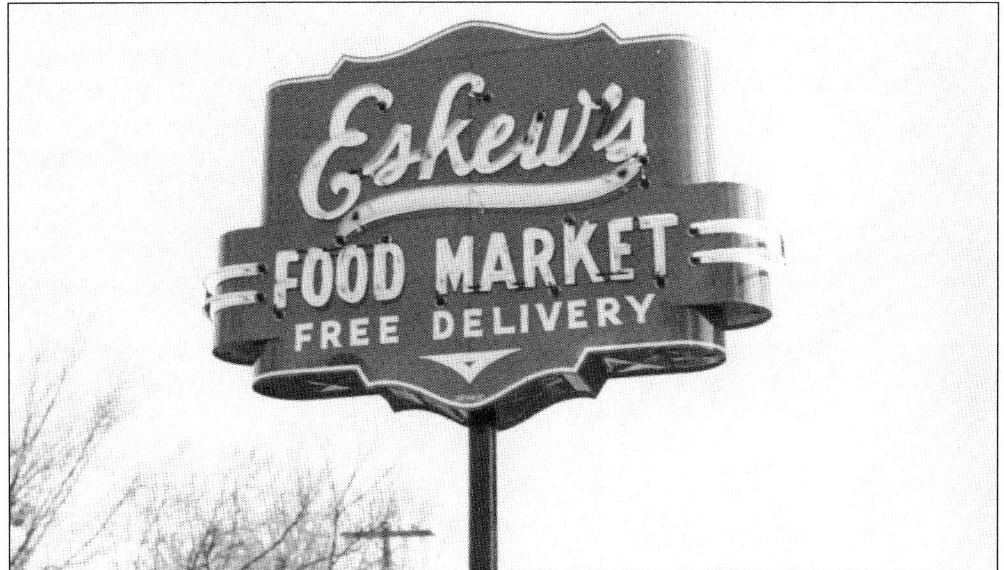

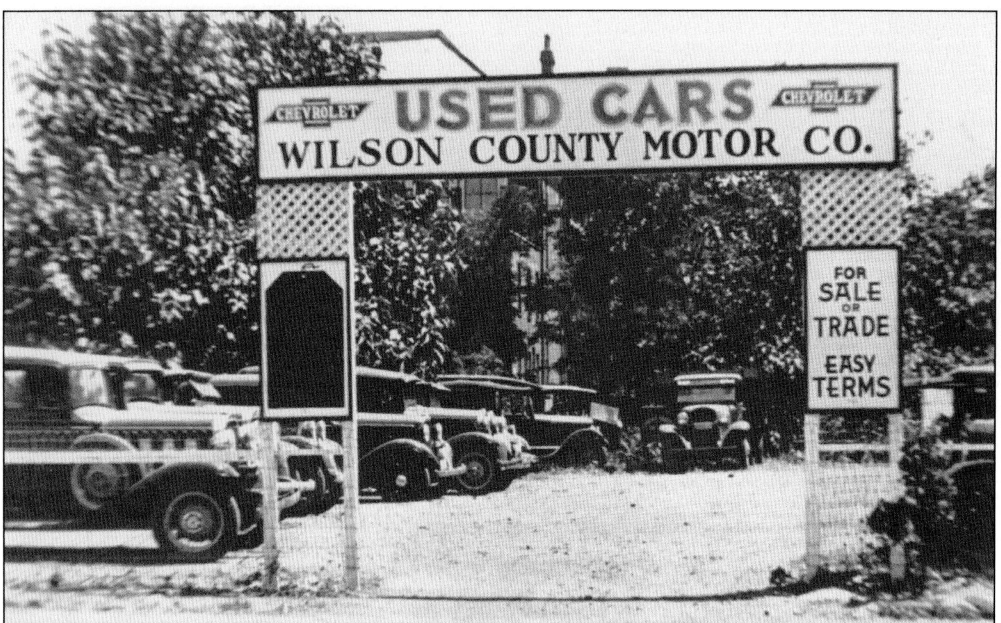

Wilson County Motors began on the corner of South Maple and Gay Streets in 1927 with Winstead Paine Bone Jr. and A.W. Hooker as original partners. Used cars were also part of the business (above). The dealership became one of the largest parts sellers in the United States during the 1940s and 1950s. A 1936 fire destroyed the building, seen below. The rebuilt dealership stayed in this location until moving to a new home on West Main Street in 1964. The photograph of the 1936 fire also illustrates the thriving business section in the area of South Maple and Gay Streets. Gay Street ended at South Maple before the completion of the new concrete bridge in the late 1920s; the opening of the street created even more buildings and new businesses. (Both courtesy of W.P. Bone.)

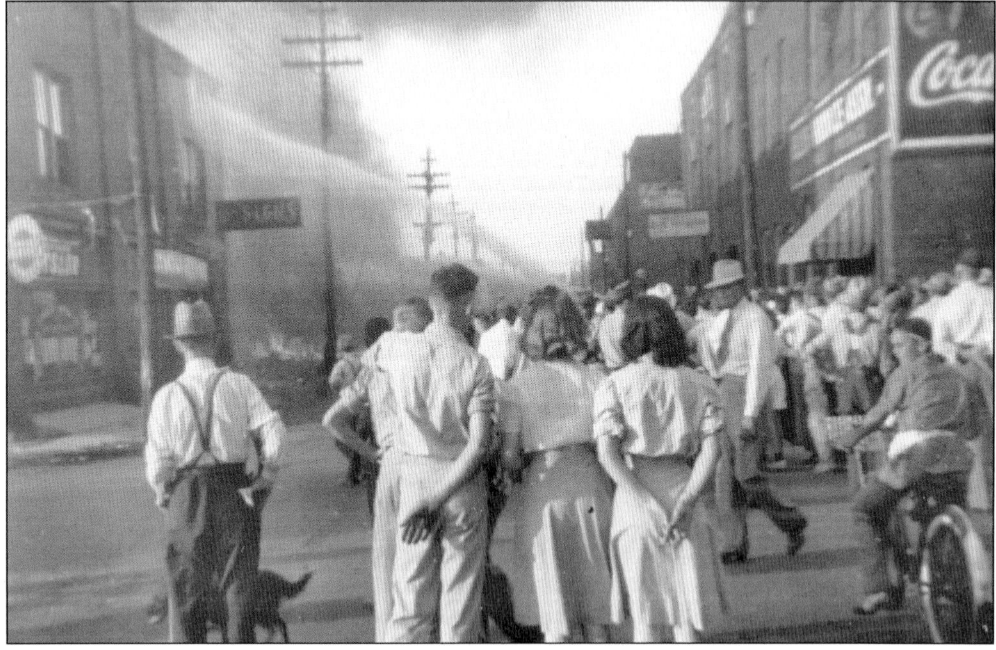

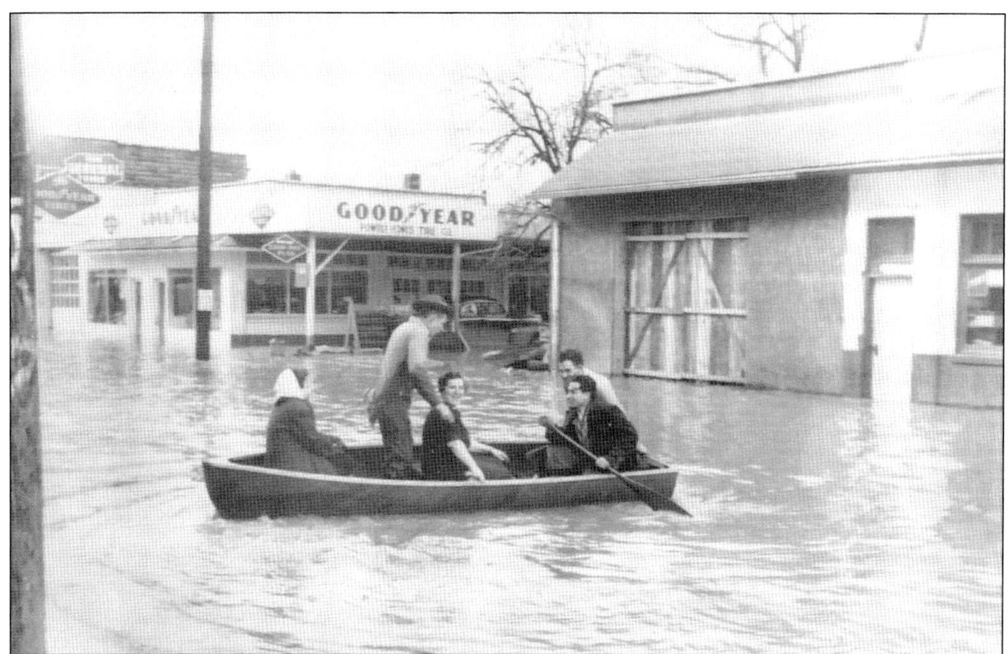

Over the years, Lebanon's downtown area has seen several floods. The flood of 1948 swamped the businesses on South Maple Street and caused workers there to use alternate modes of transportation. Using a red cedar–hulled boat made locally by Hearne Partee are, from left to right, Frances Anderson, Perry Martin, Nancy Graves, and two unidentified people. (Courtesy of W.P. Bone.)

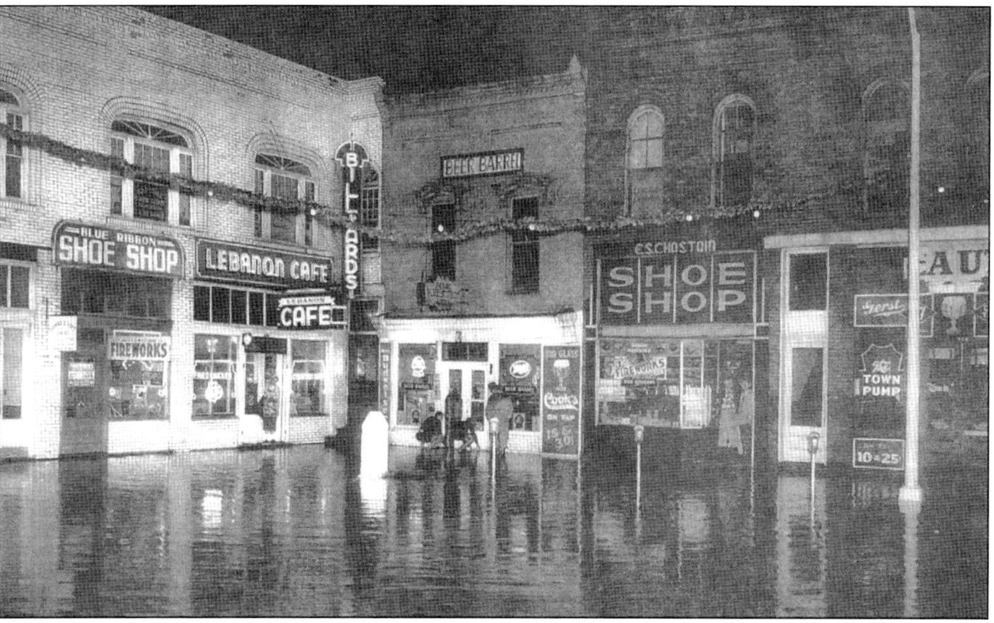

The north side of the Public Square, from the corner by the spring to North Cumberland Street, was known as the Devil's Elbow. The name perhaps came from the types of businesses located in this area: the Beer Barrel, the Town Pump, and a billiards hall in the corner. Also here were the Lebanon Café, Chastain's Shoe Shop, several attorneys' offices, and a taxi stand. (Courtesy of Thomas Partlow.)

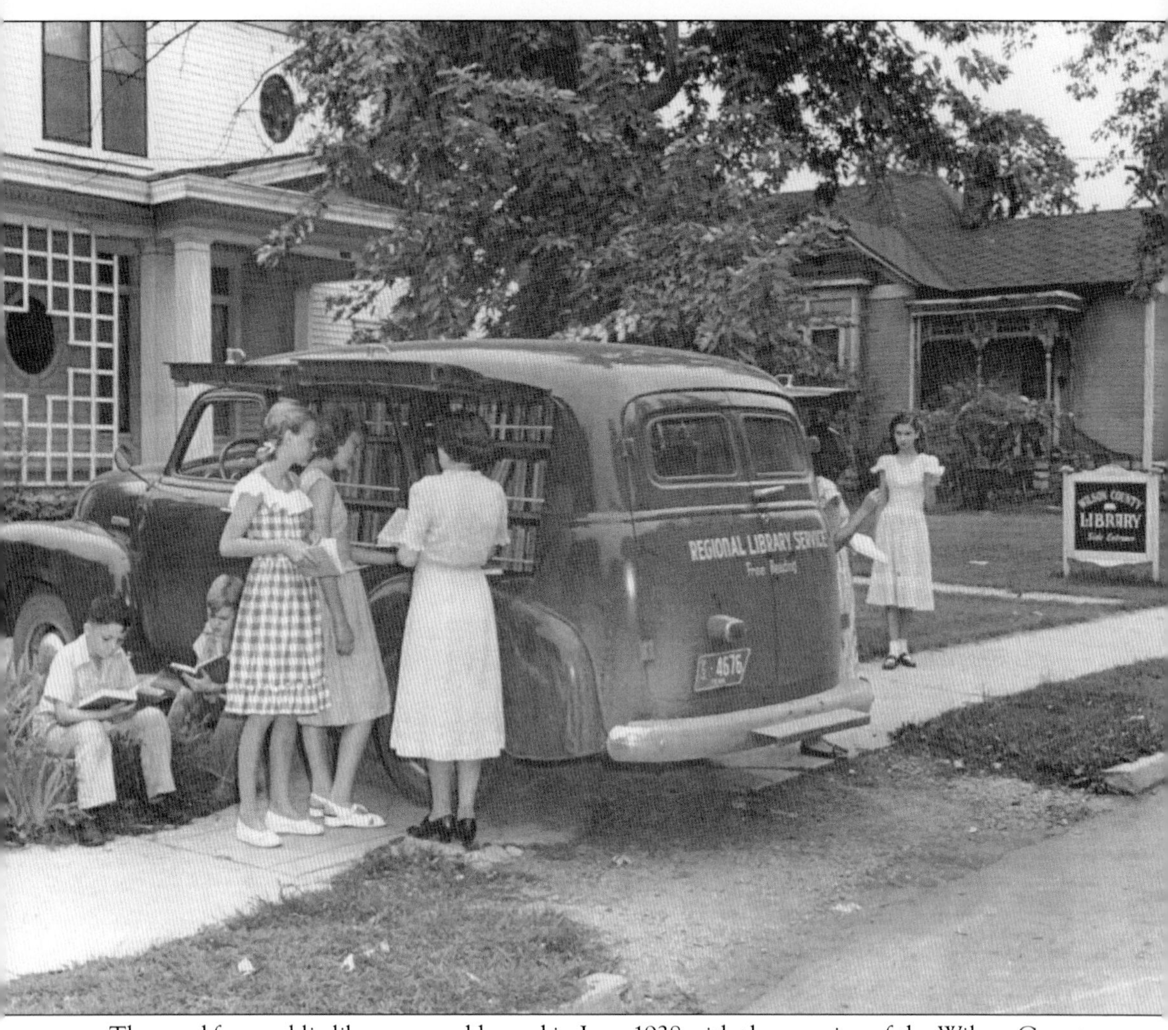

The need for a public library was addressed in June 1938 with the opening of the Wilson County Library. Funding from the state, city, and county governments and local citizens spurred its success. Housed upstairs in the former Edgar Green house on South College Street, the library stayed at this location until moving to a larger space, the former Nathan G. Robertson home on West Main Street, in 1954. Here, the library grew and donations increased. Upon her death in 1948, Mary Harkreader Carson Shipp donated land on the corner of South Hatton Avenue and West Main Street to the city for use as a public library. A new building was constructed with the cooperation of the city and the county, and the Lebanon–Wilson County Library opened at this location in 1964. This photograph shows a Highland Rim Regional Library van making a stop at the first library. The regional library system was started in 1939 by the state to supplement local systems. (CLMHC.)

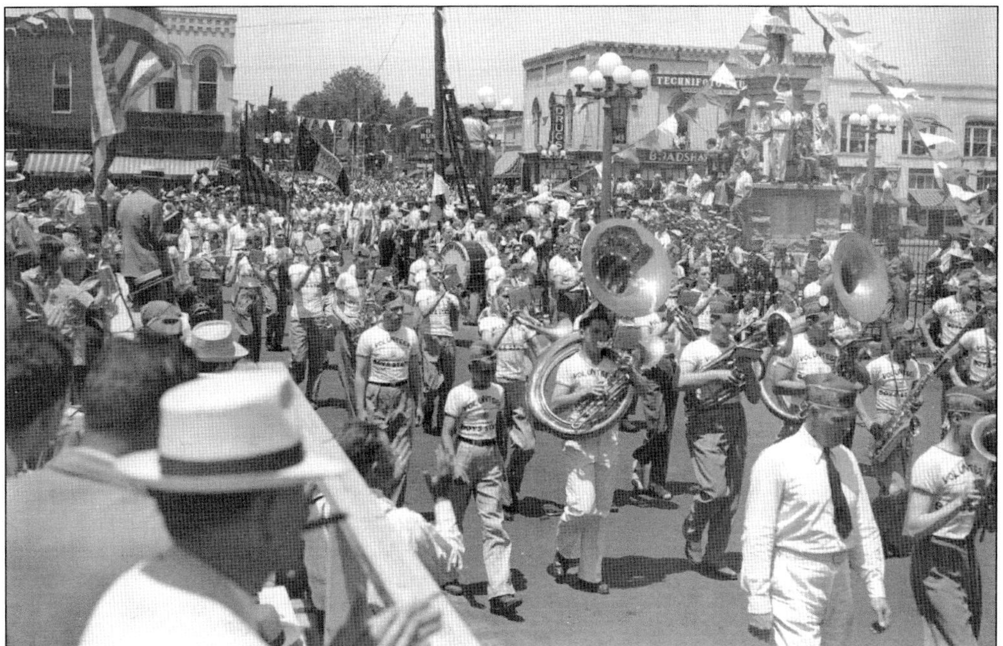

June 6, 1941, marked the first Lamb Festival in Lebanon. Staged by local business owners and civic organizations, the event was supported by the farming community. Gov. Prentice Cooper had declared the week of June 1–7 as Tennessee Spring Lamb Week. A parade attended by Governor Cooper, as well as a lamb sale, were part of the festivities. Other events on the Square that day were a pet lamb show, a wool show, and the crowning of the festival queen. Area restaurants and hotels served lamb dishes in honor of the occasion. The Volunteer Boys State Band marched in the parade (seen above rounding the Square). The Taylorsville home demonstration club's entry (below) was just one of the many floats participating. (Both, TSLA.)

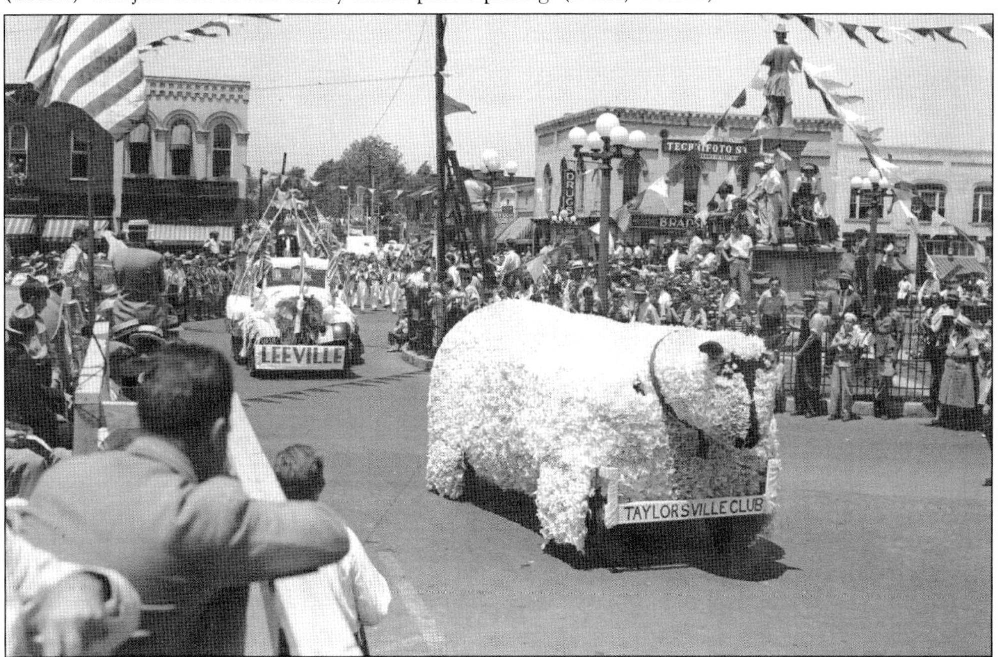

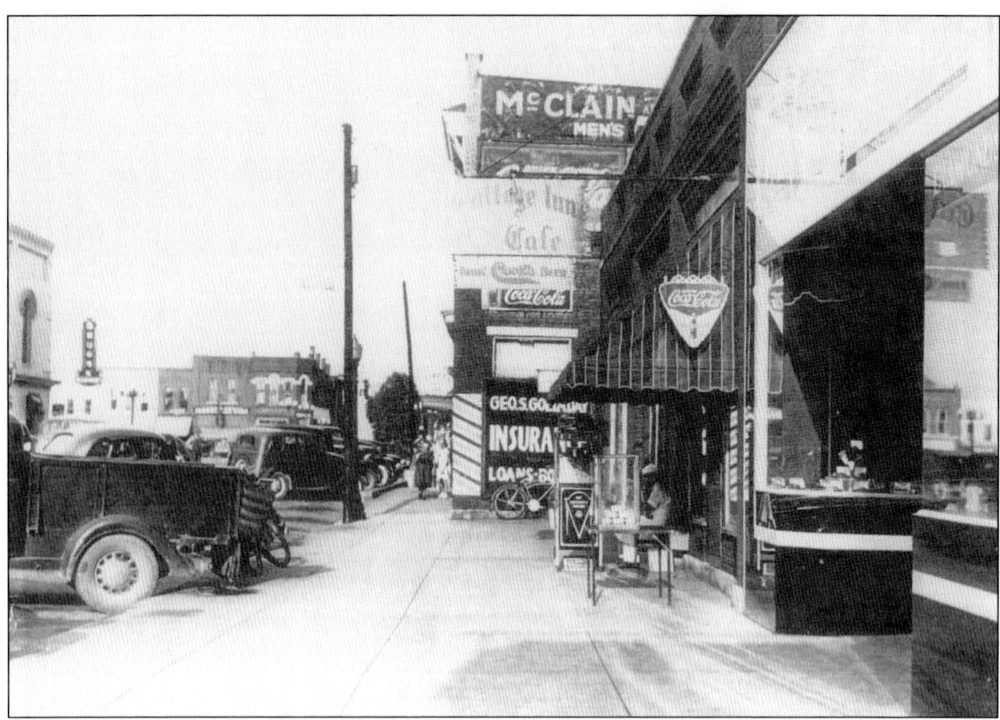

A decade certainly made a difference in this section of West Main Street, looking east from the middle of the 100 block. The photograph above, taken in 1938, shows the area before the building of the Capitol Theatre. In its place is the Village Inn Café, with food for sale on the sidewalk. The McClain Men's Store sign is on the back of the McClain Building, on the corner of the Square. The store in the foreground is Ray's Jewelry Store, located in the front of the West Side Hotel. The view below, from 1949, is after the construction of the Capitol Theatre. Note how the angled building takes up the difference in the setback of the two buildings. Bradshaw Drugs, on the left, remained the constant during this time. (Above, CLMHC; below, RWPCCU.)

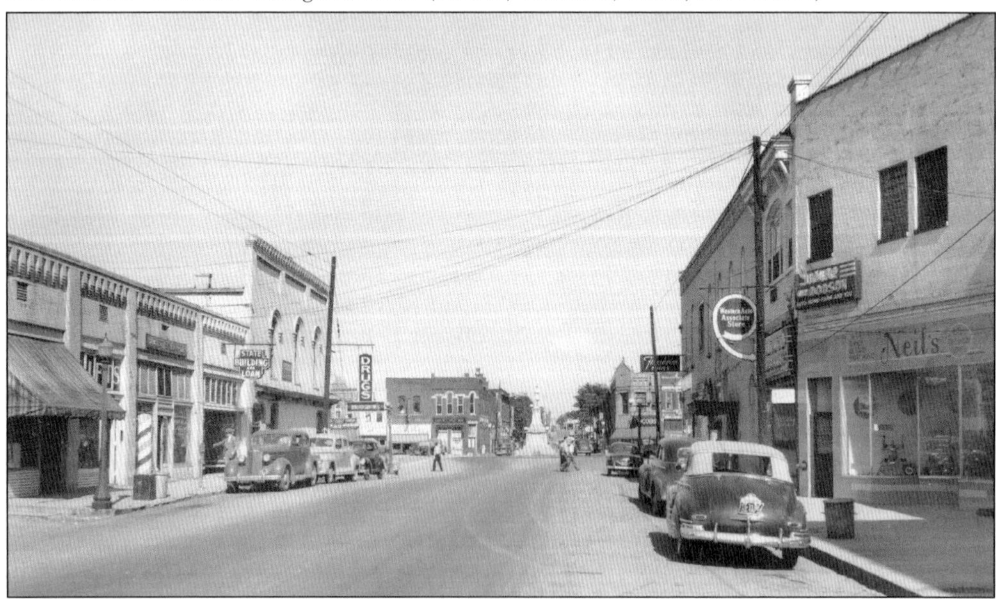

Four

Maneuvers from 1942 to 1944

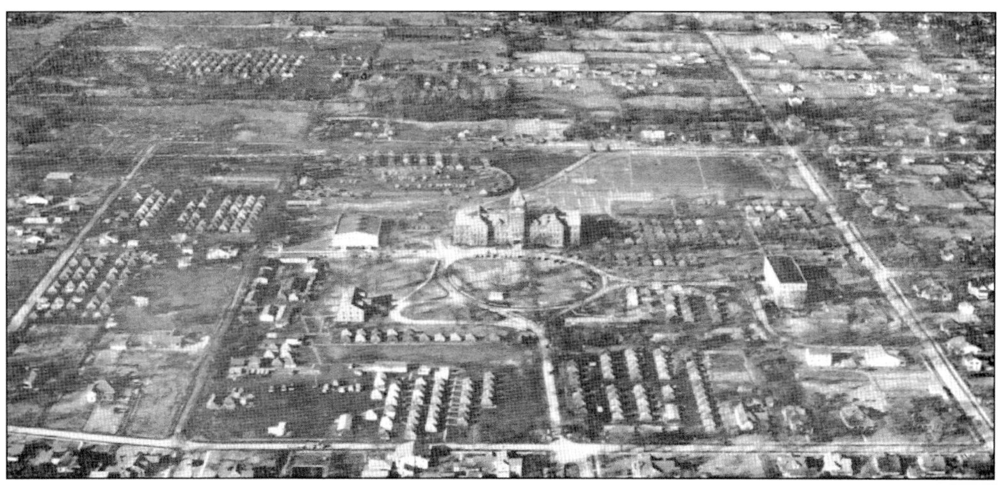

Seen here from South Greenwood Street, Cumberland University was selected as the Director Headquarters for Tennessee Maneuvers of the Second Army in September 1942. The previous year, the War Department had conducted large-scale war games around Camp Forrest, near Tullahoma. Lebanon was chosen as headquarters because of its proximity to railroads and major highways. The maneuvers trained 800,000 soldiers from a 21-county area from 1942 to 1944. Middle Tennessee was also chosen because of the similarity of the terrain to that of Western Europe. (CU.)

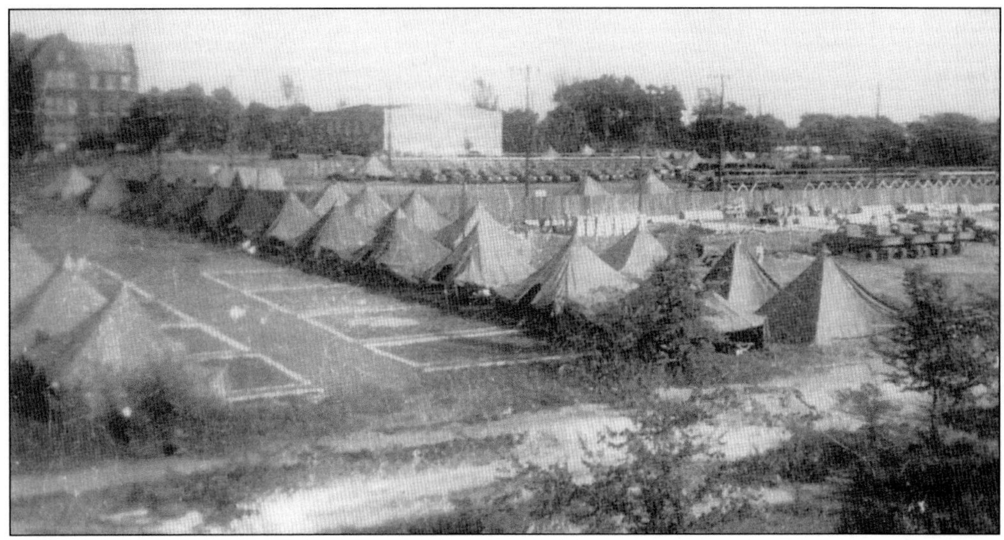

This section of Cumberland University's campus, to the rear of Baird's Chapel and the gymnasium, was known as "42nd and Broadway" during the maneuvers. The athletic field contained the motor pool for the use of Director Headquarters personal. The gymnasium housed the Second Army message center and the State Guard Armory. Men's and women's dormitories were used as quarters for officers, and the commanding general's headquarters utilized the fraternity houses on campus. Mess halls, a clinic, and hospital units were all part of the "tented city" created at Cumberland. The university also hosted representatives from nearly all the Allied nations sent to Tennessee to view the war exercise. (CU.)

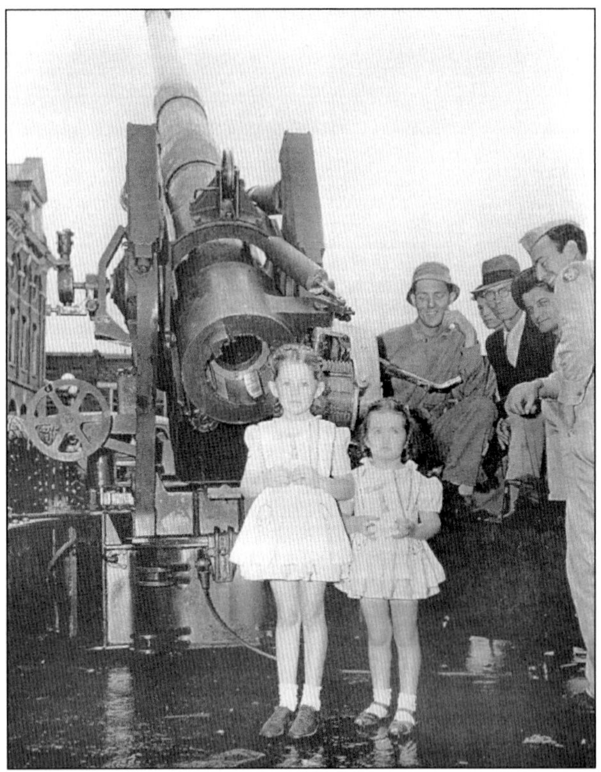

The large number of soldiers present in Lebanon during the maneuvers was a constant reminder of World War II's cost, and an aid to the sale of war bonds and stamps. Shown after purchasing their bonds on the Public Square in 1944 are Margaret Ann (left) and Beverly Sue Padgett. Bond sales were often held on the Square, with displays of military equipment such as tank destroyers, armored cars, and 155-millimeter guns. (CLMHC.)

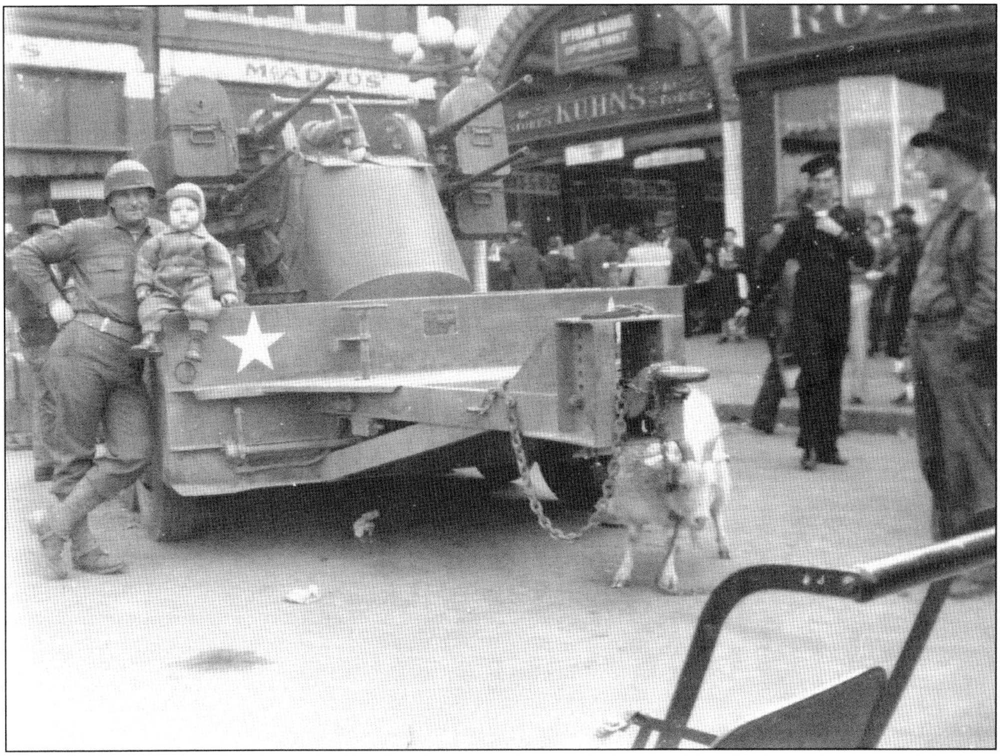

Soldiers stationed in Lebanon with the maneuvers left behind wives and families in the fulfillment of their duties. These men listened for the sound of the siren from an overhead Piper Cub to signal the completion of a problem and the start of weekend recreational time. During this time, Army wives visited, staying in local apartments. These two photographs collected in Pennsylvania show an enjoyable time on the Public Square in January 1944. It is not known if the goat accompanied this family or was a local "kid." Seen in the background is the southeast corner of the Square and the Arcade Building. (Both courtesy of T.A. Bryan.)

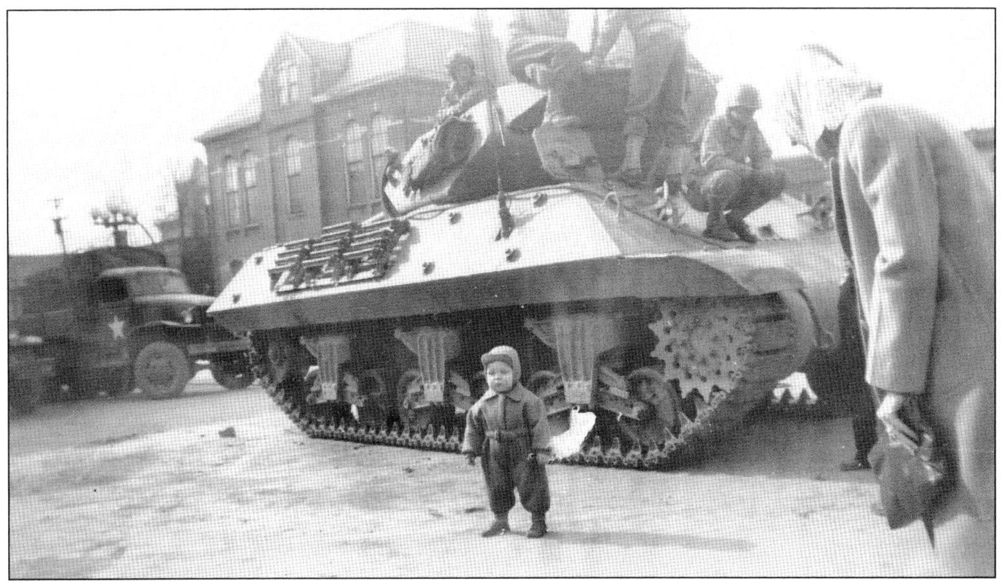

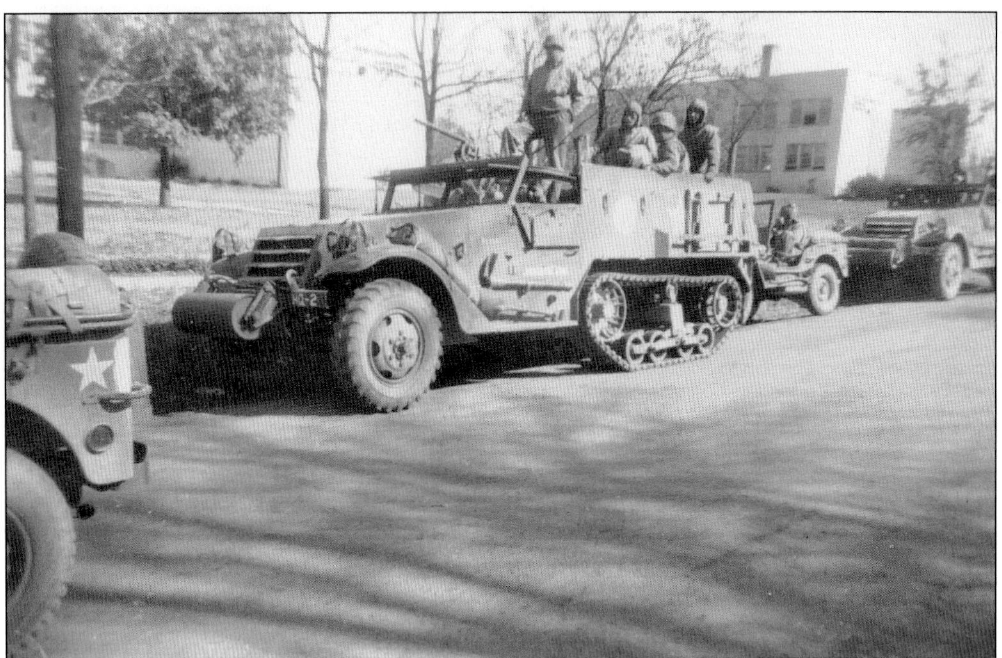

Before the start of each maneuver phase, troop trains would come into Middle Tennessee from the garrison camps of the Second Army. Motorized and armored convoys rumbled through the streets. Each maneuver exercise consisted of eight field problems for the combat troops, divided into Red and Blue armies. War games were carried out in the middle of town and in the surrounding countryside. The photograph above shows soldiers and equipment on East High Street in front of the high school. The school gymnasium was used in the winter months for the weekly critiques that followed the completion of each problem. The photograph below shows a "duck" vehicle in action. These photographs were taken in 1942 by Douglas Stone, a local high school student. (Both, CLMHC.)

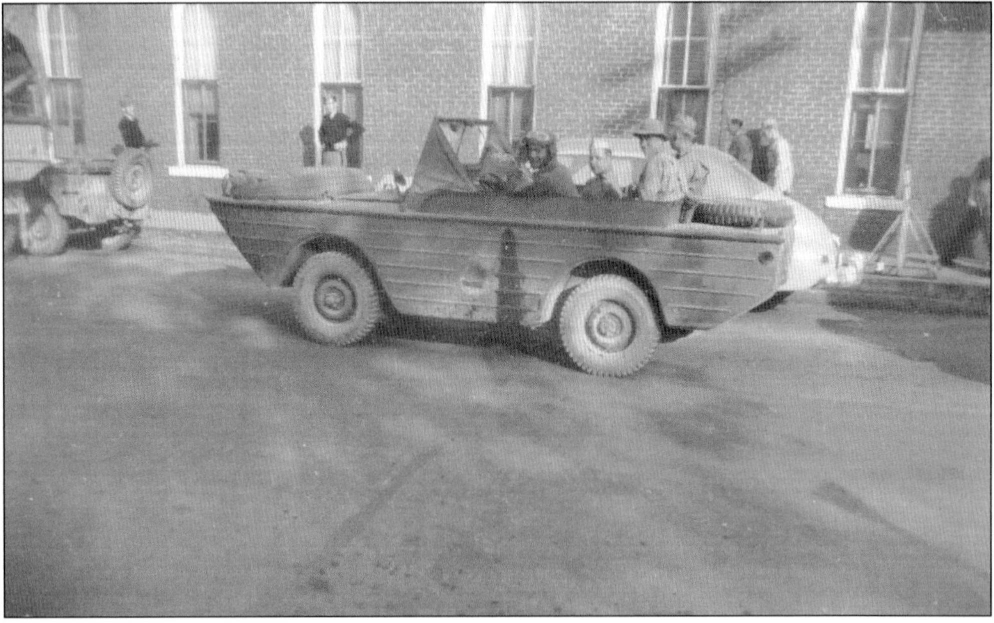

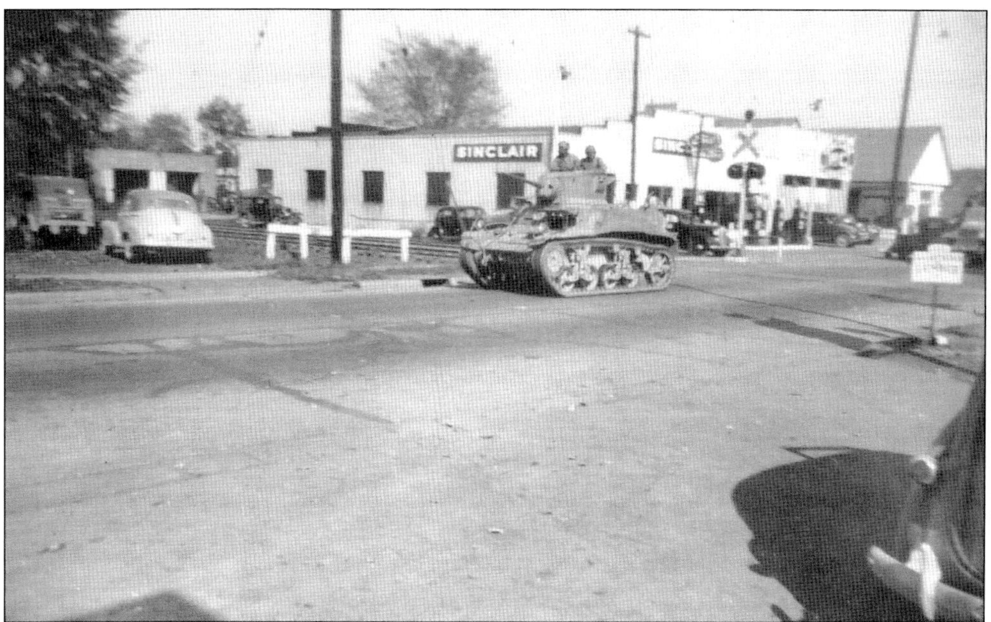

Townspeople grew accustomed to the sight of tanks on local streets, as seen above in 1942. They were also accustomed to providing hundreds of home parties and home meals coordinated by the local Red Cross chapter and the USO. Local maneuver recreation committees were in charge of entertainment and shower facilities for the troops. Weekly dances were arranged, and soldier lounges were established in available space at churches and schools. Historian G. Frank Burns described the scene: "Movie theaters and cafes were packed; drug store soda fountains were forced to shut down twice a day for cleanup." In the photograph below, equipment convoys are seen coming down University Avenue. These photographs were also taken by Douglas Stone in 1942. (Both, CLMHC.)

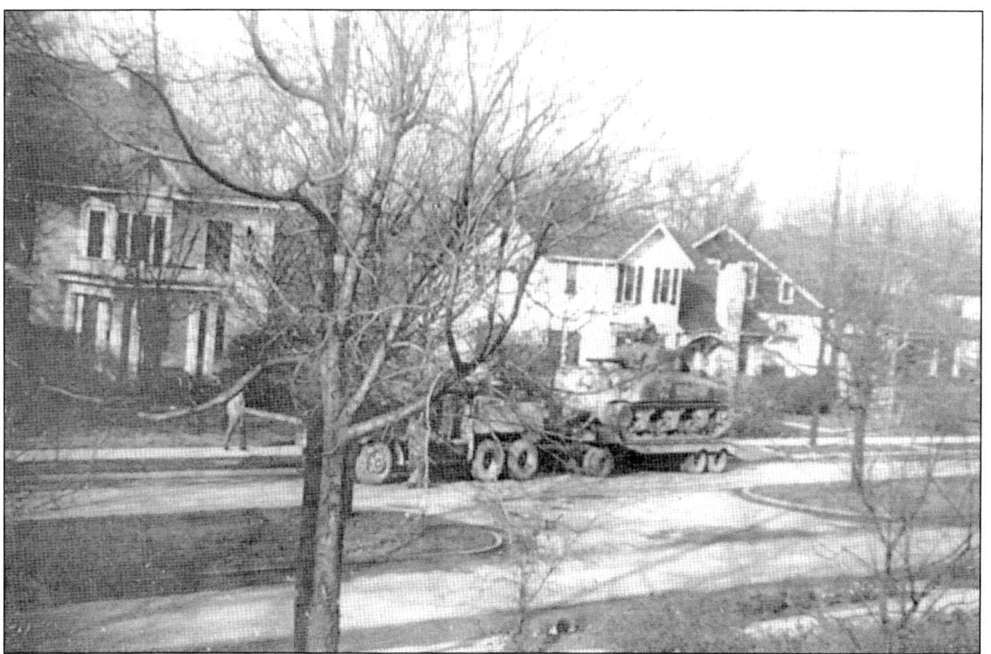

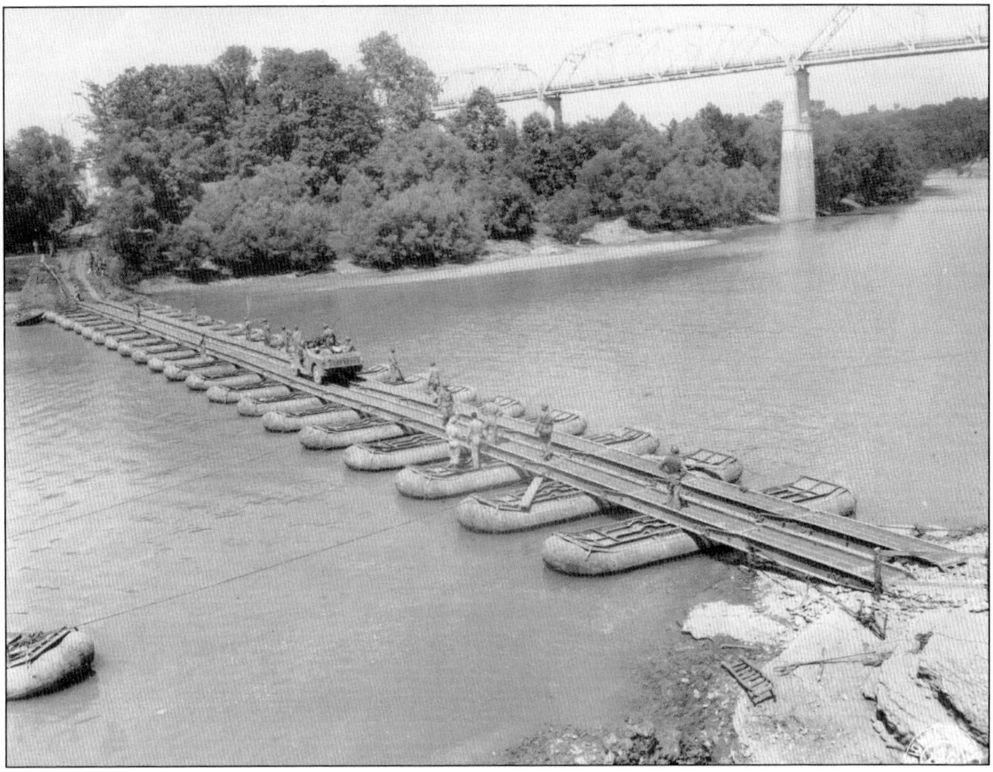

Shown in an official 164th Signal Photo Corp photograph taken on June 15, 1943, is a 5th Armored Division scout car crossing the pontoon bridge built by the 22nd engineers over the Cumberland River at Hunters Point. The Nathan Harsh Bridge, on Route 231 north, can be seen in the background. During a 1944 exercise, 21 men were killed attempting a crossing of the Cumberland River. (CLMHC.)

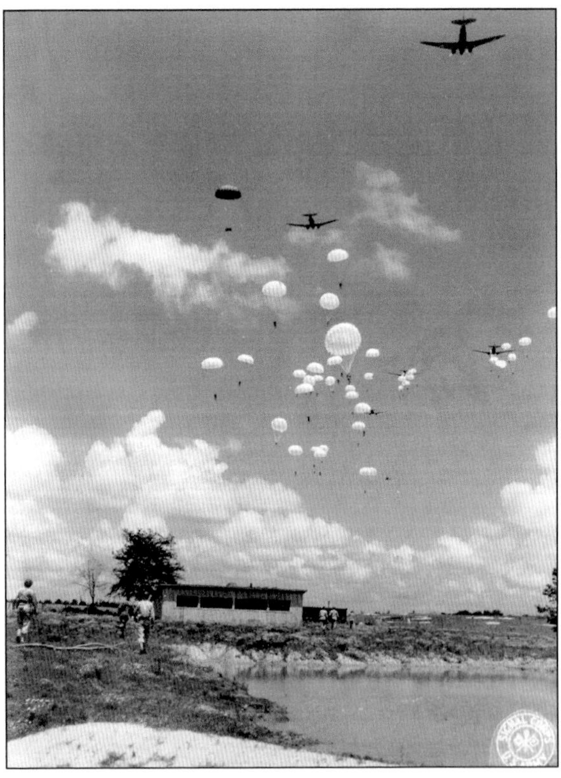

Another official 164th Signal Photo Corp photograph, this one taken on June 8, 1943, shows the 502nd Paratroops of the Second Army during an exercise. Eight days later, on June 16, the 101st Airborne Division would execute a first in the maneuvers: a jump of an entire airborne division under battle conditions. The jump occurred north of Lebanon in the Taylorsville community. (CLMHC.)

Five

Lebanon from after World War II to 1969

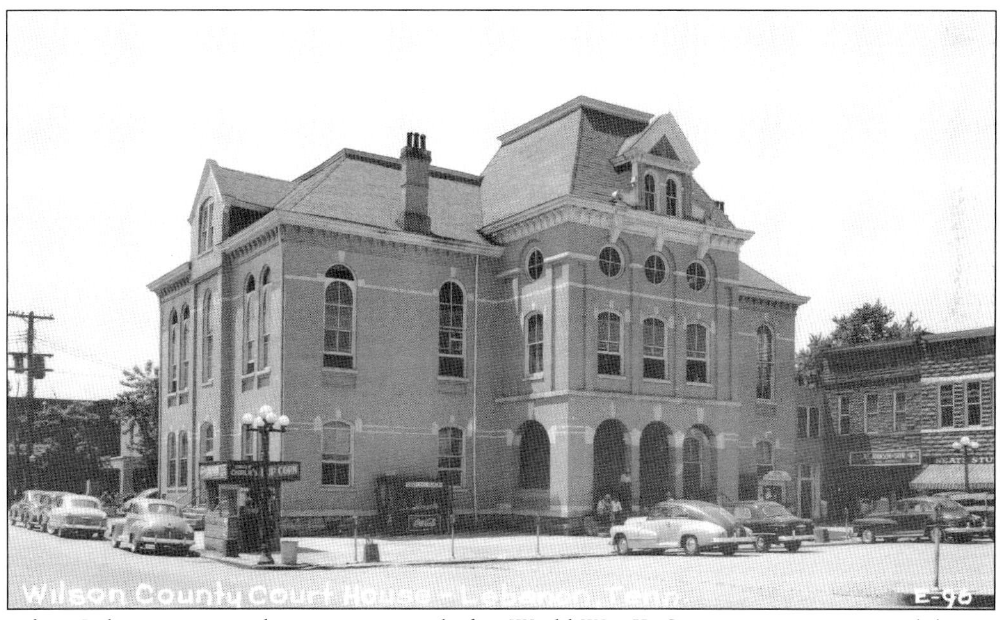

Life in Lebanon returned to a new normal after World War II. City progress interrupted during the war years began in earnest. The Wilson County Courthouse, located on the southwest side of the Square, was painted and completely remodeled in September 1948. New inlaid linoleum was installed on the floors, and central heat and air were added. The second story of the building was converted into two floors, giving the building three floors of space, with more room for offices and restrooms. (RWPCCU.)

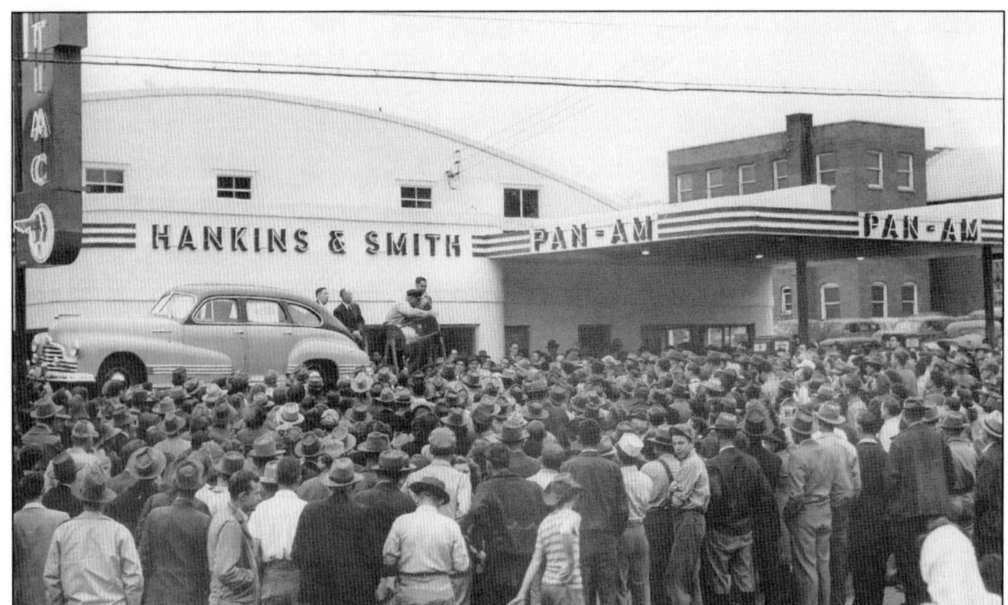

Car giveaways were popular to showcase cars produced after World War II. A halt in production of new cars during the war years made the arrival of new models a special event. In 1947 at the Hankins & Smith Motor Company on East Main Street, a crowd gathered to see the winner announced. The dealership was located between the First Methodist Church and the First Baptist Church. Employees pictured below are, from left to right, (first row) Paul Smith, Graham Williamson, Anabelle Huffman, Pete Swindell, Shorty Reynolds, John "Lightening" Height, and ? Jackson; (second row) Jim Horne Hankins, Roy Smith, H.M. Byars, Orelle Skelton, Red Reece, O.D. Dunn, Elmer Wiley, and ? McGee. (Both courtesy of W.P. Bone.)

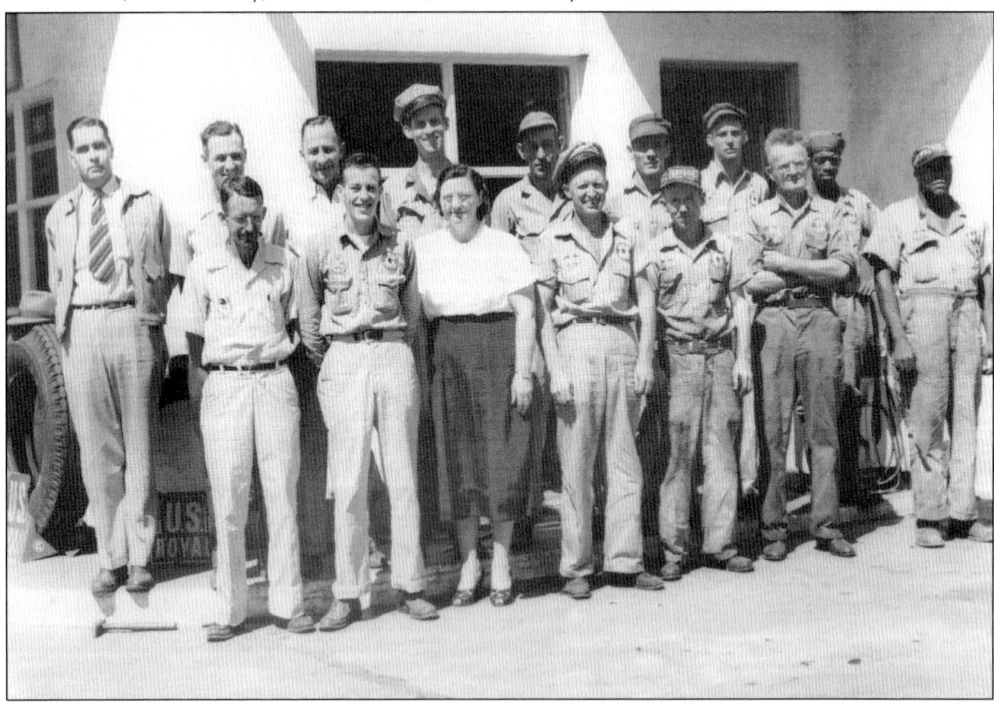

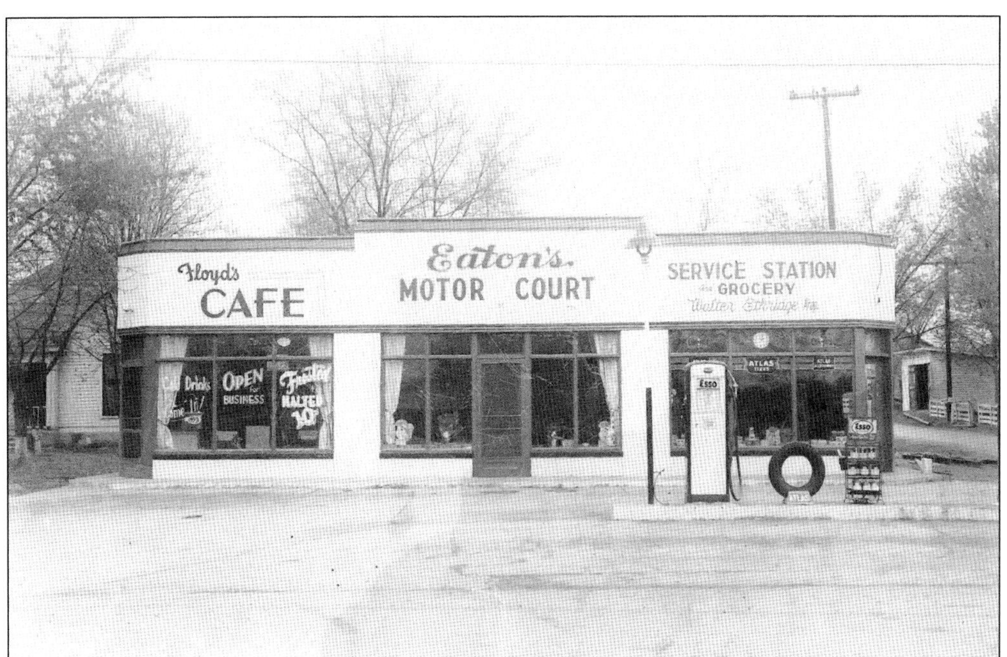

The southeast corner of Dawson Lane and West Main Street was the 1949 site of the Eaton Motor Court. The service station sold Esso gasoline for 27¢ a gallon that year. The motor court also held a variety of businesses, including a café and malt shop and a grocery. (Courtesy of Hollis McClanahan.)

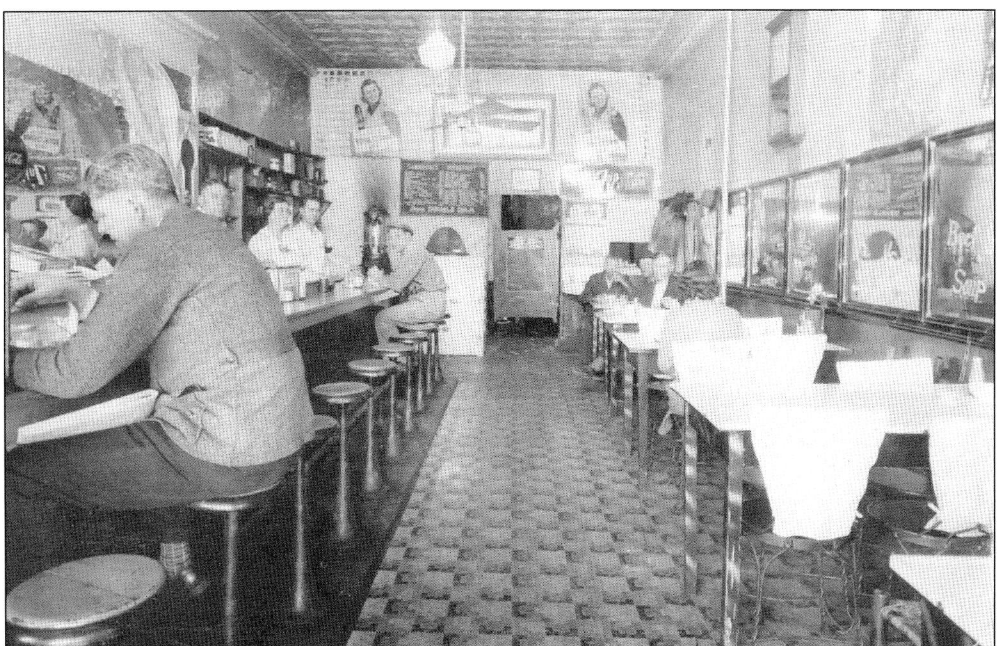

Another popular dining spot during this time was the City Café, at 106 Public Square, on the northeast side of the Square. The owner, Green Tucker, ran the diner and also set up every year at the county fair offering barbecue and hamburgers. Tucker is pictured at left, behind the counter. (Courtesy of Hollis McClanahan.)

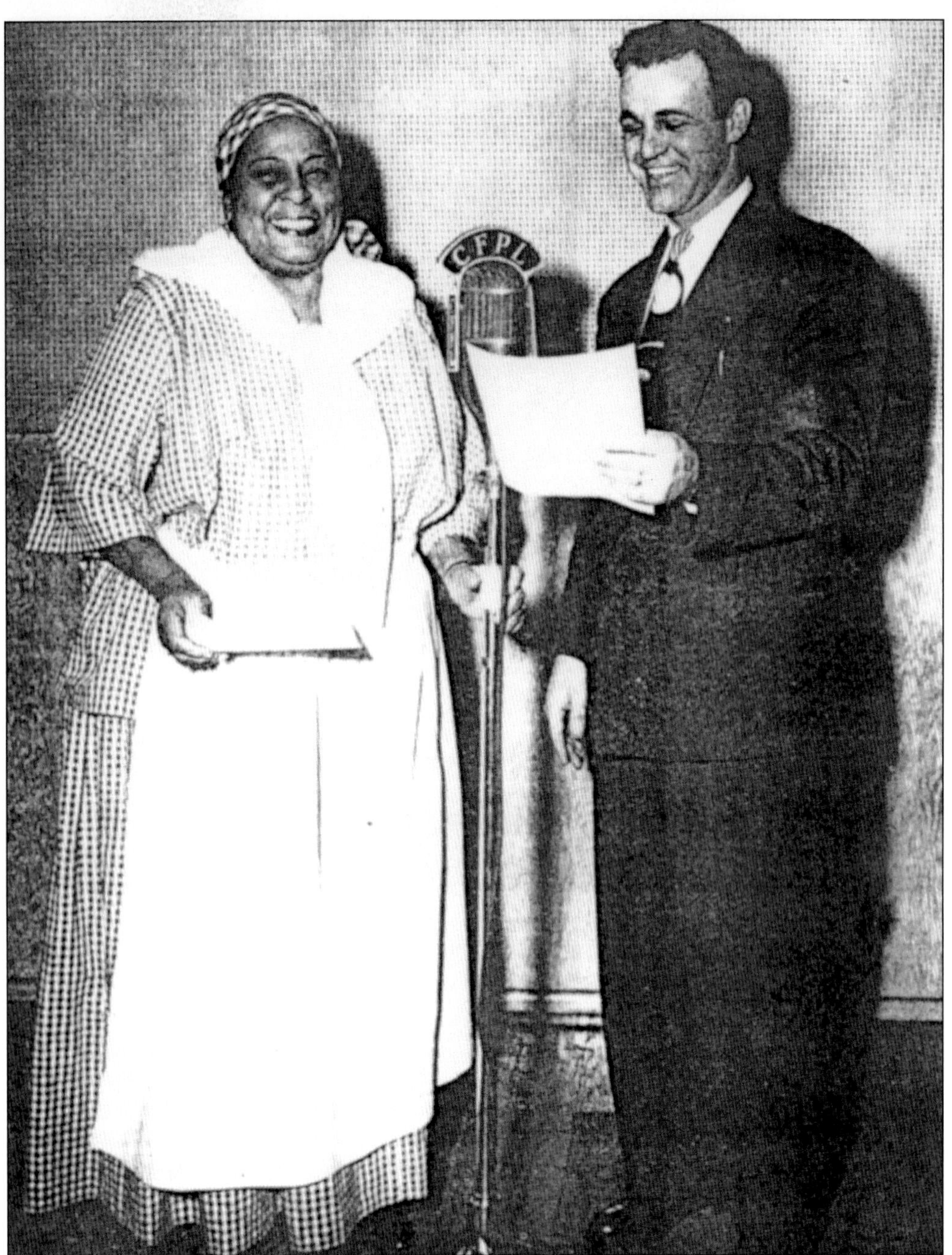

Maud Woodfork McElroy was perhaps one of Lebanon's most recognizable citizens in the mid-20th century. She assumed the role of "Aunt Jemima" for the Quaker Oats Company in Chicago in March 1947 and played the character in radio and television performances for many years. Born in Lebanon in 1892, McElroy attended Tennessee State College and studied dramatics. After graduation, she returned to Lebanon as a school teacher. She soon left for Chicago and the start of an acting career spanning 40 years. One of her first jobs was as an instructor of dramatics for the Works Progress Administration. She also participated in the federal writers' project in the 1930s. (CLMHC.)

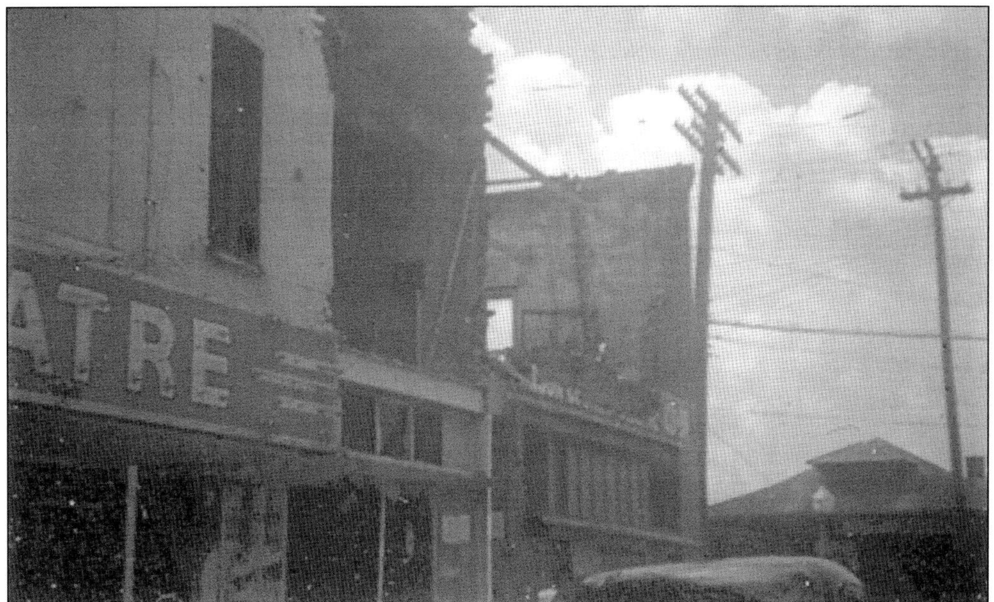

On May 22, 1949, a tornado roared through the Lebanon Public Square. The Wilson County Grange Co-Op, on the corner of South Cumberland and East Gay Streets (above), was seriously damaged. Hunter's Restaurant and the Princess Theatre, to the left of the Co-Op, also suffered a direct hit. Bradshaw's Drug Company (below), the Copelin Building, and Perfection Ice Cream Company, on the west and north sides of the Square, were also hit. Other storms occurred in May 1917 and in March and May 1933. The May 1933 tornado caused heavy damage to the First Baptist Church and homes and businesses on East Main Street. Cumberland University's Memorial Hall was struck by the storms of 1933 and 1949. In April 1944, a tornado wiped out the Lebanon airport, killing one serviceman and damaging 10 training airplanes, a B-25 bomber, and an A-25 attack bomber. (Both, CLMHC.)

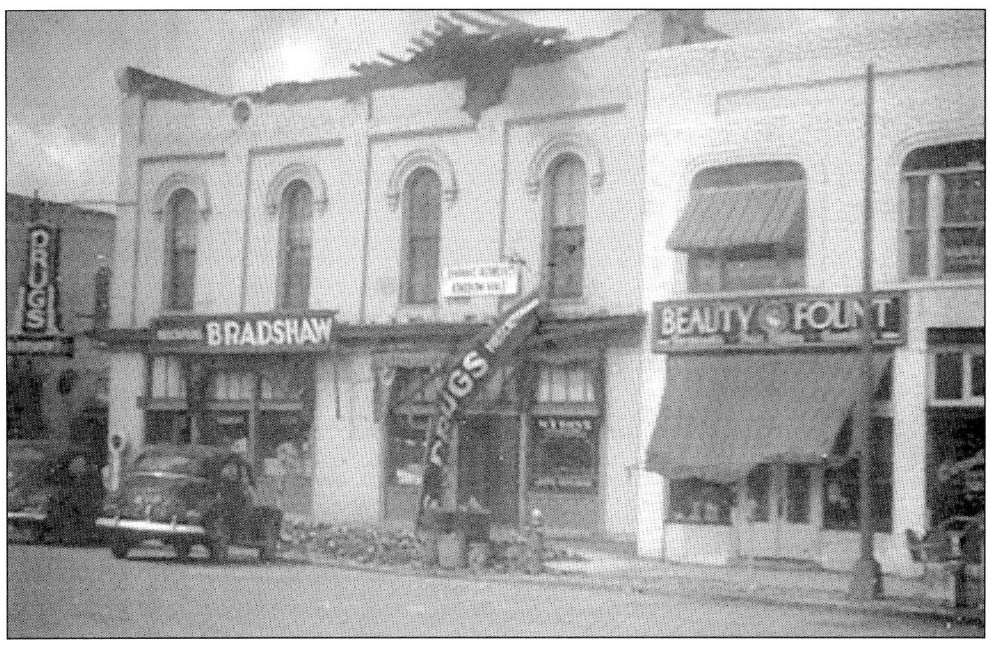

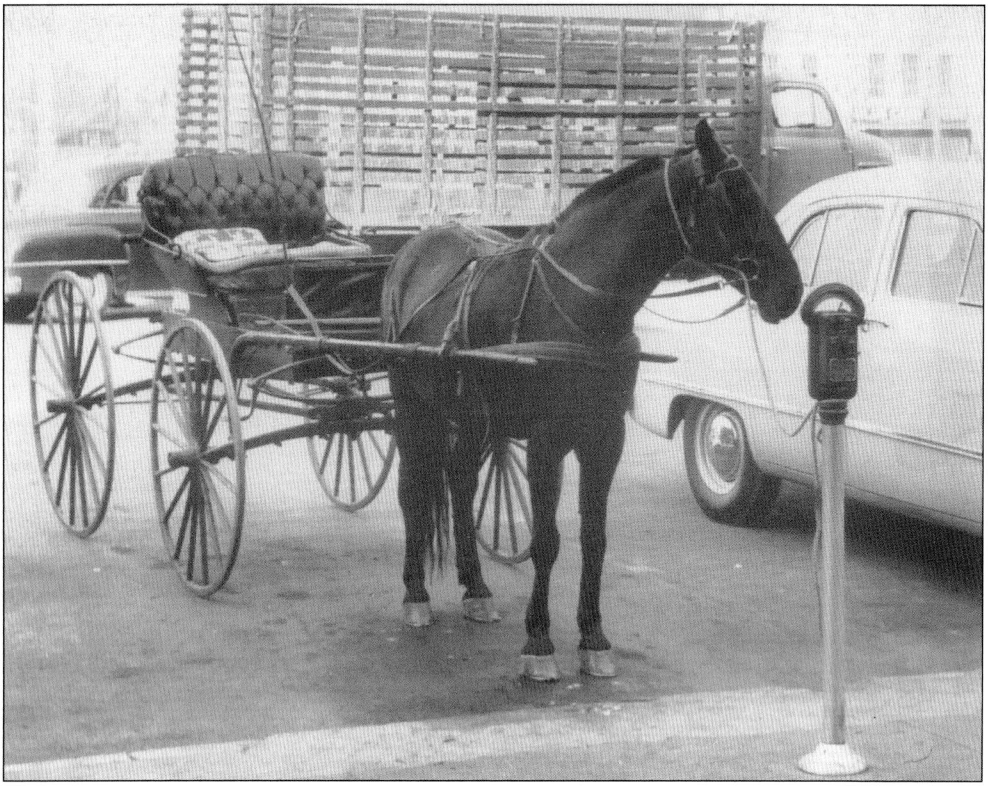

A parking meter was made useful by John Peyton for his horse and buggy on the Public Square in 1953, as seen here. Parking meters were installed in 1946. Seven years later, the Lebanon Police Department hired Frances Ashworth as a meter maid, the first woman on the police force. (CLMHC.)

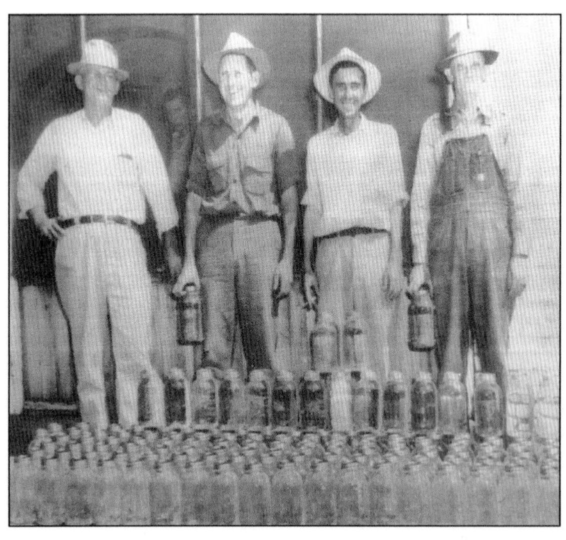

Although Lebanon liked to think of itself as a progressive city, old-fashioned problems sometimes arose. Here, Wilson County sheriff Harold Griffin (second from right), along with his posse, from left to right, Fred Carson, chief deputy J. Pat Bryan, and Ben Shorter, posed behind evidence confiscated from an illegal moonshine operation in 1952. Peering toward the camera over Carson's left shoulder is the accused. (Courtesy of T.A. Bryan.)

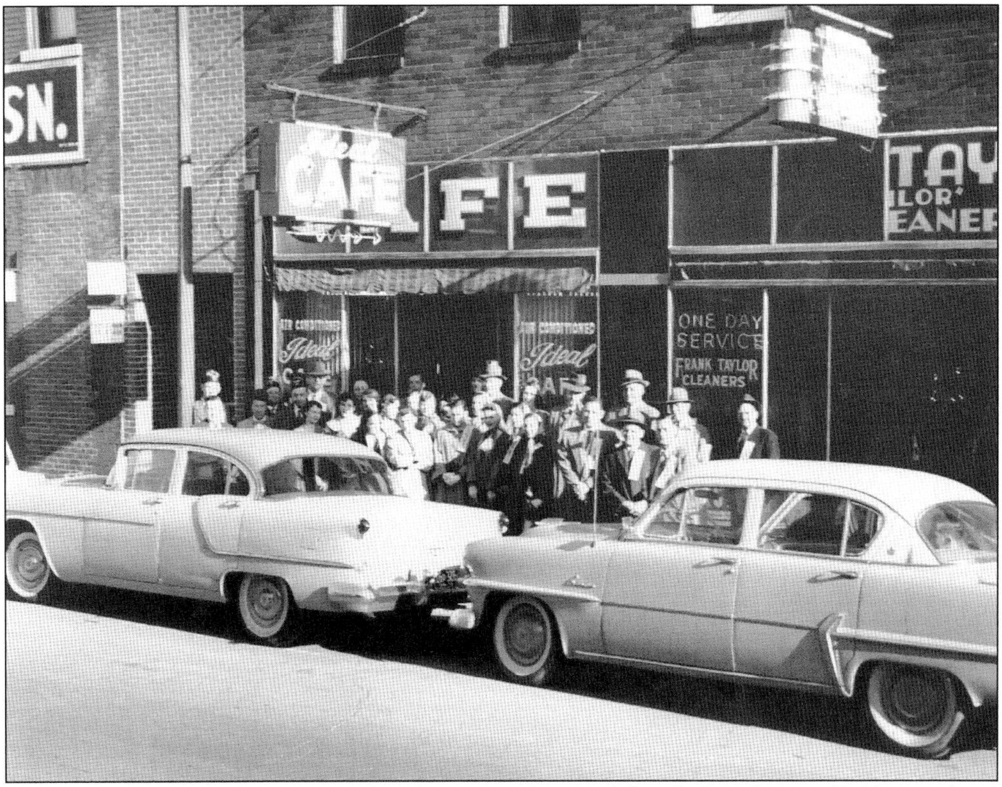

"Just What the Word Means" was the advertising slogan of the Ideal Café in 1955. Shown above is the diner at its 103 East Main Street location with a group of customers out front. The postcard view below shows the café's interior. Along with good food, the café offered tabletop jukeboxes, booths, and white tablecloths for atmosphere. Lebanon enjoyed many diners and cafés through the years; the City Café, the Dixie Café, Bennett's, Pat's, and Dewey's were all located on the Square or close by in the mid-1950s. By 1959, the Ideal Café moved to the corner of South Cumberland and East Gay Streets. (Above, courtesy of Historic Lebanon; below, RWPCCU.)

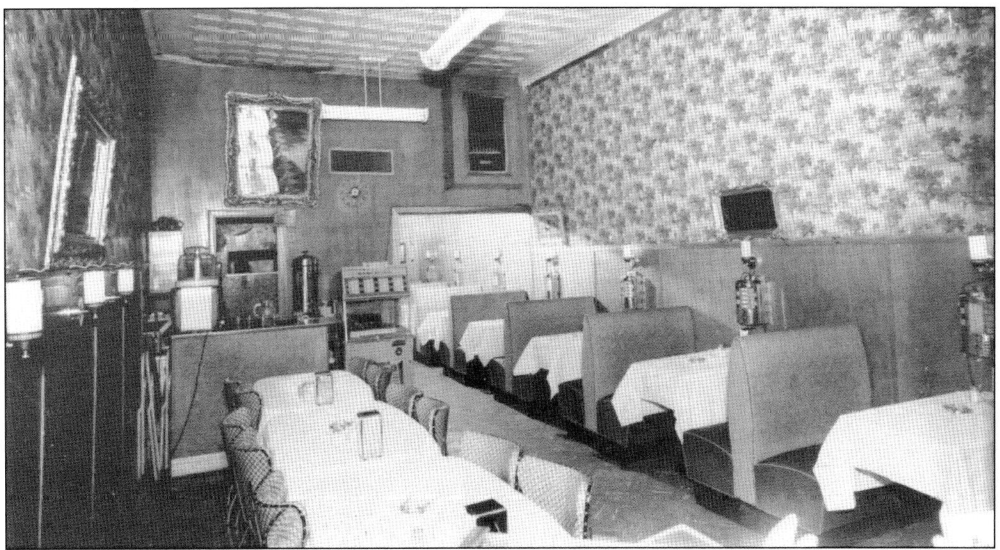

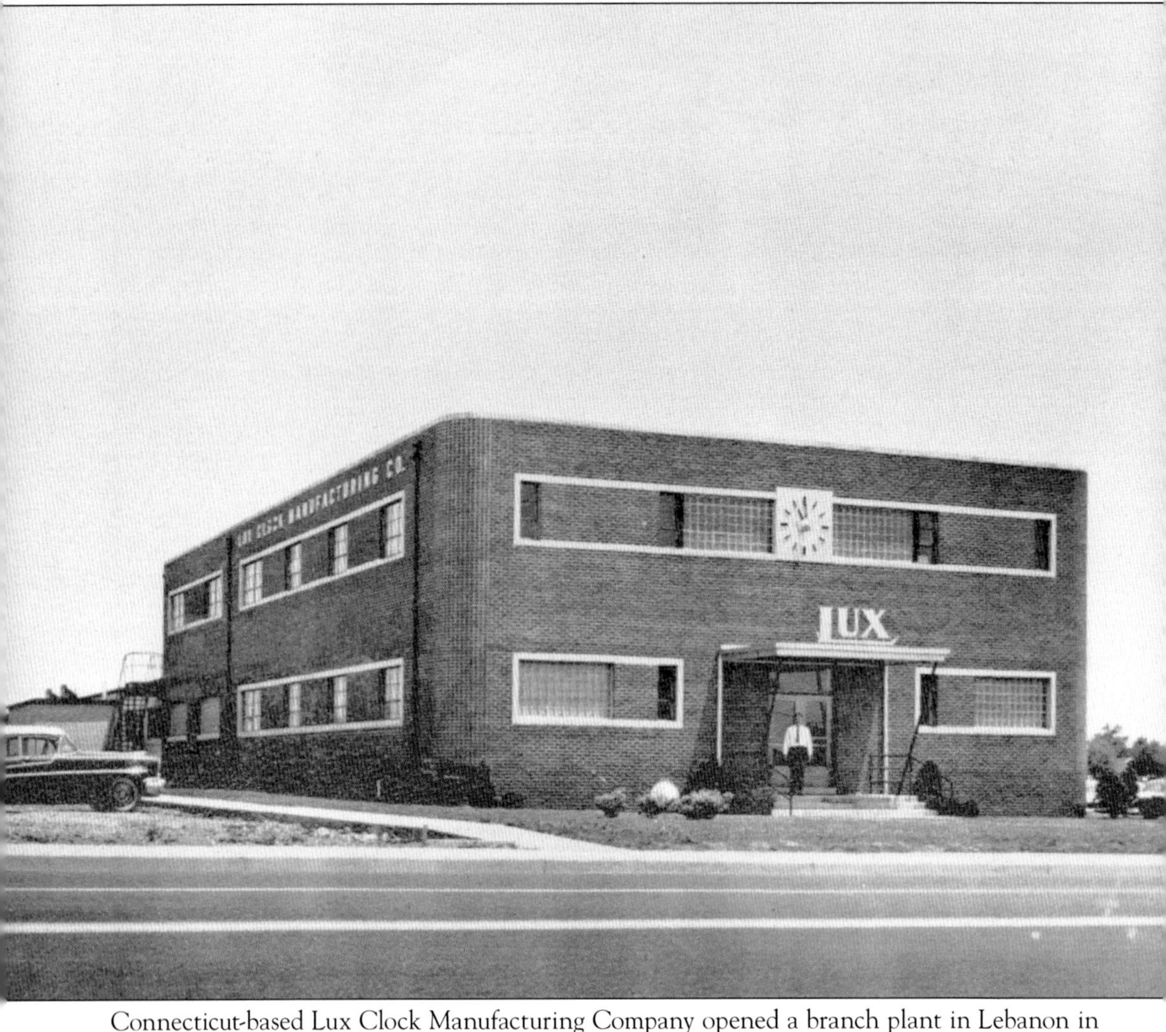

Connecticut-based Lux Clock Manufacturing Company opened a branch plant in Lebanon in June 1953 on West Main Street. The company operated under the name of Robertshaw Controls Company, Lux Time Division, after a buyout in 1961. Lebanon was chosen as a direct result of recruiting efforts by Mayor William D. Baird. When Baird took office in 1949, one of his top concerns was the out-migration of the local workforce. Lebanon at the time had only three large industrial plants and several smaller, locally owned manufacturing companies. Baird and other city leaders sought to grow the local workforce with an increase of industries by creating the first state-sanctioned industrial park, the Lebanon Municipal Industrial Subdivision. Opened in 1955, the subdivision spanned 278 acres and offered city roads, utilities, and access to the Tennessee Central Railroad line. Hartmann Luggage, in 1955, was the first to locate in the new area. Lebanon Manufacturing Company (later Precision Rubber Products Inc.) and Ross Gears & Tools Company soon followed. (CLMHC.)

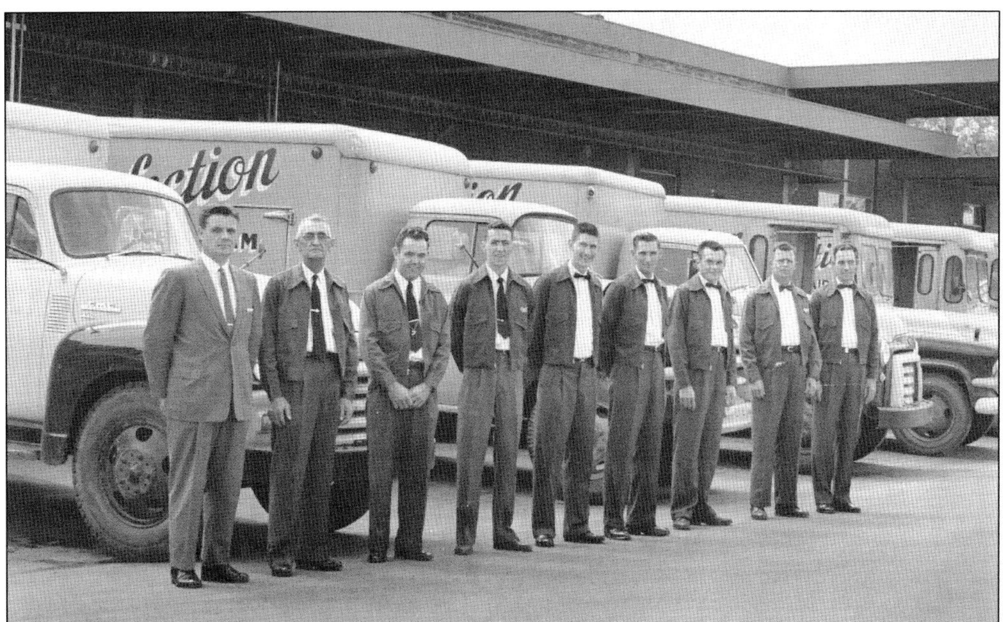

Perfection Dairy Products moved from the Square to a new, modern facility at 801 North Cumberland Street in 1960. The Scheuerman family still ran the business, now in the third generation of owners. The Perfection delivery trucks were a familiar sight. Seen in front of them are, from left to right, salesman Harry Martin, Charlie Jones, Frank Fowler, James Foster, Hugh Minchey, James Baines, Floyd Corley, Gene Edwards, and David Sanders. (Courtesy of Partlow Funeral Home.)

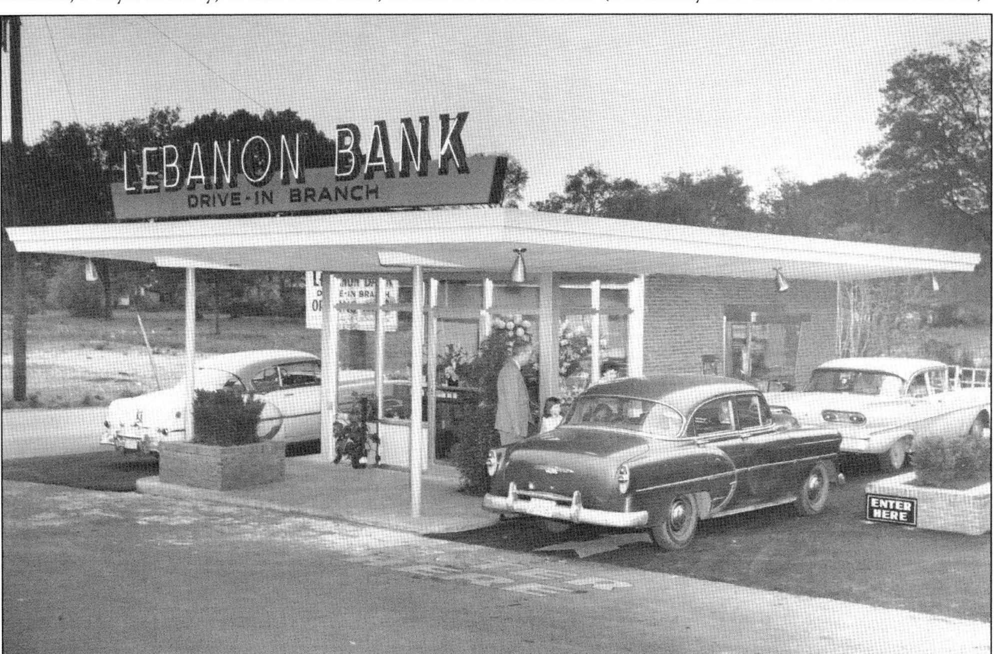

Lebanon Bank's drive-in branch was a modern addition to the town in the mid-1960s. Located at the back of the Cedars Shopping Center on West Main Street, the branch was part of business development west of the Public Square. The Cedars Shopping Center was the first strip mall in the city. (CLMHC.)

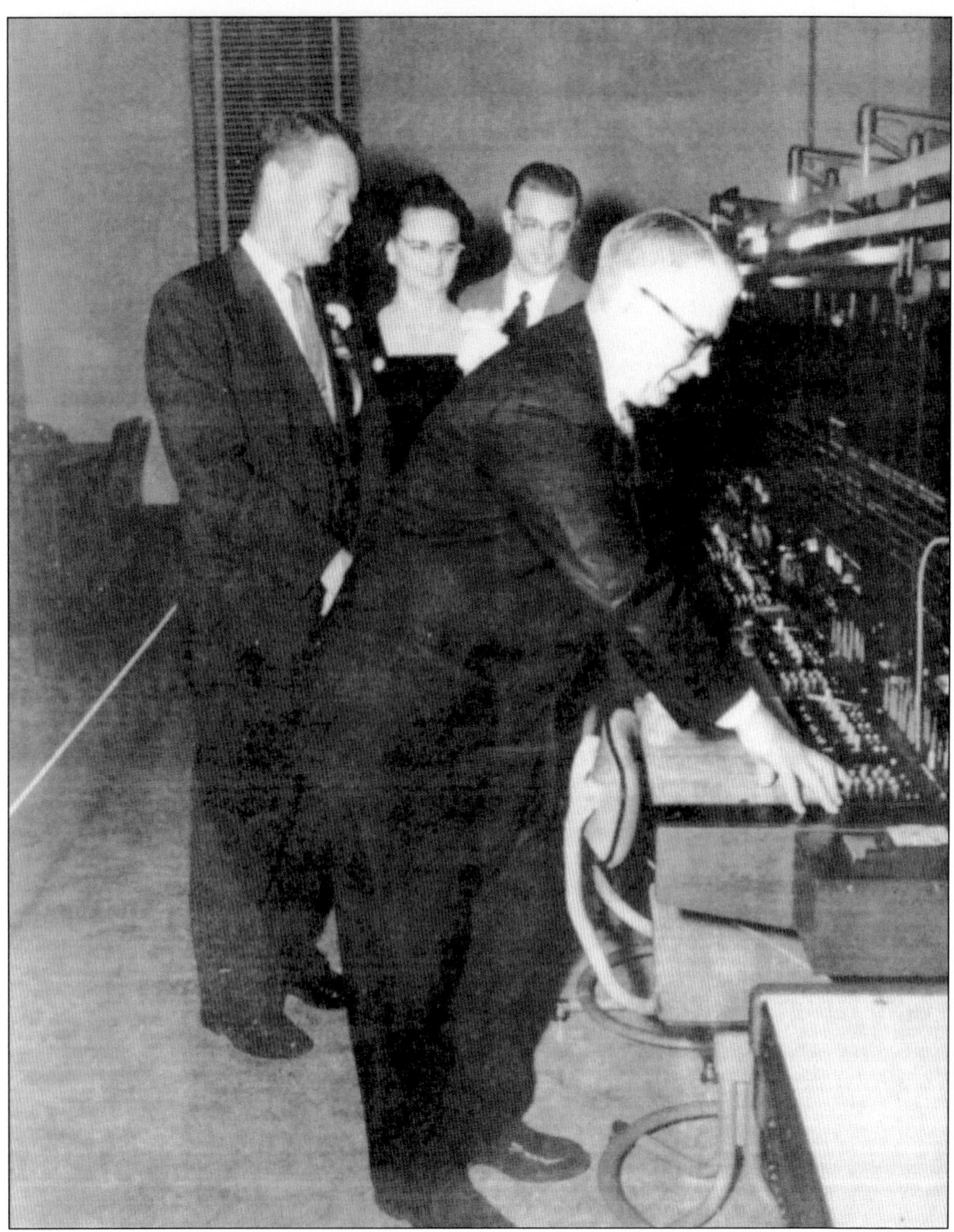

On December 15, 1957, the Southern Bell Telephone & Telegraph Company converted city lines to the dial system. Gone was the operator-assisted call. Patrons could now dial numbers themselves with the Hickory-4 exchange. Here, Mayor William D. Baird tests out the system with a phone call to Honolulu. From left to right, Hughey King, Harriet Darnell, and Ray Bryant watch the proceedings. The first telephone lines from Nashville to Lebanon were completed in 1882, with the switchboard located in the Anderson & Company Drug Store. By 1897, the city had 458 telephones installed. Another advancement came in 1937, with the change to a battery system instead of the crank system. With the installation of the dial system 20 years later, the drive-up public telephone was introduced in Lebanon. (CLMHC.)

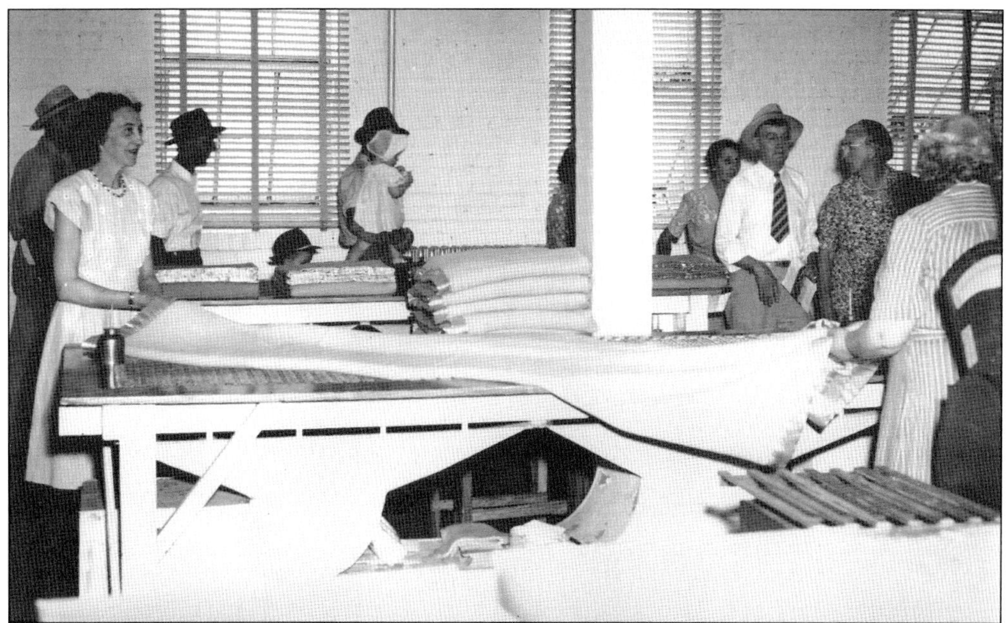

The Lebanon Woolen Mills celebrated its golden anniversary in 1958. Long known as a maker of quality blankets, the World War II years had seen production shift to the manufacturing of blankets for the Army and the Marine Corps, earning one of the first "E" awards granted. After the war, the mill's management focused on increasing efficiency and lowering costs. Old equipment was replaced, and new materials were introduced. The mill had been the sole producer in the entire country of all-wool blankets until new synthetic materials became available after the war. Folding-line employees show off their skills in the photograph above. A portion of the card room, with jack-spools, is shown below. (Above, courtesy of Partlow Funeral Home; below, CLMHC.)

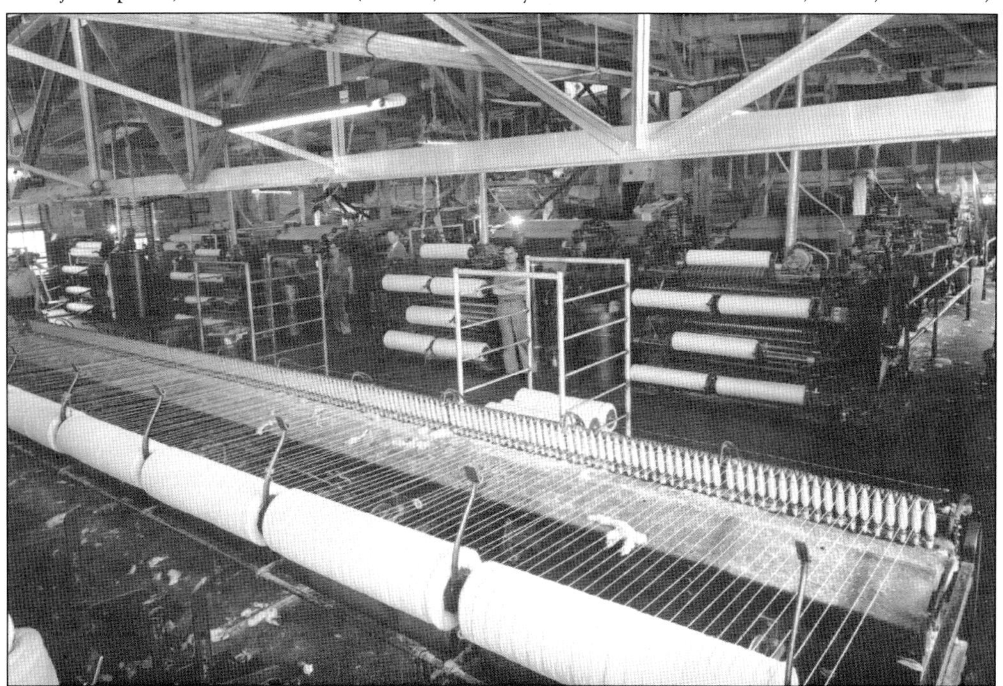

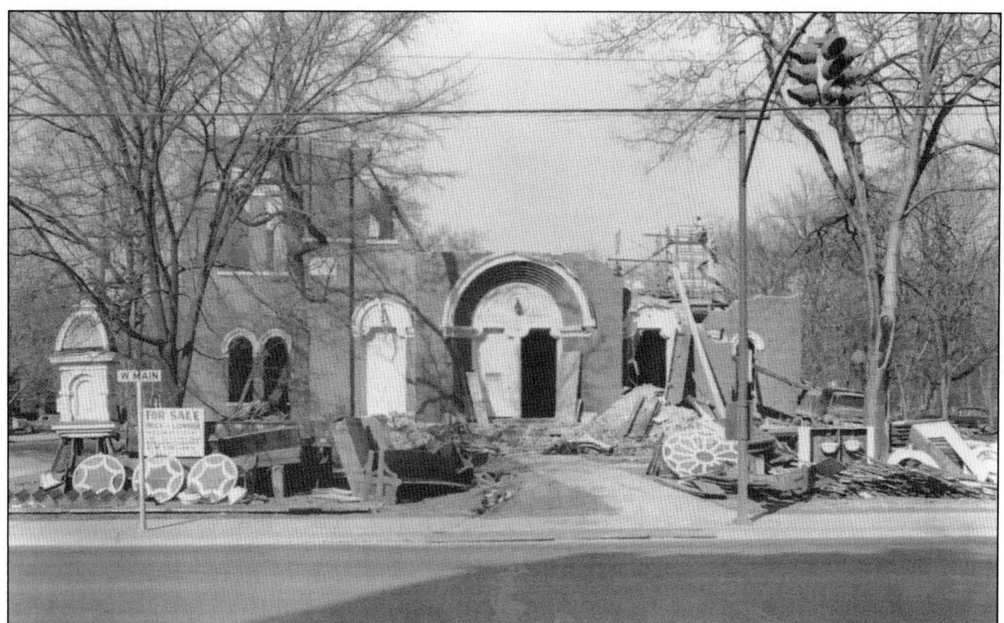

With the sale of the Cumberland University Law School to Samford University in 1961, Caruthers Hall was auctioned off in December of that year. The building was razed in 1962, and architectural parts from the building, as well as the bricks, were salvaged and sold. (CU.)

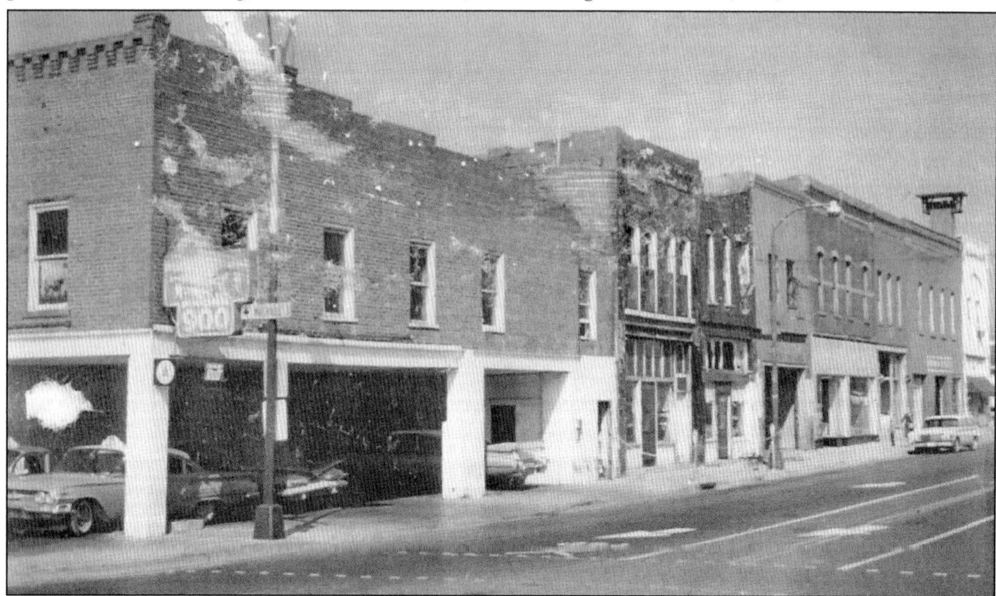

The urban renewal ideal led to the demolition of the northwest quadrant of the Public Square in February 1967. Buildings razed included the Perfection Ice Manufacturing Company, facing West Market Street; the former city hall and fire station, on North Cumberland Street; and the area known as Devil's Elbow. Commerce Union Bank had recently purchased all of the properties. Bank president William Earthman stated in the *Lebanon Democrat* on February 4, 1967, "Commerce Union Bank desires to be in a position to be a part of the future growth and development of Lebanon . . . and to help improve the general appearance of the downtown shopping area." (CLMHC.)

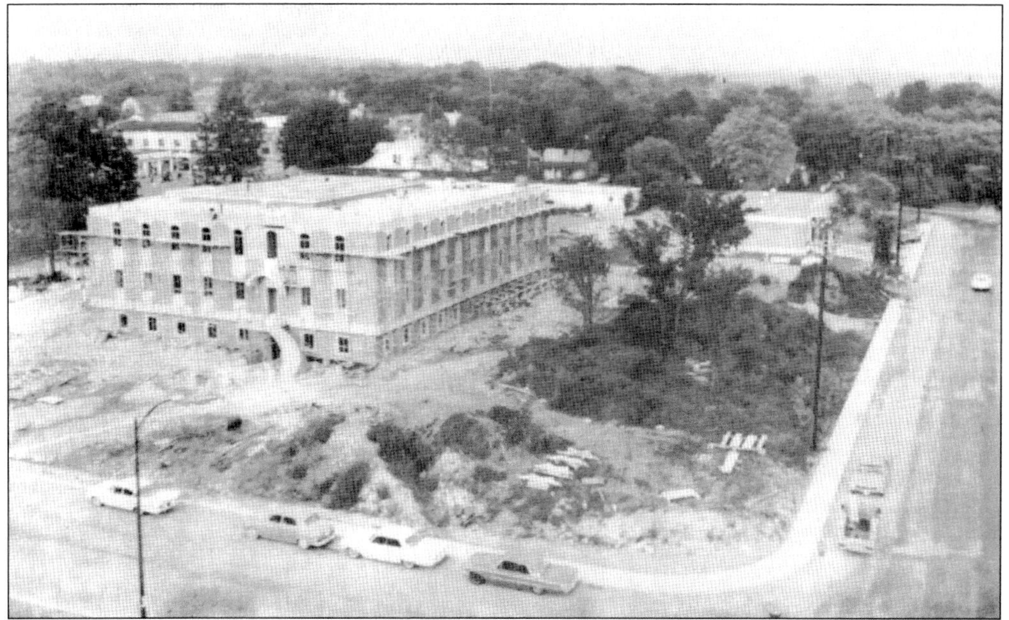

The Wilson County Courthouse moved off the Public Square in 1968. Community leaders hoped development of the business district would follow to the higher, less flood-prone area on East Main Street. The new courthouse, shown here in a view from Gay Street, was completed at a cost of $1.2 million. (CLMHC.)

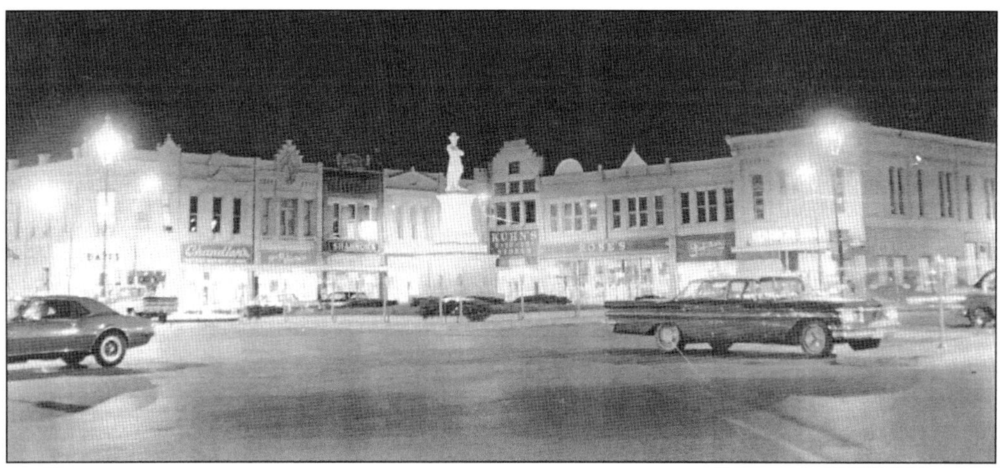

During the late 1960s, the Public Square changed dramatically. The traffic pattern was altered with the addition of parking around the General Hatton monument. The courthouse and northwest corner were gone, replaced with Potter's Park and a parking lot, respectively. This night scene looking into the southeast corner shows the new look. A project to rework parking and traffic patterns on the Public Square is slated to begin in the fall of 2014. (CLMHC.)

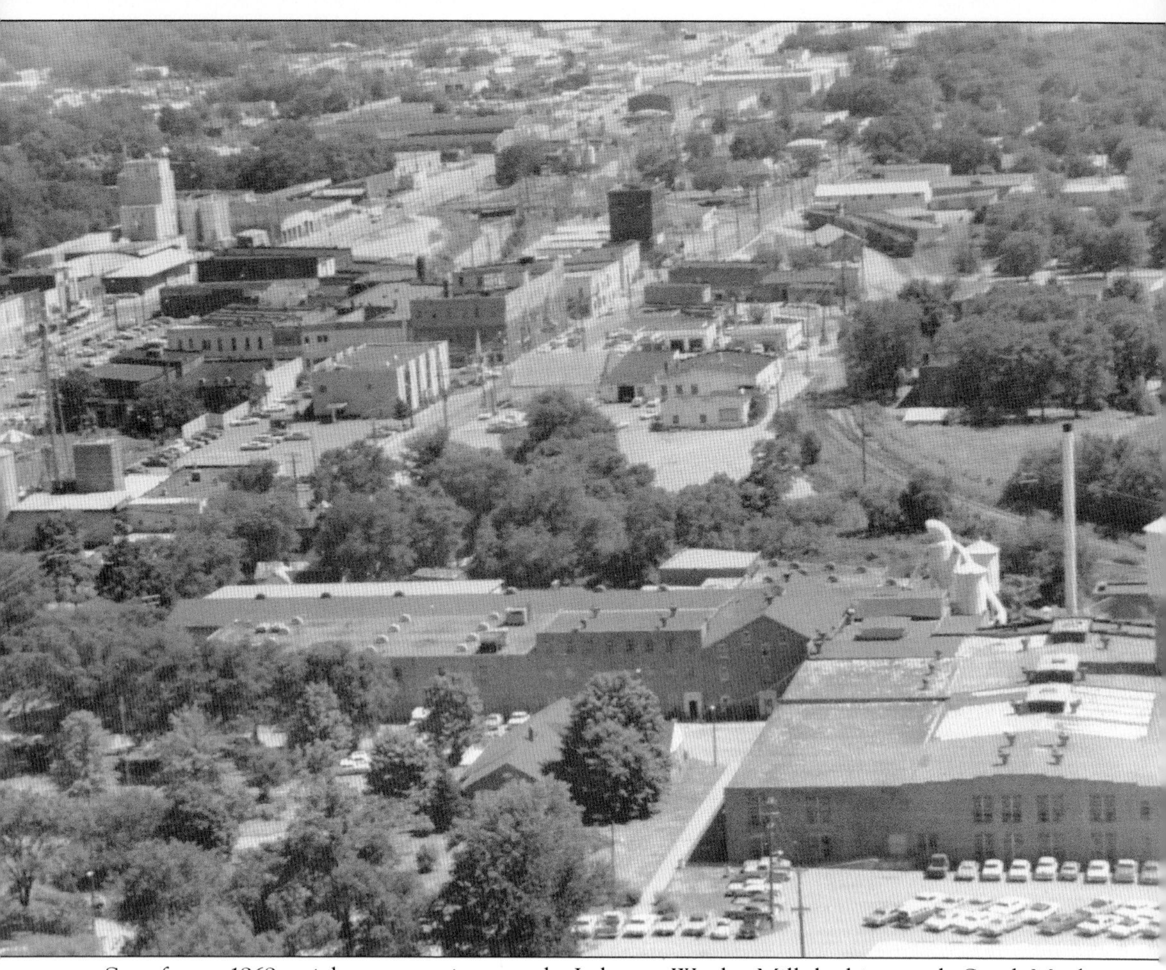

Seen from a 1969 aerial vantage point near the Lebanon Woolen Mills looking south, South Maple Street and the southwest side of the Public Square still contain landmark buildings. The West Side Hotel and the three-story mill, near the present-day farmers' market, are both still standing. The Princess Theatre, on South Cumberland Street, has its marquee and tile facade. Lebanon had seen many improvements by this time. The Square and main streets in town were first paved beginning in 1924, causing the removal of trees from the Square. After a valiant attempt to save its life, the lone tree, a survivor of an 1888 beautification program, was removed in 1949. In May 1948, a new, modern "whiteway" was installed throughout the city. The new lighting system was accompanied by the addition of electrical meters on homes. (CLMHC.)

Six

Uniquely Lebanon

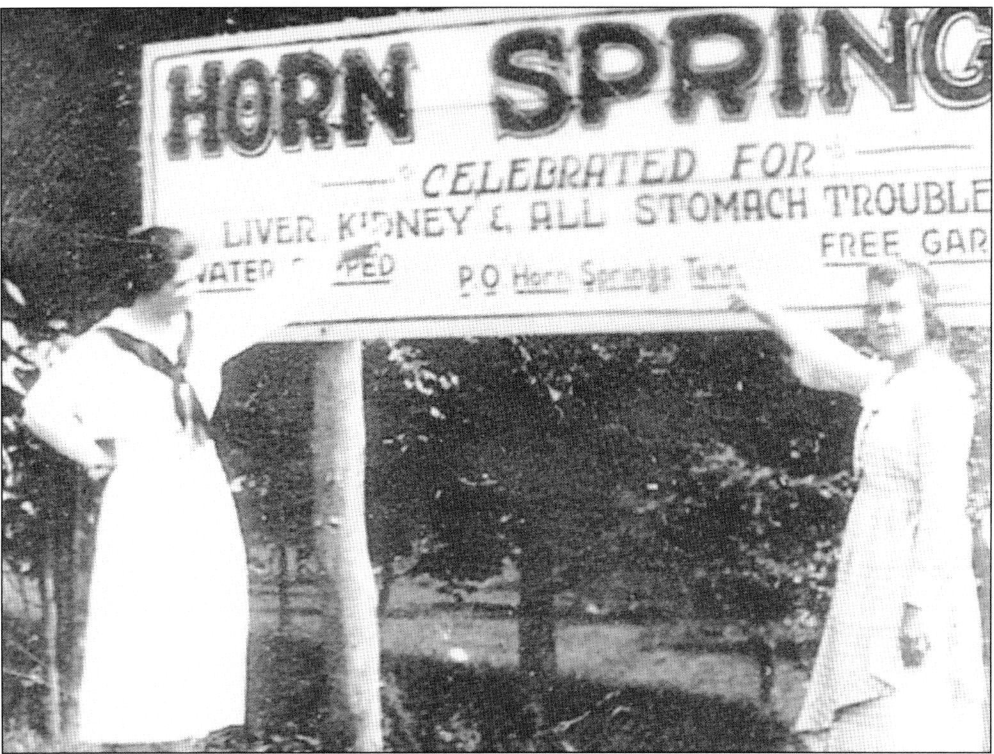

James Horn discovered peculiar-tasting water flowing from a spring on his property, four miles west of Lebanon, in 1870. Soon, he was marketing and bottling the water, which tests had shown to contain several trace minerals, as a cure-all for ailments. The water was shipped throughout the eastern United States advertising the newly established Horn Springs Resort. The resort was located on picturesque rolling hills that were part of a 640-acre land grant to Ethelred Horn, James's father. Horn Springs was very popular with families, with many coming every summer to escape the heat of the city and to partake of the healing waters. The resort sign is seen here in the 1920s. (Courtesy of Charles and Elaine Bell.)

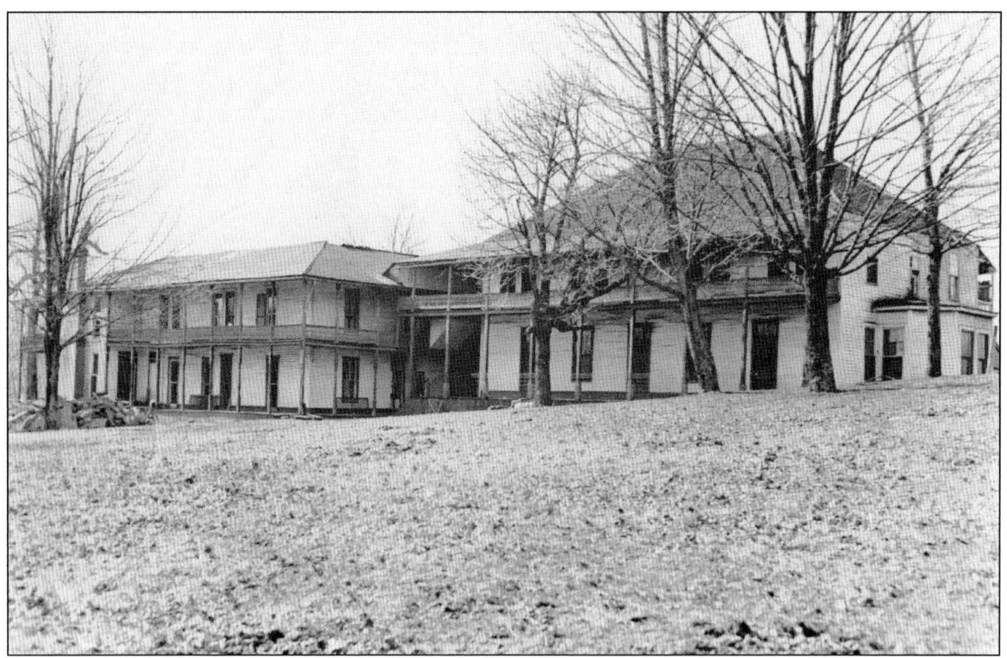

James Horn passed away in 1893, leaving the resort to his son Jim. Under Jim's direction, the resort added a dance hall, a dining room, a bowling alley, and additional guest rooms. This same year, the Tennessee Central Railroad added a stop just steps from the hotel. The photograph above shows the hotel building in 1899. Below is the view from the train stop. Visitors could step off the train and take the sidewalk straight into the resort. Advertisements touted the "3,000 feet of porches" for the enjoyment of guests. (Both courtesy of Charles and Elaine Bell.)

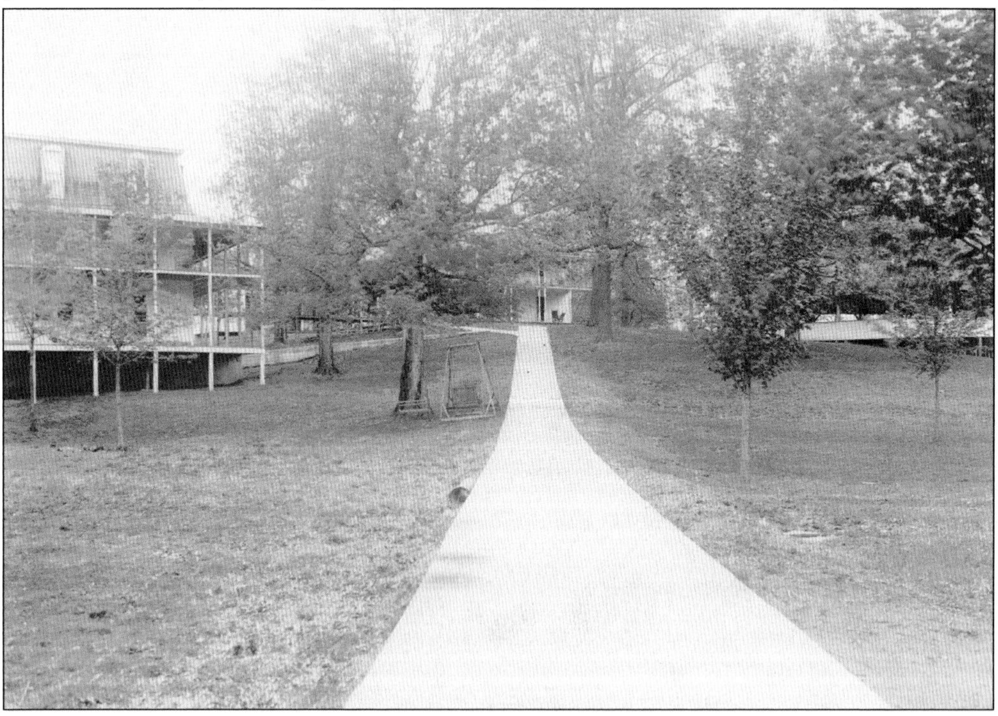

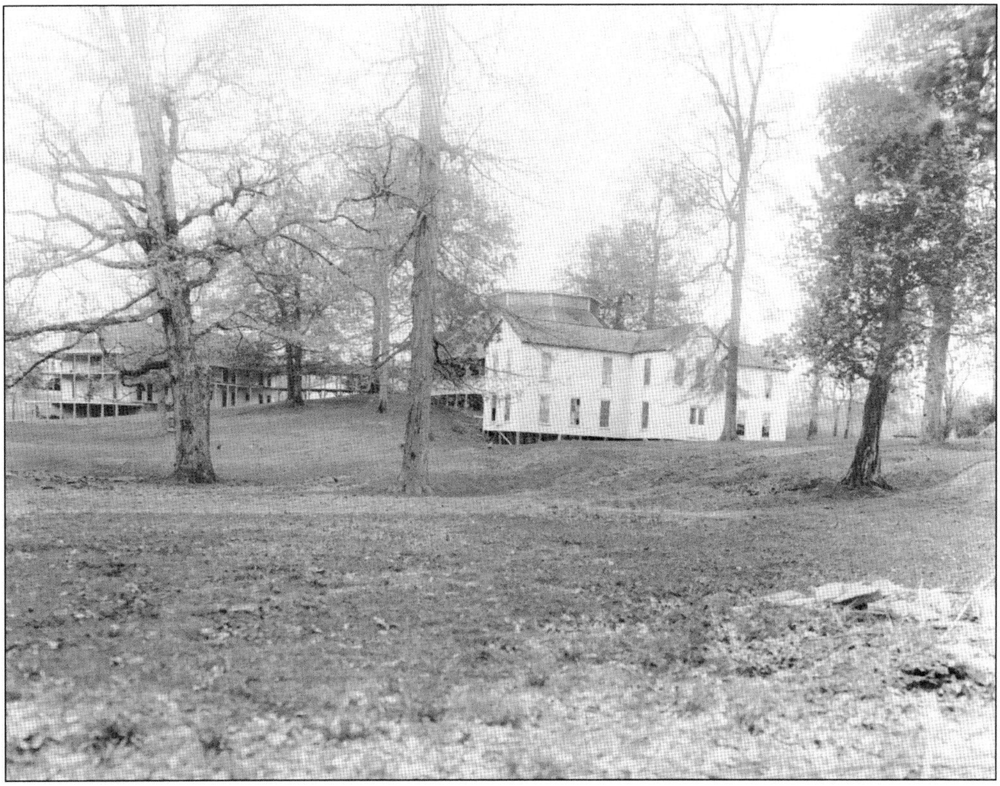

The new annex and pavilion, or amusement hall, can be seen in the background above. These were added to the resort in 1907. The late 1890s through the late 1920s were the heyday for Horn Springs. During this time, Horn Springs had its own post office. Guests could stay in touch with relatives and friends while spending the summer months at the resort. The photograph below illustrates the actual spring that powered the whole idea of the Horn Springs Resort. Also seen are the tennis courts, to the right, just one of many activities offered. The stock market crash of 1929 and the death of Jim Horn in the 1930s led to the downsizing of the hotel and control of the property shifting to Horn's son, Joseph. (Both courtesy of Charles and Elaine Bell.)

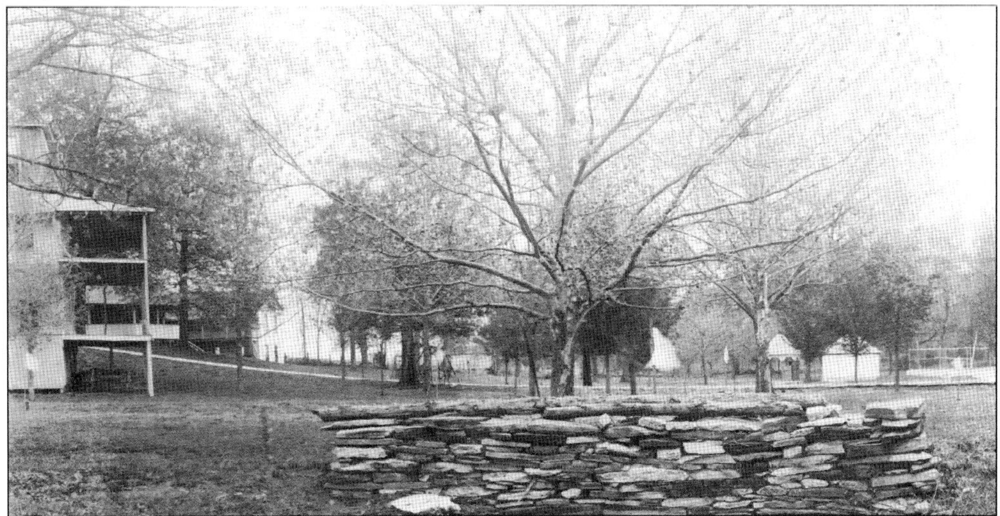

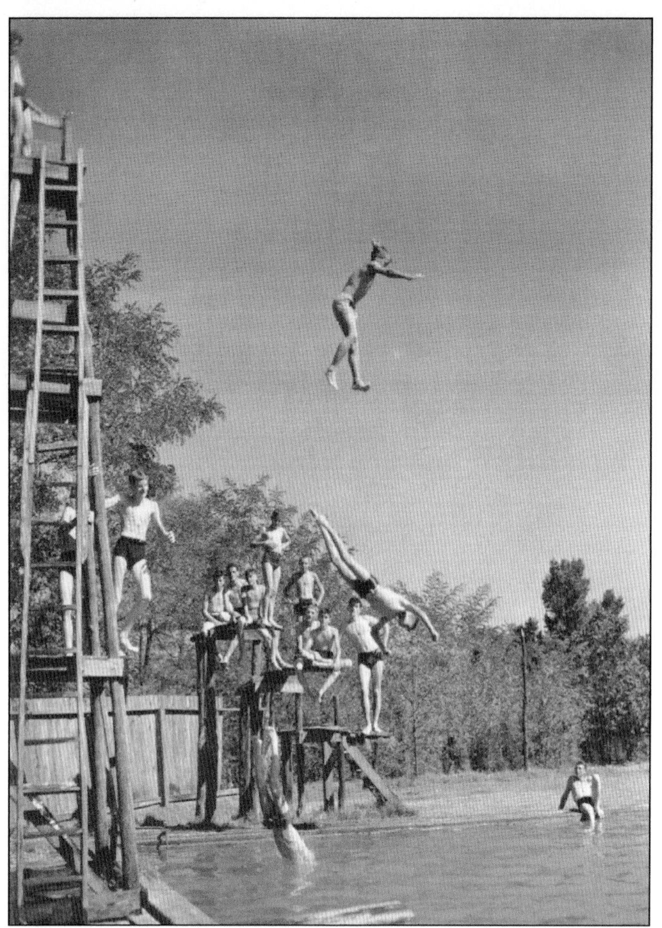

The Horn Springs pool was added in 1935. Swimmers are seen at left enjoying a jump off the diving platform. The postcard view below shows the pool house. The pool is remembered as having the coolest water even in the heat of summer, because it was filled with spring water. The hotel was now being used as an event center, hosting dinners, lunches, and dances. Although not as prestigious as in its heyday, the resort still had its share of famous visitors, including Pres. Harry Truman, who signed the guest register in 1949 when in Lebanon for the dedication of a Cordell Hull portrait at Cumberland University. Dr. R.D. Wilkerson purchased the property in 1937, adding a miniature golf course. The Horn Springs hotel burned down on June 26, 1949. The pool continued to operate until the mid-1970s. (Left, courtesy of Charles and Elaine Bell; below, RWPCCU.)

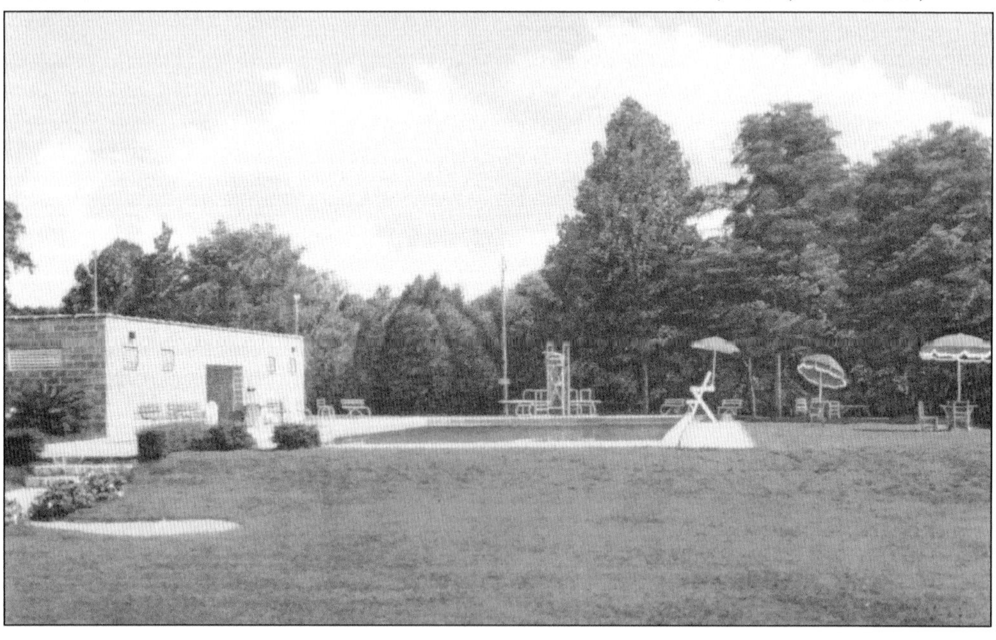

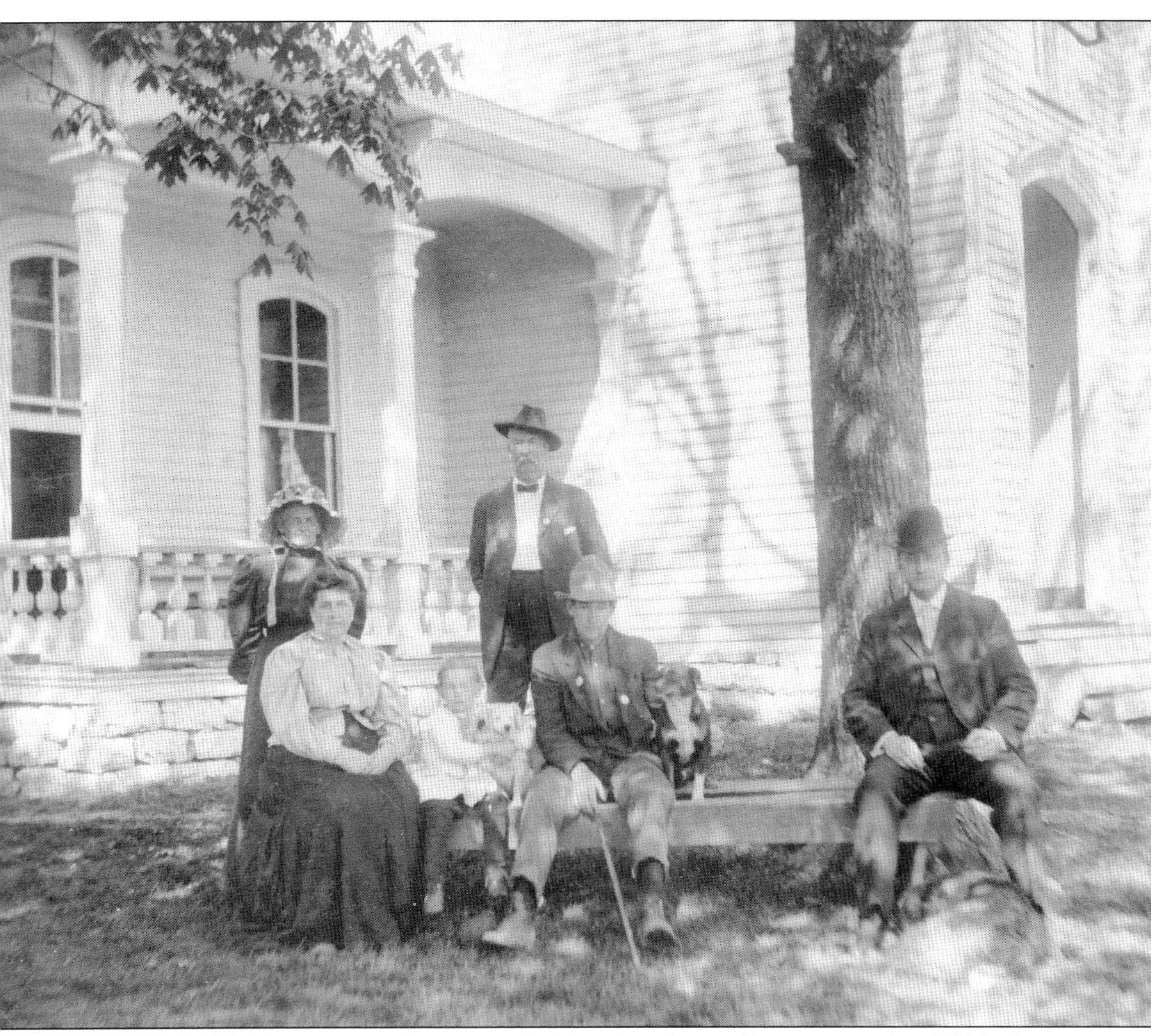

A competitor of the Horn Springs Resort was the Hamilton Springs Resort, opened in 1898 by Jim Hamilton. This mineral spring water resort was located only a few hundred yards up the road. It also had a stop on the Tennessee Central Railroad line, although its stop was not quite as close to the hotel as its neighbor's. The competition between the two resorts was never friendly. According to oral histories, the two owners only spoke to each other one time, at a political rally in 1912. The moderator asked the two to speak on their respective resorts. Horn spoke first, extolling the benefits of his spring's water as the best. Hamilton countered that it should be good, since the spring at the Hamilton Springs Resort was the water's source. Hamilton Springs Resort ended operations in 1932, when the hotel burned down. Shown in this photograph is Jim Hamilton, in the center rear. (Courtesy of Charles and Elaine Bell.)

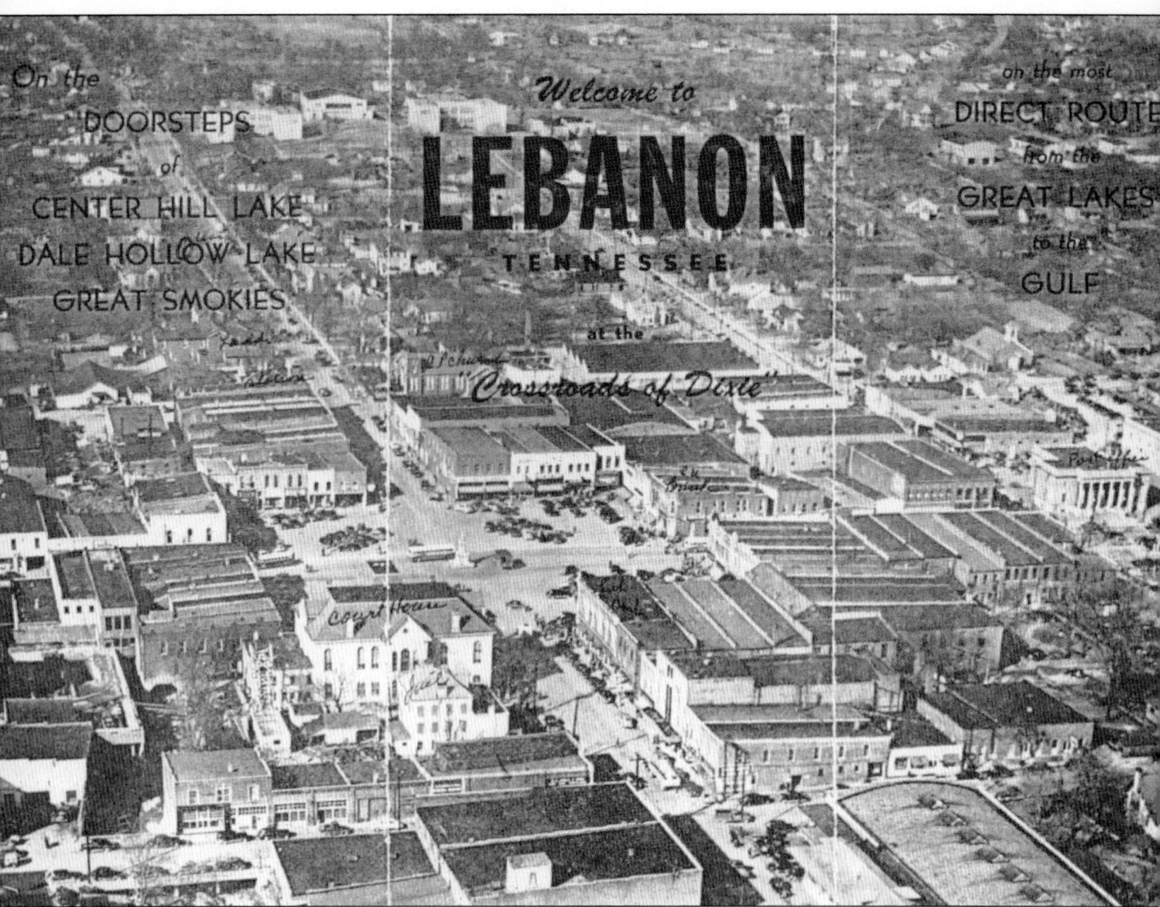

Lebanon's role as county seat has always influenced the number of hotels in the town. In 1887, there were at least five operating hotels. The town's location on the Hermitage Turnpike, now Highway 70N, also increased the need for lodging. This highway was crucial for tourists, linking Lebanon to all parts of the United States. The first steps for a federal, paved highway system began in 1915. That year, the Bristol-Memphis Highway Commission led a caravan of motorists through town in a campaign for the new system. Highway 231 entered Tennessee at the Kentucky state line, passing through Lebanon's Public Square and continuing on to the Alabama border. The brochure cover shown here features an aerial photograph of Lebanon looking north from just south of Gay Street, crossing over South Cumberland Street, in the early 1950s. (CLMHC.)

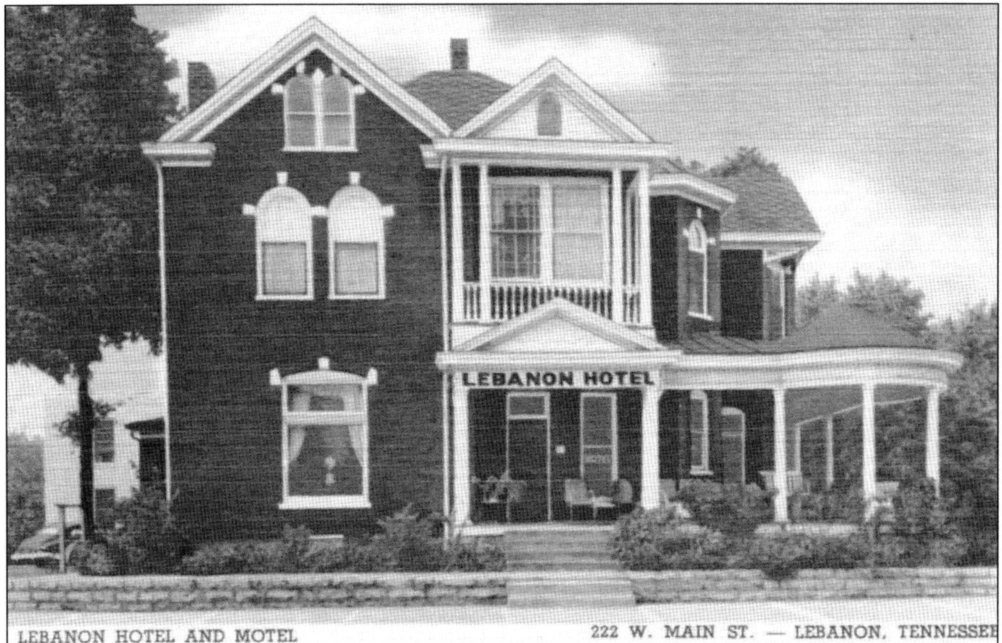

J.D. Barton built this brick structure at 222 West Main Street in 1903 on the site of the former Corona Institute. By 1907, the building was in use as the Lebanon Hotel. At the time of this postcard view, the hotel was owned by C.H. Ligon. Rooms with a bath started at $2, and parking was free. The building passed through several owners until it was razed in the 2000s. (RWPCCU.)

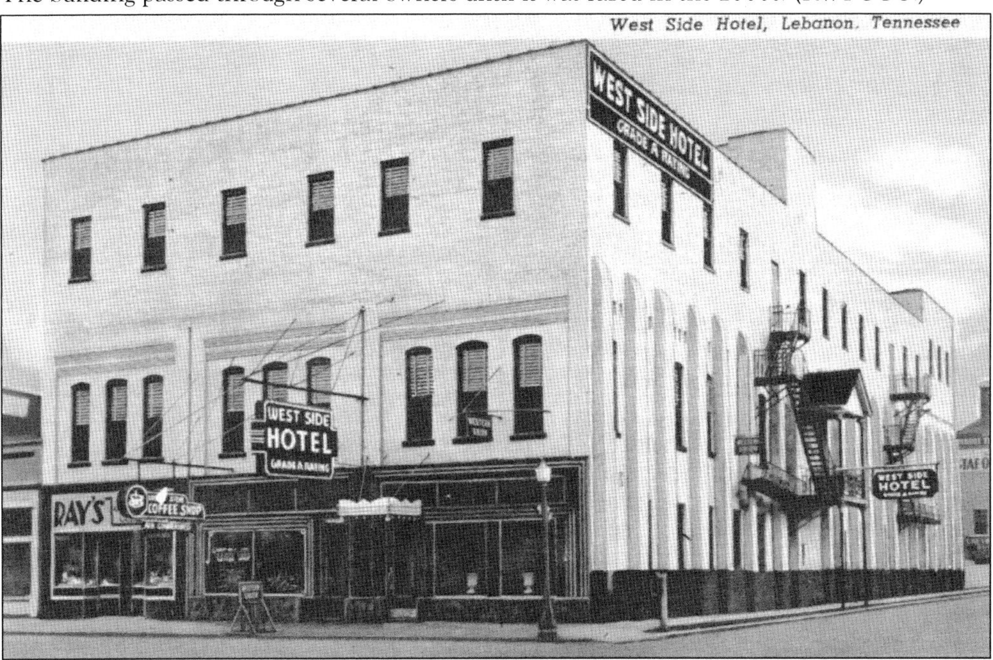

The West Side Hotel and Opera House was built in 1887 on the corner of West Main and South Maple Streets. It was originally a two-story, redbrick building. Extensive remodeling in 1949 added a third floor and a white coat of paint. On the night of July 30, 1982, an arsonist set the hotel ablaze, destroying the building and causing the death of fire chief Wendell Organ. (RWPCCU.)

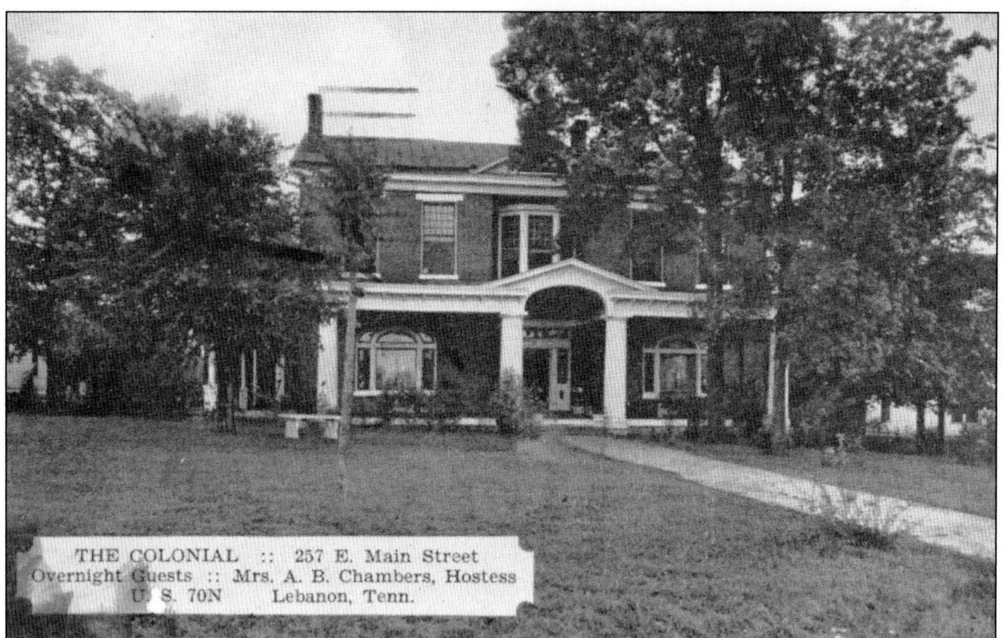

In 1937, this redbrick home operated as the Colonial, a guest house run by Mrs. A.B. Chambers. Located at 257 East Main Street, it was the home of Jordan Stokes during antebellum years. By 1912, it was used by the local chapter of the Knights of Pythias. (RWPCCU.)

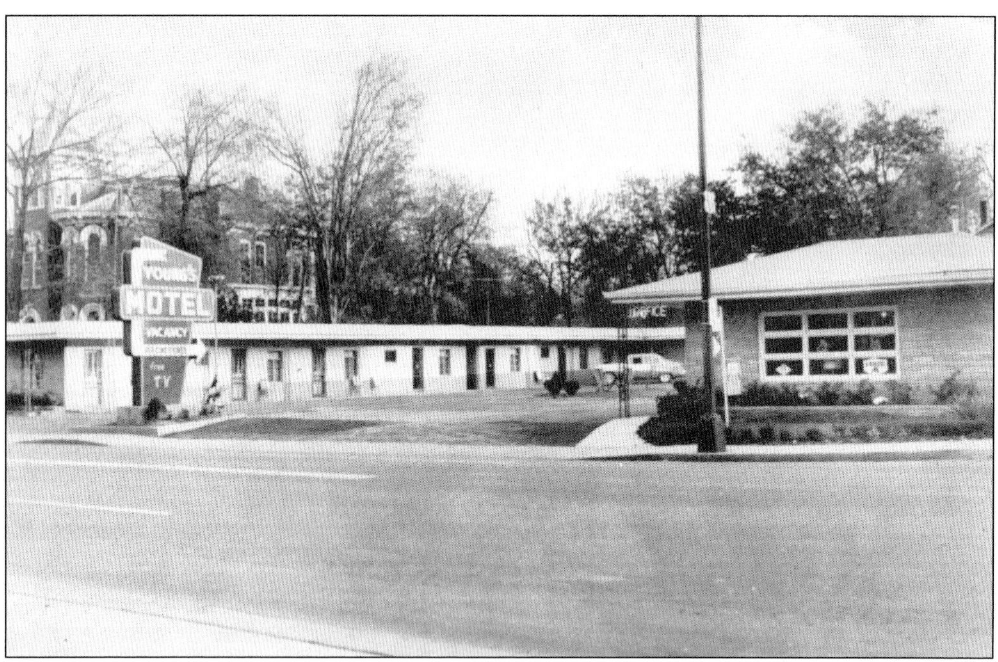

Young's Motel was on the corner of West Main and South Greenwood Streets, opposite Caruthers Hall. Built in the 1950s on the site of the former Rufus McClain home, it was a short-lived operation. By 1969, the location was the parking lot for the new Peoples Bank. To the left is the N.G. Robertson house, built around 1870. (RWPCCU.)

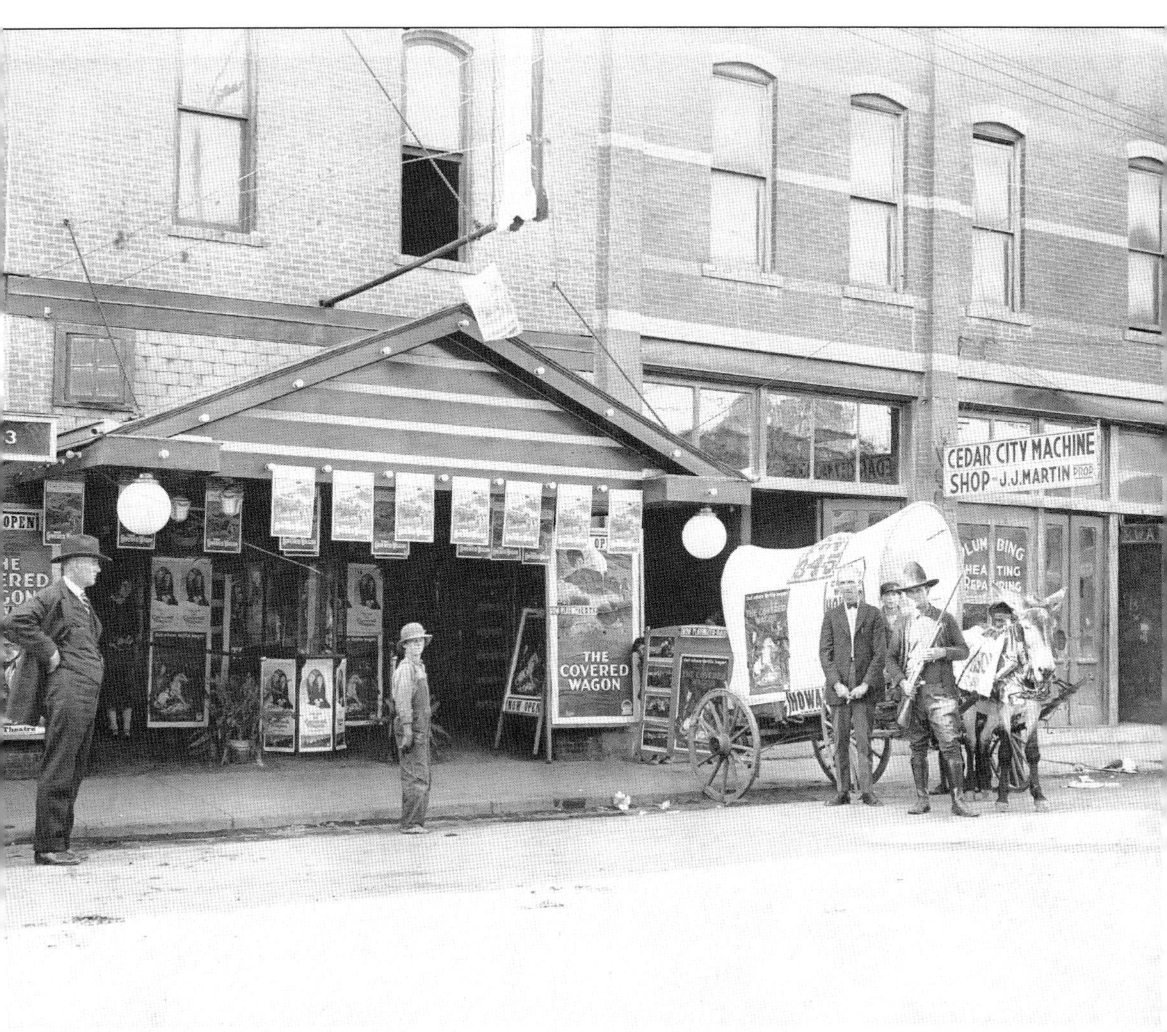

The Howard Theatre on North Cumberland Street, seen here in 1923, was not the first theater in Lebanon. That honor goes to the Nickel-O Theatre, located on the west side of the Square in 1908. John R. Hatcher Sr., standing to the left of the man holding the rifle, became manager of the Nickel-O in 1912 and thus began his long career in Lebanon's entertainment industry. The Lebanon of the early 20th century was full of theaters; the Lyric Theatre also opened in 1908 on South Cumberland Street, and a few years later, the Bijou and Custer Theatres were built side-by-side just north of the Lyric. Other theaters were the Star, upstairs on the corner of East Main and North College Streets; the Airdrome, on South Maple Street; and the Ritz, on North Cumberland Street. In the mid-20th century, locals had another option to enjoy the movies: the Cedar Drive-In Theatre on Rome Pike. (CLMHC.)

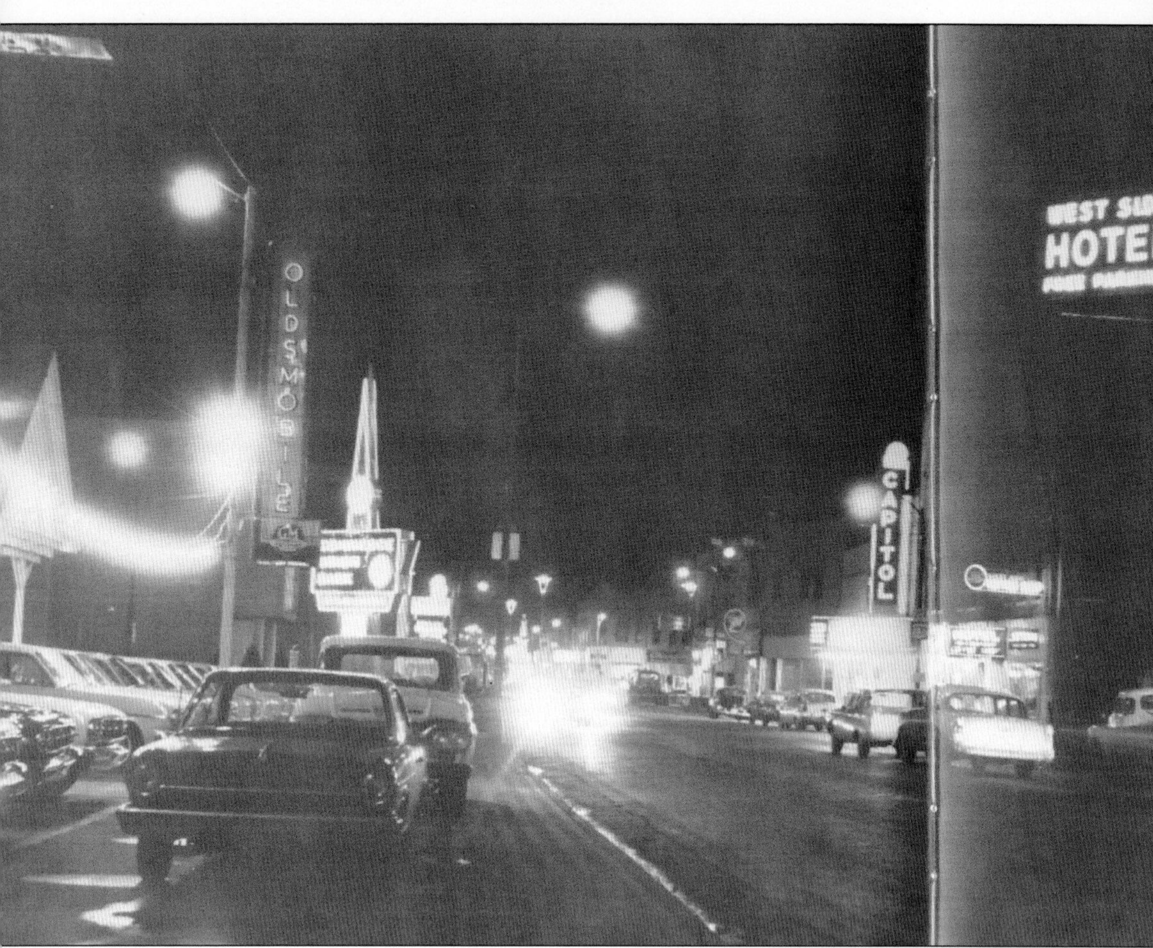

With its dramatic neon sign and marquee, the Capitol Theatre, at 110 West Main Street, is a landmark in downtown Lebanon. Built in 1949 by the Crescent Amusement Company, the theater was the last of the "picture show" houses to survive in town. The theater had seating for 1,000 in the auditorium, as well as balcony space. It featured a "crying room" for parents with fussy babies. Closed in the early 1980s, the building had various businesses move in for short periods of time but sat empty and neglected for many years. Now fully renovated, with the lobby carefully restored, the Capitol is once again a center of social life in Lebanon. (CU.)

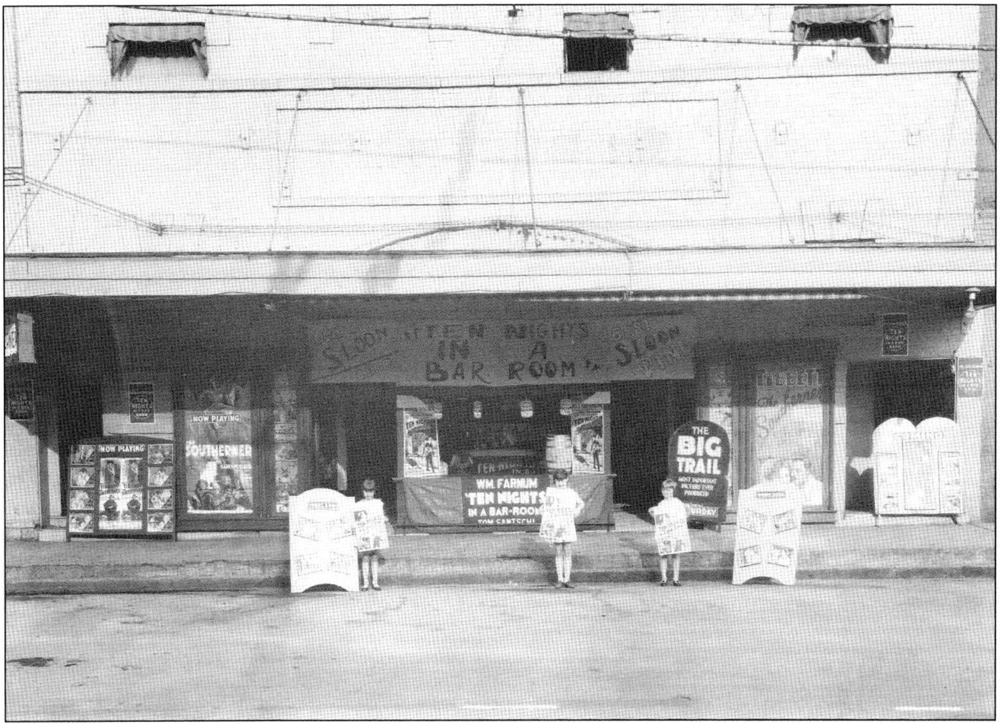

Tony Sudekum bought the Lyric Theatre from John Hatcher Sr. in 1927, extensively remodeled the building, and renamed the theater the Princess. A modern sound system was installed for the new "talkie" motion pictures, a first for Lebanon. Seen above in 1931, the theater kept this look until 1937, when the facade was reworked with stripes of blue vitrolite tile, shown in the image below to the left of the old courthouse. Another renovation took place in 1942. The Princess Theatre operated together with the Capitol Theatre until it closed in 1959. (Above, CLMHC; below, courtesy of T.A. Bryan.)

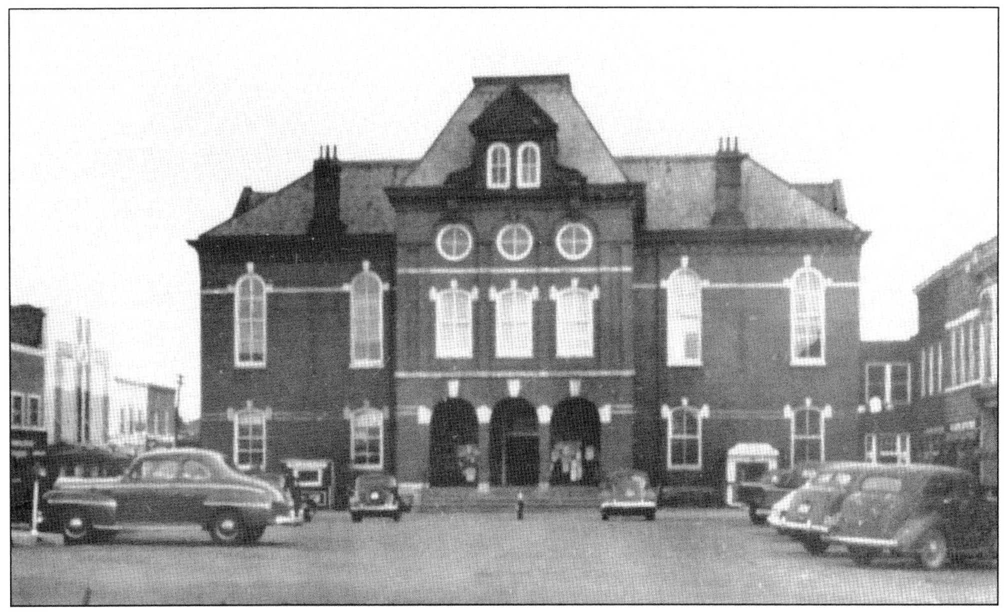

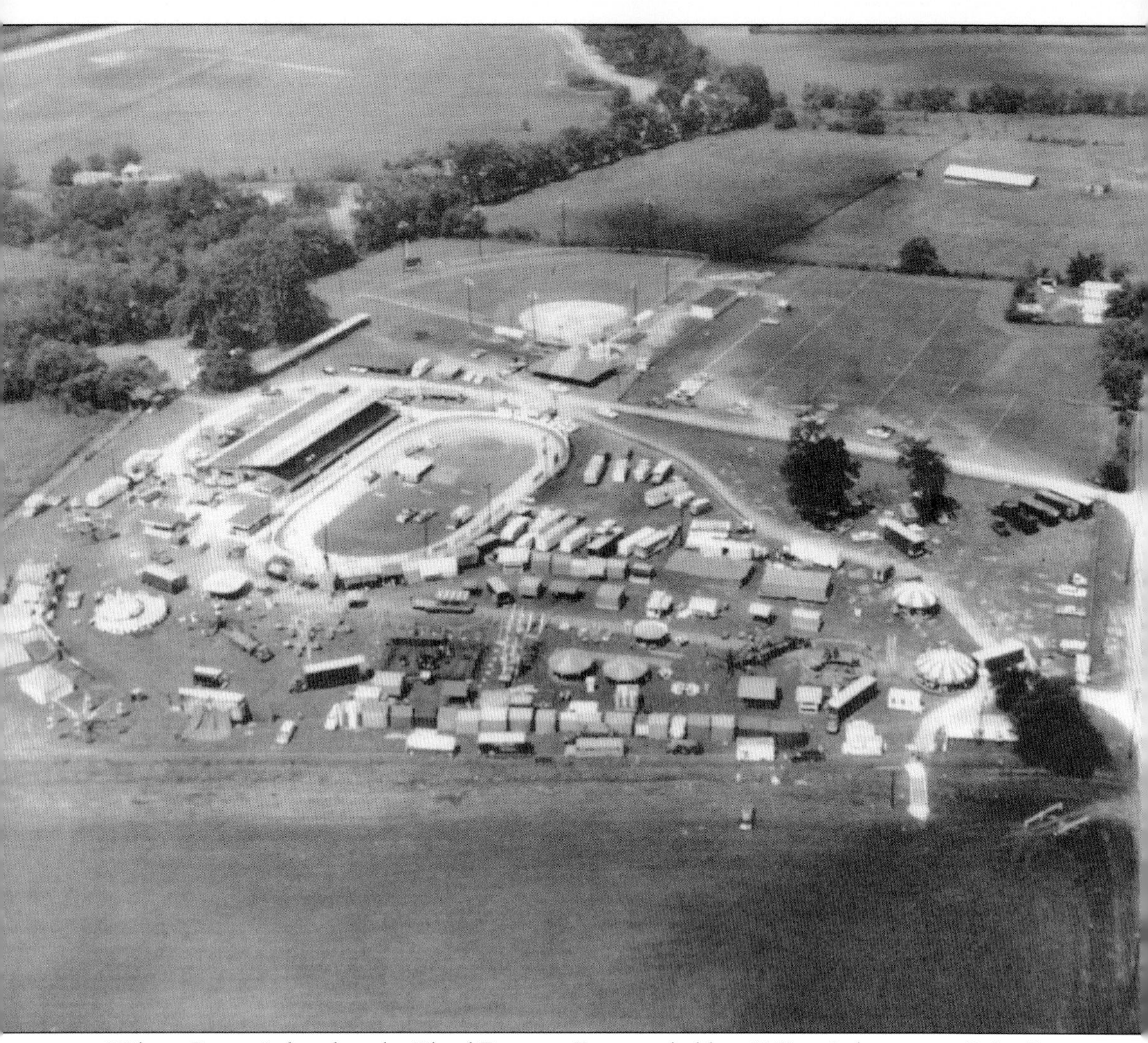

Wilson County's first fair, the Third Division Fair, was held in 1853 in Lebanon on Coles Ferry Pike, the site of the Jimmy Floyd Center today. Annual fairs were held on this property until 1884. Other fairs may have been held intermittently, but the fair was not reorganized as an annual event until 1919. By 1920, a grandstand, stables, and a cattle barn had been built on the fairgrounds and fair attendance was over 20,000 people. The Wilson County Fair would continue as an annual event until 1969. The Coles Ferry Pike site is seen here. In 1973, the Lebanon Jaycees revived the fair for two more years at the Coles Ferry Pike fairgrounds before moving it to the James E. Ward Agriculture Center. In 1979, Wilson County Promotions formed to continue the Wilson County Fair. (Courtesy of Wilson County Promotions.)

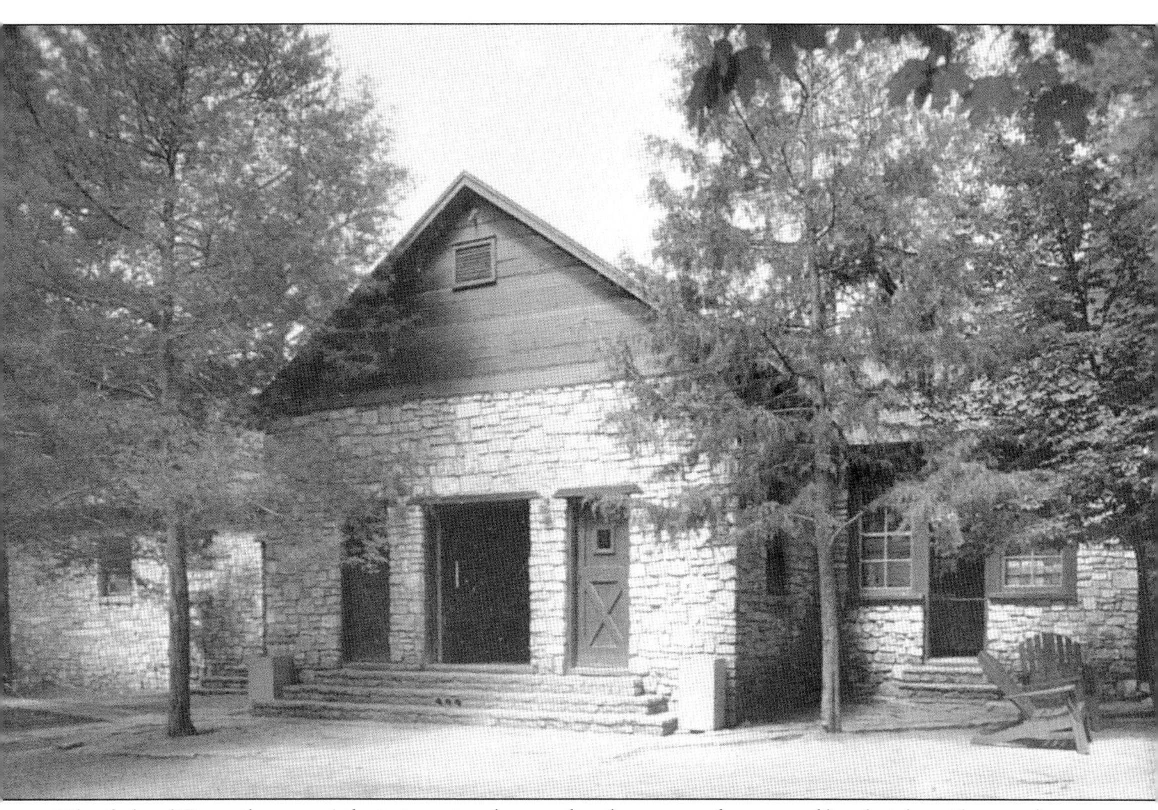

The federal Resettlement Administration began development of a tract of land eight miles south of Lebanon on both sides of Murfreesboro Pike in 1935. This land had been logged for years by the local cedar industry. By 1937, thousands of cedar seedlings were planted in a reforestation effort. During this same time, within Cedar Forest, the Works Progress Administration (WPA) built roads, trails, a swimming pool, picnic areas with shelters, and a main lodge building, seen here, built of native stone and cedar. Although still federally owned, the Tennessee Department of Conservation leased the land and operated the park as Lebanon Cedar Forest. The park was officially deeded to the State of Tennessee as a state park in 1955. The flora of the cedar glades was another reason to visit the park. As early as 1901, botanists discovered rare species known to grow only in this habitat. Elsie Quarterman's research in the 1960s led to the Cedar Forest's designation as a National Natural Landmark in 1973. (RWPCCU.)

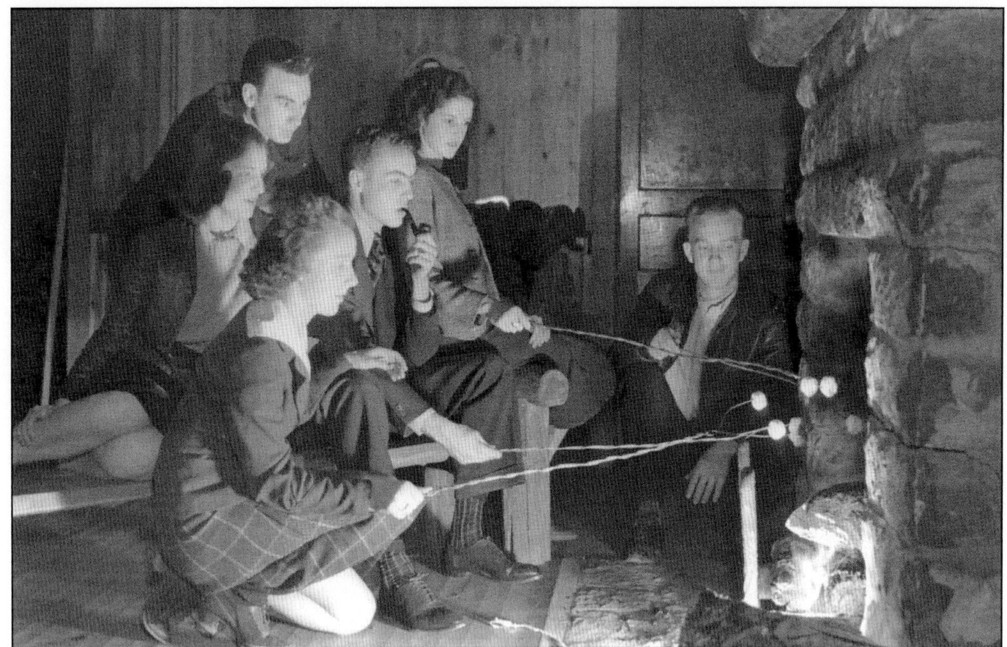

Campers and locals have enjoyed many activities at Cedar Forest, or, as it is officially known, Cedars of Lebanon State Park. A 1939 marshmallow roast in the Main Lodge is shown above. The Main Lodge was also the site of square dances and card games. This structure and others built by the WPA in the 1930s and 1940s were listed in the National Register of Historic Places in 1995. A dance is in full swing in the photograph below. Other activities in the park were horseback riding, hiking, picnics, camping, and swimming. Spelunking was also available, as the park contained several caves. (Both, TSLA.)

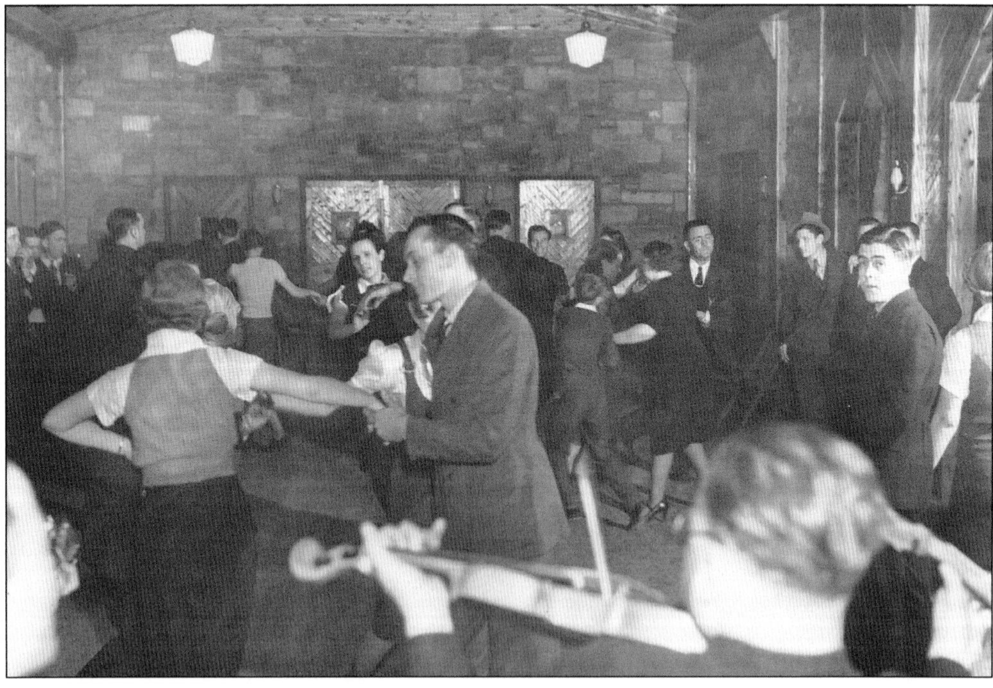

Seven

Cracker Barrel Old Country Store

Cracker Barrel Old Country Store began in 1969 off of Highway 109 in Lebanon. Dan Evins (1935–2012), the founder, envisioned people eating in the restaurant, relaxing on the front porch's rocking chairs, and filling up their cars' gas tanks. The first Cracker Barrels had overall-wearing attendants to pump customers' gas. (RWPCCU.)

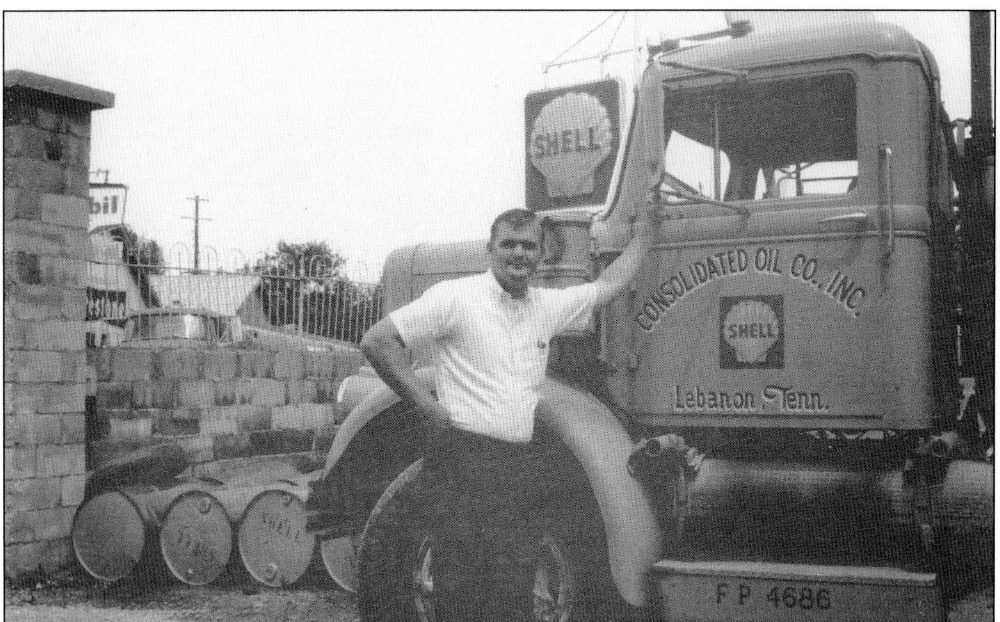

Dan Evins visualized the restaurant business as a way to sell more gasoline during his work as a Shell Oil "jobber," pictured above. The federal interstate system was well underway, and Evins knew travelers would want a familiar place to stop during their trips, something similar to the small-town country store, a place in the community where everyone gathered to shop, eat, relax, and reminisce. Also part of the experience were the artifacts and memorabilia that decorated the store and were for purchase in the gift store. The old-fashioned cash register, seen in the original store's setup below, was part of the charm. (Both courtesy of Cracker Barrel Old Country Store.)

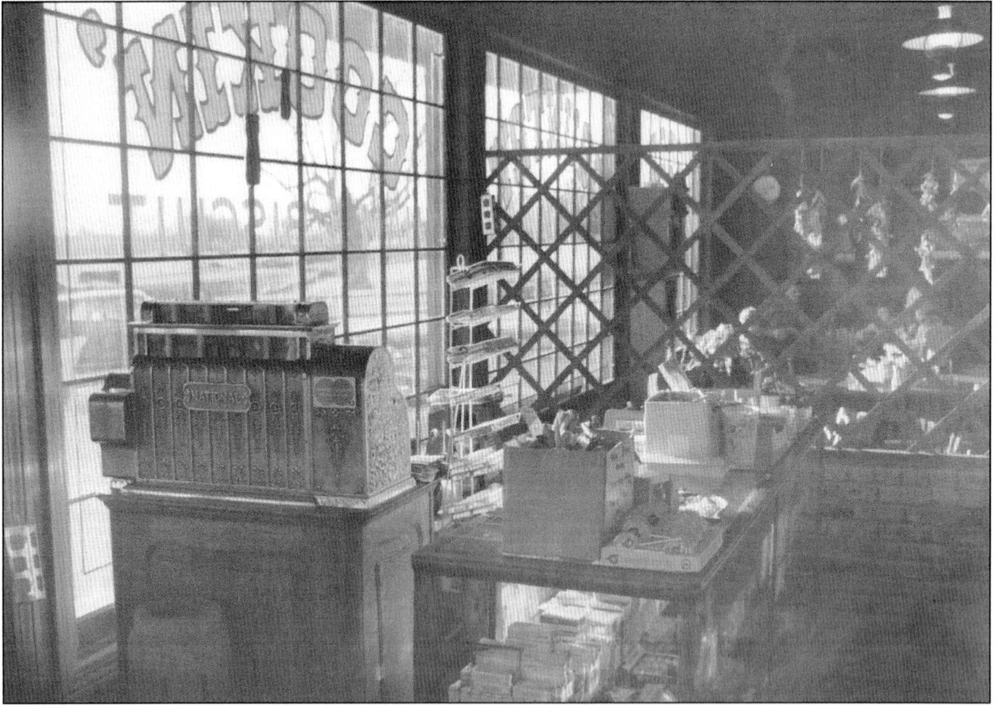

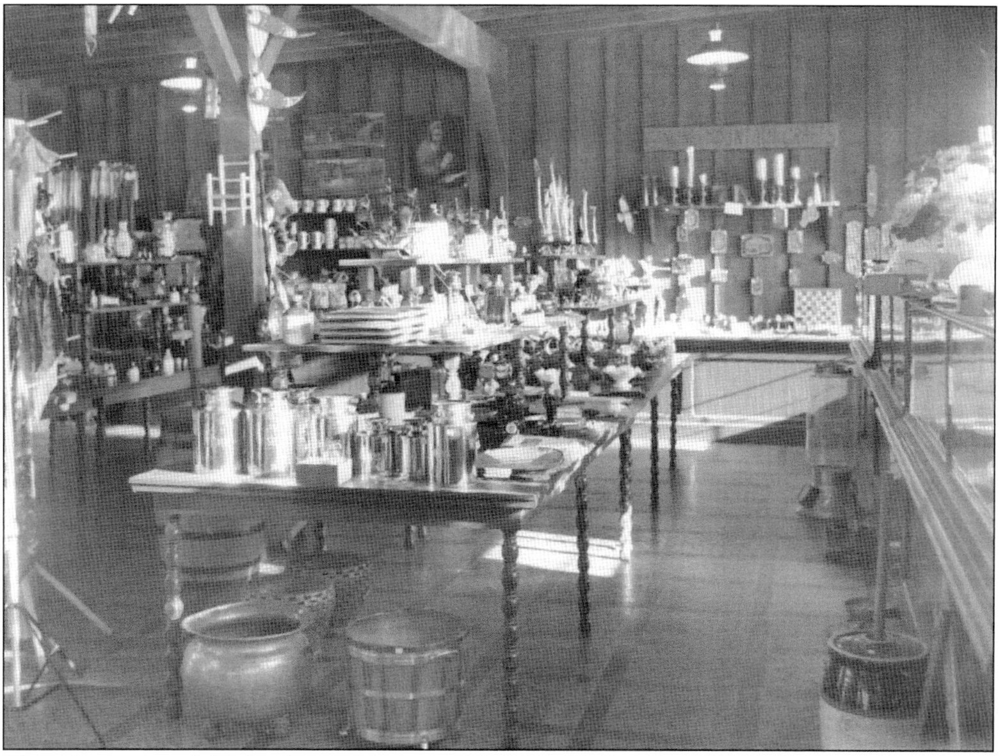

The gift store was full of early American reproductions of glassware, toys, and cast-iron cookware. Also available were soaps, candles, candies, and jellies. Authentic items hung on the walls of the gift store and restaurant, including farm implements, advertising posters for products of an earlier era, portraits, and in the Lebanon store, autographed photographs of top country music artists. Other celebrities in town for WSM's Grand Ole Opry would often stop by. Below, actor George Burns poses with employees. The waitresses also wore a country uniform, with bandana kerchiefs, denim skirt jumpers, and a bandana print blouse. (Both courtesy of Cracker Barrel Old Country Store.)

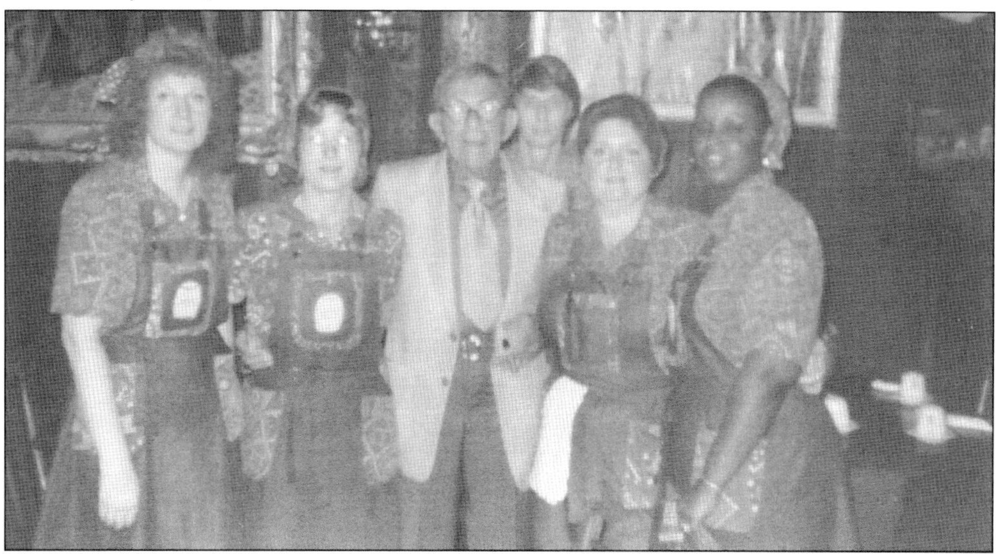

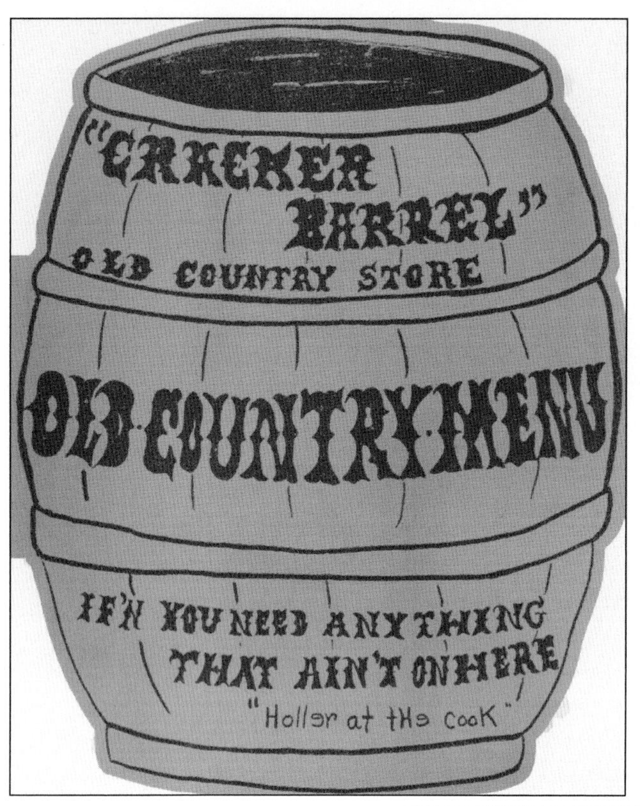

Cracker Barrel's simple country cooking concept was based on food found in households across the South, familiar food one's grandmother might have prepared. The original menu's "Southern" phonetic spelling featured items for breakfast, lunch, and supper. In February 1970, Evins incorporated the company and sold 10 blocks of 20,000 shares at 50¢ a share. The first investors were mainly from the local community. Evins commented on the reason for the restaurant's appeal to Bill Carey in Carey's book *Fortunes, Fiddles, and Fried Chicken: A Nashville Business History*, saying, "You might have a lady in a fur coat sitting next to a guy in overalls with muddy boots on. She's there because she thought it was quaint. He's there because he was hungry." (Courtesy of Cracker Barrel Old Country Store.)

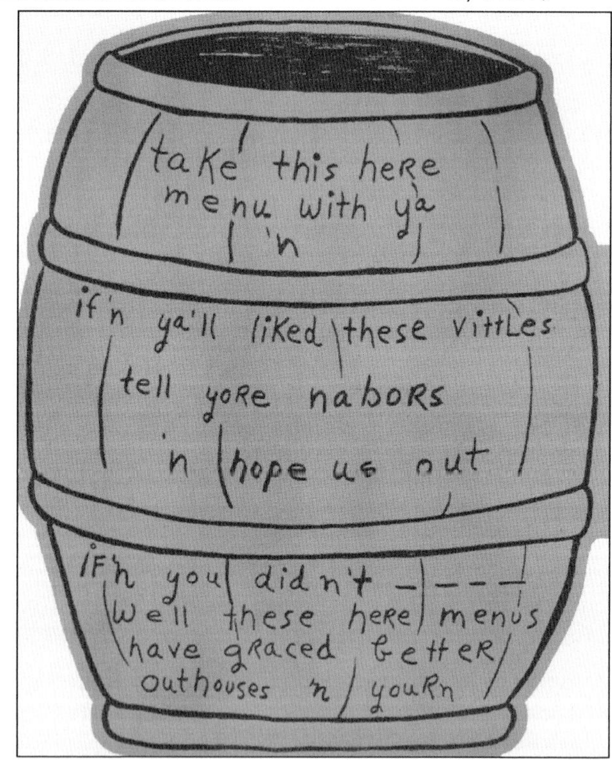

Juices and beverages

Orange — .25
grapefruit — .25
'mator — .25
out House prune .25
Coke, tab, sprite and .15 + 25
orange — .15
coffee — .15 + 25
cow juice — .15
Tea
Shakes — .30

CRACKER barrel brakfast

1 Hen aig — .50
2 hen aigs — .65
hickory smoked bacon — .40
Country sausage — 40
City ham — .50
*Cracker barrel sausage — .55
griddle cakes — .70
Red eye Gravy — .15
cracker barrel saw mill gravy and bisuits — .30
*Lasses and homemade biscuits — .30

ALL ORDERS WITH HOMEMADE Biscuits hominy grits, and the BEST jelly you ever 'et — we sell it in the store we even eat it ourselves.

*"Cracker barrel Country Boy Brakfast"
"just tell us how you like your aigs AND — Loosen your belt"
1.75

sanwiches

Sho nuff hambergers — .55
Sho nuff cheeseburgers — .65
skillet grilled cheese — .40
smoked bacon, lettuce and 'mator — .60
Country ham — .85
City ham — .65
City ham and cheese — .70
skillet fried hot dog — .35
FRENCH FRIES — .25
Onion Rings — .35

"CRACKER Barrel Specialties"

*Country ham and homemade buiscuits — 1.45
county line cheese and crackers — .40
lonies and crackers (Bologna to you yankees) .35
*Bowl of beans in hamhock and cornbread — .55
onions - homemade pickle relish - hot sauce
Greens and hawg jowl, fresh cornbread — .55

DESSERT

soft ice cream and homemade fried pies .25
— other stuff when you can get it — or when the cook aint sik.

Turnip greens and hog jowl with fresh cornbread was also on the original menu, pictured above. Staples such as grits, country ham and biscuits, and "lonies" and crackers have been offered from the start. Homemade freshness has always been a guiding principle at Cracker Barrel. Items are made from scratch in the kitchen and on a typical day, the restaurant chain uses 70,000 pounds of flour for biscuits and dumplings as well as 151 million eggs for its breakfast platters. Another staple on the tables in the restaurant is the peg game. To date, over 10 million peg games have been produced exclusively for Cracker Barrel. Below, line cooks serve up a bowl of beans in the restaurant kitchen. (Courtesy of Cracker Barrel Old Country Store.)

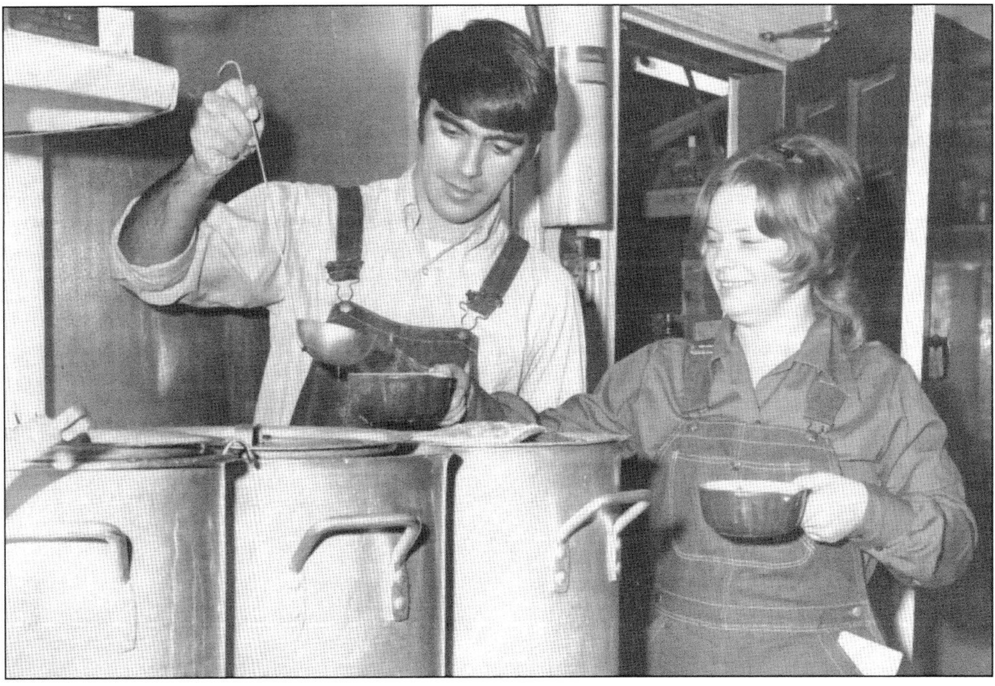

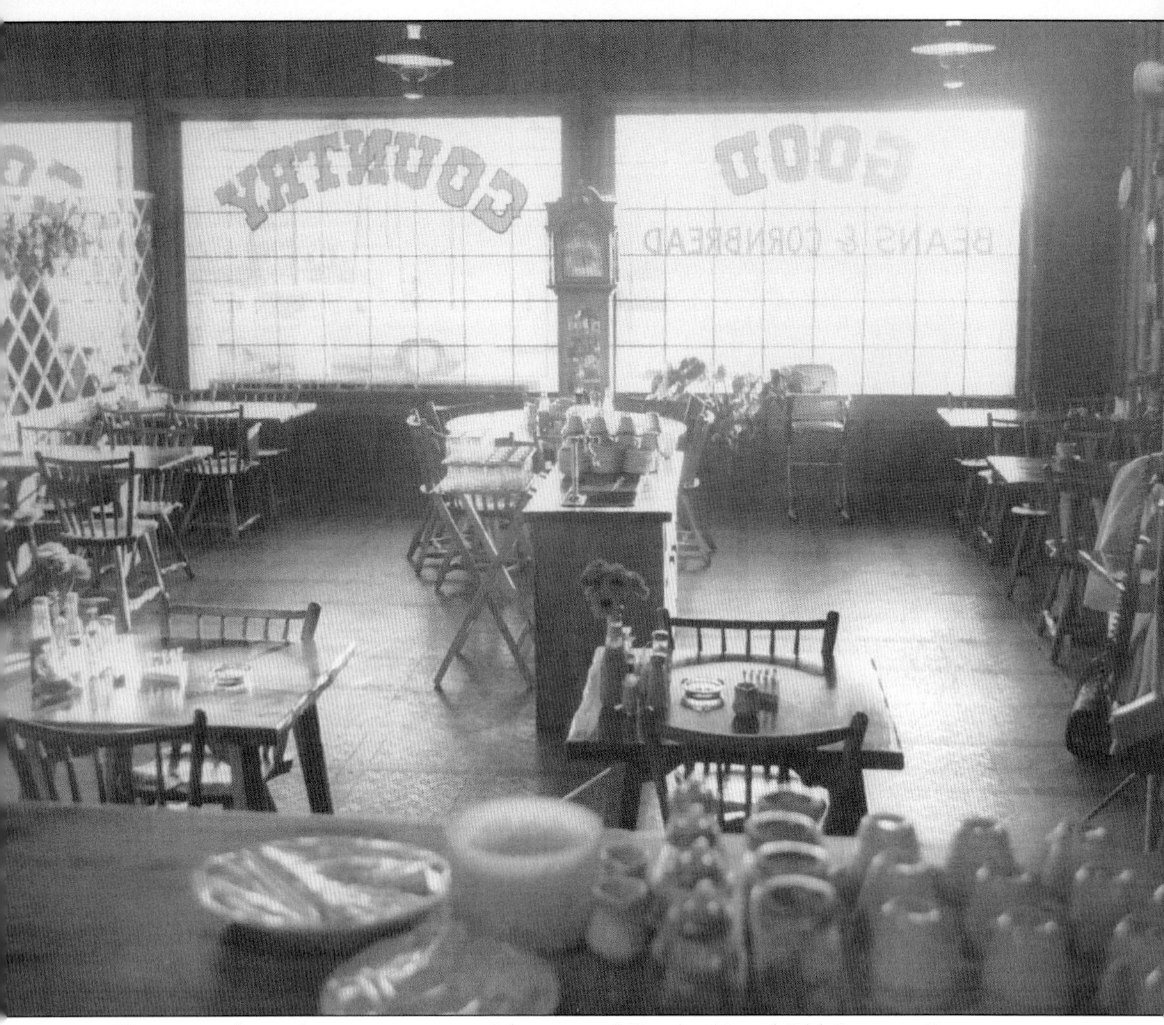

This image shows the interior setup of the original Cracker Barrel Old Country Store restaurant. Cracker Barrel's unique look has been achieved with the use of over 600,000 artifacts through the years. The Décor Warehouse on the main headquarters campus houses more than 90,000 artifacts. Each item is restored and archived by a warehouse team led by Larry Singleton. Each new store's interior is carefully designed by Singleton and his team. The items are first laid out in a full-size replica of the restaurant's interior, photographed, then packed and shipped to their new location. Approximately 1,000 artifacts are used to create each store interior. Even with rapid expansion, maintaining control over the image of its restaurants and stores has been an important aspect of the Cracker Barrel philosophy. To achieve this, Cracker Barrel retains ownership of all its locations. (Courtesy of Cracker Barrel Old Country Store.)

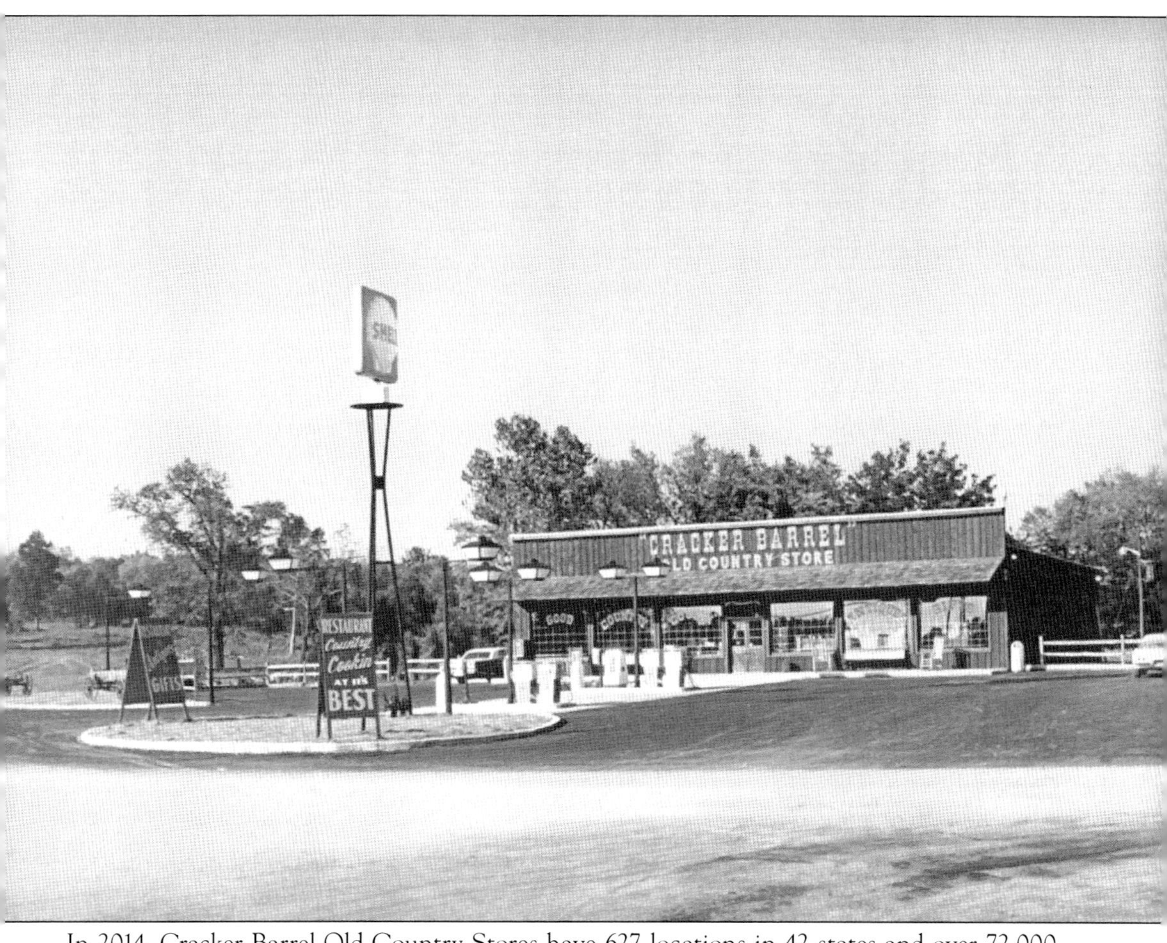

In 2014, Cracker Barrel Old Country Stores have 627 locations in 42 states and over 72,000 employees. Corporate headquarters is still located in Lebanon. Evins often stated he could never have imagined the success when he and local contractor Tommy Lowe first laid out the store at Highway 109. The company continued to grow, with the opening of 84 stores from 1980 to 1990; the stores no longer had the gas pumps out front, a result of the 1970s oil crisis. Continued growth prompted the offering of the company's stock to the public in 1981. Evins was CEO from 1969 to 2001 and continued as chairman until his retirement in 2004, when he became chairman emeritus. Cracker Barrel reached the milestone of its 500th store opening in May 2004. The corporate plan of placing restaurants close to the interstate for travelers as well as locals, keeping the food simple, and appealing to all has proven successful for the company. (Courtesy of Cracker Barrel Old Country Store.)

Bibliography

Bone, Winstead Paine. *A History of Cumberland University, 1842–1935*. Lebanon, TN: self-published, 1935.

Burns, G. Frank. *Phoenix Rising! The Sesquicentennial History of Cumberland University*. Lebanon, TN: Cumberland University Board of Trustees, 1992.

Burns, G. Frank. *Wilson County, Tennessee County History Series*. Memphis, TN: Memphis State University Press, 1983.

Castle Heights Military Academy Catalogs. Lebanon, TN: 1930 and 1961.

Clay, Eddie S. *Memories of Yesteryear*. Lebanon, TN: self-published, 1992.

Crutchfield, James A. *Hail, Castle Heights! An Illustrated History of Castle Heights School and Castle Heights Military Academy*. Lebanon, TN: Castle Heights Alumni Association, 2003.

Drake, James Vaulx. *The Life of General Robert Hatton*. Nashville, TN: Marshall & Bruce, 1867.

History Associates of Wilson County, Dixon Merrit, ed. *The History of Wilson County: Its Land & Its Life*. Lebanon, TN: County Court of Wilson County with cooperation of Commerce Union Bank, First Federal Savings & Loan Association, and Lebanon Bank, 1961.

The *Lebanon Democrat*, Sesquicentennial Edition. Lebanon, TN: The *Lebanon Democrat*, September 26, 1969.

Lockett, Patricia Ward and Mattie McHollin, with the Wilson County Black History Associates. *In Their Own Voices: An Account of the Presence of African Americans in Wilson County*. Lebanon, TN: The *Lebanon Democrat*, 1999.

McMillian, Woody. *In the Presence of Soldiers, the 2nd Army Maneuvers and Other World War II Activity in Tennessee*. Nashville, TN: Horton Heights Press, 2010.

Moss, Brenda and James Jordan. *The Wilson County Fair, Tennessee's Big County Fair*. Lebanon, TN: Wilson County Promotions, 2009.

Schlink, Ellen T. *"This Is The Place": A History Of Lebanon, Tennessee, 1780–1972*, Vols. 1–2. Nashville, TN: Blue & Gray Press, 1975–1976.

Sloan, Gene. *With Second Army: Somewhere in Tennessee*. Murfreesboro, TN: Middle Tennessee State College, 1956.

The Phoenix yearbooks. Lebanon, TN: Cumberland University, 1895, 1896, 1897, 1903, 1904, 1911, 1915, 1938, 1948, 1949, 1958, 1962, 1965.

ABOUT THE ORGANIZATION

Historic Lebanon is a nonprofit whose mission is to actively pursue the revitalization of Lebanon's Public Square and surrounding neighborhoods. The organization seeks to achieve these goals by implementing activities and programs which:

EDUCATE the public on Lebanon's rich historic identity within its boundaries in Wilson County and in the context of the greater Middle Tennessee region,
CREATE a center of activity on the Public Square with an economic restructuring plan, beautification plan, and promotion plan,
FOSTER a sense of community pride, and
PURSUE the preservation of Lebanon's unique cultural and architectural heritage.

Historic Lebanon is grateful for the continued support of the community and of our annual sponsors: Cumberland University, Ligon and Bobo Funeral Home, CedarStone Bank, the Thackston Family Foundation, Wilson Bank and Trust, City of Lebanon, and the Wilson County Commission.

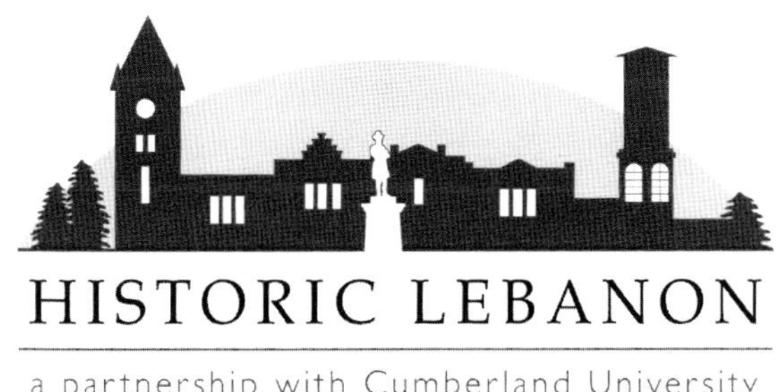